Wisdom
for
Today's Decisions

Don,

Thank you for the opportunity to play harmonica for Big River. It was both fun and educational for me, primarily thanks to your leadership and guidance.

As "Tom" would say, it was a "Thunderation-al" time, and I would have "Waded" knee deep in blood" to be a part of it.

Thanks so much.

Mark Juick

Wisdom
for
Today's Decisions

But the path of the
righteous is like the
light of dawn, that
shines brighter and
brighter . . .
—Proverbs 4:18

A Fresh Look at Proverbs

Mark Quick

Pleasant Word
A Division of WINEPRESS PUBLISHING

Printed in the United States of America

Packaged by Pleasant Word, a division of WinePress Publishing, PO Box 428, Enumclaw, WA 98022. The views expressed or implied in this work do not necessarily reflect those of Pleasant Word, a division of WinePress Publishing. Ultimate design, content, and editorial accuracy of this work are the responsibilities of the author.

ISBN 1-4141-0104-X
Library of Congress Catalog Card Number: 2004

Dedication

I am thankful for the support and encouragement of my wife and the patience of my three daughters (for sharing the computer with me). I am also thankful to the scores of dedicated and fascinating Christian men and women who have attended my Sunday school class over the past 13 years for sharing their insights and beneficial dialogues with me. Most of all, I dedicate this work to the loving Father we all share, who orchestrated the bringing of all these people together.

Table of Contents

Preface

This is not a pretty work. It contains repetition and frequently jumps from concept to concept.

This book was not written for any particular age range. It is intended for serious disciples of any age.

Structurally, the work may be labeled as a commentary. However, the purpose of the book is devotional. It was written with the intention of helping Christian readers see connections between Proverbs and the whole of biblical scripture.

Above all, it is intended to challenge the reader to apply God's principles to every aspect of life.

It is the author's hope that you will truly find wisdom for all of your decisions and that you will learn what it truly means to fear the Lord, to walk in His ways, and to fall ever more deeply in love with Him.

Proverbs 1

1:1 The proverbs of Solomon the son of David, king of Israel:

Knowing the author lends credibility to the text. The authorship is clear and undisputed for chapters 1–22:16 (see also 1 Chronicles 28:9, 2 Chronicles 1, and 1 Kings 3:9–11). Chapter 30 is attributed to Agur and chapter 31 to King Lemuel. We know very little about either man. All we really know is what we can glean from the internal evidence within these two chapters.

Proverbs 25:1 states, "These also are proverbs of Solomon which the men of Hezekiah . . . transcribed." All we can really know from this statement is that some portions of the book of Proverbs were compiled after Solomon's death.

Some scholars believe the phrase "Hear the words of the wise" from Proverbs 22:17 provides additional internal authorship evidence. However, I have seen no adequate evidence to believe such a reference implies an author other than Solomon himself. Other than chapters 30 and 31, I attribute the entire book to Solomon himself.

1:2–6 To know wisdom and instruction, to discern the sayings of understanding, to receive instruction in wise behavior, righteousness, justice and equity; to give prudence to the naive, to the youth knowledge and discretion, a wise man will hear and increase in learning and a man of understanding will acquire wise counsel, to understand a proverb and a figure, the words of the wise and their riddles.

The purpose of Proverbs is outlined here. How do we assess and judge things? By what principles shall we live? There is something for everyone, regardless of age, maturity, or intellectual ability. Proverbs has something for each of us!

Sometimes we think that only "smart" people can be wise, or perhaps we assume that smart people *are* wise. The wisdom spoken of here in Proverbs is not restricted to mental capacity or intelligence. In fact, smart and intelligent people can (and often do) behave foolishly, while mentally challenged individuals may behave and make decisions that demonstrate great wisdom. Moral wisdom trumps mental intelligence when it comes to living a godly life. Wisdom is available to all, but certainly not all will hear her voice. While you read through Proverbs, the question to simply ask yourself is: Will you hear and heed her voice? In other words, are you open to change and growth?

As we continue through the book of Proverbs, you will become aware of a deeper purpose not specifically mentioned in the above list (although it could be argued that the word *righteousness* covers what I am about to suggest). The ultimate purpose of Proverbs is to enable us to walk with God and to live out the two great commandments to love God and to love men.

1:7 The fear of the LORD is the beginning of knowledge; Fools despise wisdom and instruction.

"Fear [*yir'ah* in Hebrew] of the LORD" is the key to understanding Proverbs. *Yir'ah* seems to be a combination of fear, reverence, awe, and total awareness of His presence.

12

Genuine fear of God ultimately allows us to perceive the power and capabilities of God. Having a state of mind full of fear, we understand clearly that He can and will do as He says. He is faithful in His promises, but His promises include judgment. However, this in turn helps us establish a firm foundation for faith and trust in God. We know He is trustworthy. That is why we fear Him. But it is also why we can trust Him. He alone is worthy of our fear, as Jesus expounded in Matthew 10:26–33.

Fear of God causes us to come to grips with our relationship with God. Fear of God allows real faith in God to blossom because it allows you to cast out *all other fears.* Try the following experiment. Read the paragraph, then close your eyes and try to visualize this encounter with God Almighty.

Imagine God. Now imagine Him seated on a great throne. You are attempting to see His face, but the brilliance is blinding. You hear the words, "Come closer, My child"—but fear grips your heart. You remember an unkind word you said. You remember a time in which you were a poor witness and when you had a bad attitude. Again you hear the thunder: "Come closer, My child."

To the right-hand side of the throne there is a movement, and the shadow of a figure crosses your eye, enabling you to stop blinking. Now you can stare more carefully than before. You stumble forward and utter the words, "Holy, holy, holy, O Lord God Almighty, forgive me."

Thunder rumbles again and you hear, "Be still, My child, your sins have already been covered and forgiven."

This exercise illustrates to a small and imperfect degree what fear of God *feels* like. Fear of God is a total awareness of the *reality* of God, and it is an attitude that encompasses our entire being. Our acute awareness of God and the state of mental and spiritual readiness it produces allows us to begin to grasp knowledge.

By contrast, fools despise this entire idea, because they don't value wisdom and knowledge, or having a deep relationship with God.

1:8–9 Hear, my son, your father's instruction, and do not forsake your mother's teaching; Indeed, they are a graceful wreath to your head, and ornaments about your neck.

How do you honor your father and mother? Listen to them. Fathers and mothers are not infallible, but they have your best interests at heart. We shall see many comments about the fifth commandment elucidated throughout Proverbs.

Keep in mind that these verses precede the passage about peer pressure and sin. There is a learning hierarchy that Solomon is teaching us. Learn from God first and from parents second. Later he will add the voice of wisdom and also counselors (or advisors) to this list. The basic principle is to be open and ready to receive instruction.

1:10 My son, if sinners entice you, do not consent.

The two verbs to consider here are *entice* and *consent*. Both speak to the freedom of one's will. Sinners desire others to sin along with them. In Genesis 4:7 God warned Cain, saying, "Sin is crouching at the door; and its desire is for you, but you must master it."

Moral dilemmas exist at all stages of our lives, from early childhood through old age. We live in a world full of temptations. Even before the fall of Adam, choice and temptation were real. If choice were *not* to exist, then God would have developed a robotic, deterministic system.

Actually, there are many people who believe we *do* live in a deterministic setting. Extreme behaviorists (such as B. F. Skinner) believe that people act only from conditioned responses, and in essence, therefore, do not really choose. Some who believe in fate, karma, or chance may believe that choice is just an illusion. Even some radical ultra-Calvinists use language suggesting we have no control or free will at all.

Proverbs is full of advice. The whole point of advice is that people can take the advice and use it to improve their lives, because we do have freedom concerning our will. While it is beneficial for us to wrestle with and find a balance between the concepts of free will and the sovereignty of God, the simple thrust of this verse is "Do not consent." Choose to choose wisely.

> 1:11–14 If they say, "Come with us, let us lie in wait for blood, let us ambush the innocent without cause; Let us swallow them alive like Sheol, even whole, as those who go down to the pit; We shall find all kinds of precious wealth, we shall fill our houses with spoil; Throw in your lot with us, we shall all have one purse,"

In order to demonstrate the principle of self-control, Solomon presents a hypothetical situation. It has been suggested by some that the most powerful word in the English language is the word *we*. The world knows how powerful this is. The simple phrase "Come with us" brings a flood of emotions and thoughts. If I don't go, will I miss out—or worse, will I forever be excluded in the future? Will I be mocked? If I am not "one of them," perhaps they will turn on me and attack me in the future.

A spectrum from desire to fear plays on our will at vulnerable times. In such times confusion reigns rather than wisdom. When the final argument of easy wealth appears, it is difficult to argue against. The *future* and any potential consequences may become forgotten in a hazy mist of *present* self centered concerns.

Maturity may be defined in part by future orientation. Individuals who are mature tend to look down the road and plan and prepare for possible future eventualities. Immature individuals tend to live only in the present. Thus, when an immature person makes a choice, he often lacks the benefit of understanding the consequences of the decision.

> 1:15 My son, do not walk in the way with them. Keep your feet from their path.

This verse represents the second primary theme of Proverbs chapters 1–9. First, we are to fear the Lord, and second, we should watch carefully the path upon which we tread. We shall see as we continue through Proverbs that there is God's way or there are other paths. All paths except God's path eventually lead to destruction. The Hindu idea that all paths lead to the top of the mountain is simply not biblical. If you are a fatalist, the book of Proverbs will drive you crazy.

> 1:16–19 For their feet run to evil, and they hasten to shed blood. Indeed, it is useless to spread the net in the eyes of any bird; but they lie in wait for their own blood; they ambush their own lives. So are the ways of everyone who gains by violence; it takes away the life of its possessors.

These verses illustrate the principle of reciprocity. Stated concisely, what you reap is what you sow. This passage implies that evil individuals are blinded by their own corruption. In a sense, they are more bird-brained than real birds. At least a real bird will avoid a snare it has witnessed being laid. But these individuals lay their own snares for themselves.

This passage also illustrates another common biblical theme, "For the wages of sin is death" (Romans 6:23).

> 1:20–21 Wisdom shouts in the street, She lifts her voice in the square; at the head of the noisy streets she cries out; at the entrance of the gates in the city, she utters her sayings:

Wisdom is shouting, will you listen? The main point here is that wisdom can be found anywhere if we have an attitude of openness to hear it.

> 1:22 How long, O naive ones, will you love simplicity? And scoffers delight themselves in scoffing, and fools hate knowledge?

Three causes for *not* listening to wisdom's voice are suggested here: 1) being naïve; 2) having the attitude of a scoffer; and 3) simply hating knowledge.

Being naive is defined for us as loving simplicity. The word *simplicity* here can also be translated as *foolishness*. This is the immature person who is just not ready to learn.

The primary motivation for a scoffer (as revealed in this verse) is humor. This is the class-clown type of person. This individual attempts to see the funny side of everything. He takes delight in poking fun at everything.

The third type of nonlearner is the fool who simply hates to learn anything. Perhaps he cannot understand how the knowledge will be used. Maybe the thought of learning smacks of work, and his overt laziness will not tolerate such a condition. Regardless of his internal motivation, he hates knowledge.

The interesting question that remains unanswered is the question of how long these people will refuse to learn. Educators understand that they cannot "learn" anyone. They can only teach.

The question to ask yourself is, are you ready to learn?

1:23 Turn to my reproof, behold, I will pour out my spirit on you; I will make my words known to you.

This represents a conditional promise. If we listen *and* heed wisdom's reproof, then we will begin to attain it. Notice how important reproof is, or actually how important it is to be able to accept it. One of the hardest things to do in life is to embrace reproof. It is also one of the healthiest things we can do, as it is often the first step toward humility and needed change.

1:24–27 Because I called, and you refused; I stretched out my hand, and no one paid attention; And you neglected all my counsel, And did not want my reproof; I will even laugh at your calamity; I will mock when your dread comes, when your dread comes like a storm, and your calamity comes on like a whirlwind, when distress and anguish come on you.

17

No man has an excuse. No one is able to claim that wisdom did not beckon him. It is interesting to note that the same is true regarding God Himself (see Romans 1:21–25).

The latter part of the passage deals with judgment. Solomon's father David pointed out a similar thought: "The wicked plots against the righteous . . . the LORD laughs at him; for He sees his day is coming" (Psalm 37:12–13).

> 1:28–32 Then they will call on me, but I will not answer; They will seek me diligently, but they shall not find me, because they hated knowledge, and did not choose the fear of the LORD. They would not accept my counsel, they spurned all my reproof. So they shall eat of the fruit of their own way, and be satiated with their own devices. For the waywardness of the naive shall kill them, and the complacency of fools shall destroy them.

This passage deals with hypocrisy. We cannot find true wisdom on our own terms. We cannot hate knowledge, refuse to fear God, neglect counsel, disregard reproof, and then "pretend" to seek wisdom and find it.

There is a very close connection between Solomon's concept of wisdom and the theological concept of salvation. In regard to salvation, God will always offer grace to each of us. But in regard to natural consequences, a price must be paid for wayward behavior. To be *wayward* means to be off the path or way, and this always leads to trials, problems, or destruction that would have been otherwise unnecessary.

> 1:33 But he who listens to me shall live securely, and shall be at ease from the dread of evil.

Those of us who listen have no need of worry, for our peace rests in God. The promise of judgment is intended to bring about the healthy fear of the Lord and begin the learning process. Here the promise of security and blessing and peace should make us all grateful to God.

18

Proverbs 2

2:1 My son, if you will receive my sayings, and treasure my commandments within you,

Throughout the book of Proverbs the theme of obeying commandments is repeated and expanded upon. Often people think of the word *obey* as a word that implies dos and don'ts and regulations. What Christianity actually teaches is that we "treasure" the commandments. Obedience then becomes joyful and we discover that real freedom and abundance of life comes through this process.

Solomon is clearly the author here, but how are we to understand the phrase "My son"? One explanation is that these words were written specifically to an actual son such as Rehoboam. Another possibility is that Solomon penned these words of his wisdom poem as if they were the actual words of God Himself addressed to all His children, which we can all read specifically as His "son." I leave such debates to others, but I believe that all scripture can be profitable for each of us and that the applications apply to each of us. I therefore feel safe in exhorting any reader to treasure the commands of God.

2:2–5 Make your ear attentive to wisdom, incline your heart to understanding; for if you cry for discernment, lift your voice for understanding; if you seek her as silver, and search for her as for hidden treasures; then you will discern the fear of the LORD, and discover the knowledge of God.

Do we just leave this issue of wisdom up to God? No, we must take an active role. Our role in the process of acquiring wisdom includes active listening, heartfelt desire for it, prayer, the active seeking of it, and valuing it above wealth.

Here Solomon repeats the primary theme of fearing the Lord, which is what the quest for wisdom is all about. Notice also how God utilizes the "discovery" method of learning. When God in His supernaturalness breaks through into what for us is "natural," we observe a miracle. Often we see Him teaching in the Bible through miracles and through spokespeople who have received a direct (i.e., miraculous) message. But even more often He uses the discovery method. Jesus used this with His parables, and when John the Baptist asked, "Are you the coming one?" Jesus replied in a manner that implied John should observe the signs and come to a proper conclusion based on these signs (Matthew 11:2–6). By doing this, John could discover the truth for himself.

2:6–8 For the LORD gives wisdom; from His mouth come knowledge and understanding. He stores up sound wisdom for the upright; He is a shield to those who walk in integrity, guarding the paths of justice, and He preserves the way of His godly ones.

God is the ultimate source of all wisdom. It is not *nature*, as some propose, lest we worship the creature rather than the Creator (Romans 1). Notice as you read these verses how intimately the concept of peace and divine preservation are tied into the concept of wisdom. In difficult times, Romans 8:28 may not seem to be in full operation, but if we maintain a godly perspective, eventually we will see how powerful our "blessed hope" truly is! As

John recorded, "He who overcomes, I will grant to him to sit down with me on My throne" (Revelation 3:21).

Consider the phrase "He preserves the way of His godly ones." The "way" is the path toward God. Solomon is going to continue to develop this theme of the "way" so that we may understand both His role and our role in the covenant. In Proverbs, wisdom involves walking on the "way."

2:9 Then you will discern righteousness and justice and equity and every good course.

To begin to see as God sees is one of the greatest blessings He can grant us. As wisdom becomes more and more a part of us, what is it that we focus on? Let us compare this verse to Paul's exhortation: "Whatever is true, whatever is honorable, whatever is right, whatever is pure, whatever is lovely, whatever is of good repute, if there is any excellence and if anything worthy of praise, let your mind dwell on these things" (Philippians 4:8). This verse represents a beautiful promise of discernment and guidance.

2:10 For wisdom will enter your heart, and knowledge will be pleasant to your soul;

In addition to receiving salvation and being changed forever *positionally* in our relationship to God, as we accept Him we are changed *internally* as well. Paul said that we are "new creatures" (2 Corinthians 5:17). Unlike a fool (see Psalm 14:1), knowledge becomes pleasant to us.

2:11 Discretion will guard you, understanding will watch over you,

God will continue to watch over us, but as we draw near to Him and allow Him to impart godly attributes to us (such as righteousness and wisdom, etc.), we should begin to make better choices. Thus our own discretion (which we actually acquired from Him) will guard us.

2:12–15 To deliver you from the way of evil, from the man who speaks perverse things; from those who leave the paths of uprightness, to walk in the ways of darkness; who delight in doing evil, and rejoice in the perversity of evil; whose paths are crooked, and who are devious in their ways;

This passage points out the extremely *practical* reasons for accepting the path of wisdom. Not only will this path lead to salvation for our souls, but even while we are here on earth we may receive deliverance from many forms of evil.

2:16 To deliver you from the strange woman, from the adulteress who flatters with her words;

Wisdom can deliver you from sexual troubles if you listen to her "voice." Another point of advice is this: beware of flattery. Flattery always contains hidden motives.

2:17–18 That leaves the companion of her youth, and forgets the covenant of God; for her house sinks down to death, and her tracks lead to the dead;

The metaphorical "adulterous woman" is a *type*. This is the person who believes in personal happiness above commitment. The illustration points out that she does not commit to man or God. Her path leads to death, and often those around her (i.e., "her house") must also suffer because of her choices. Our current society has even developed language to mollify the grieving conscience of individuals who struggle with self-centered behavior. Popular psychology often states things such as the following: "You should be happy . . . don't feel sorry for other people, they knew what they were doing . . . you can't be bound by vows you made 10 years ago . . . you have a right to be happy. Your happiness is more important than _____." These worldly-wise platitudes and others can be seen nightly on nearly any situation comedy, and they reflect the social climate of our times. Proverbs reveals the end result of such thinking and behavior.

> 2:19 None who go to her return again, nor do they reach the paths of life.

Furthermore, she takes those who go to her down the same path of death. One of the first things to learn about the different paths spoken of in the Bible is that while you may find yourself at a crossroads, you cannot be on two different paths at the same time. You may switch paths, but this act is a result of a willful choice rather than chance. 1 Corinthians 2:14–15 points out that "a natural man does not accept the things of the Spirit of God; for they are foolishness to him, and he cannot understand them, because they are spiritually appraised."

> 2:20–22 So you will walk in the way of good men and keep to the paths of the righteous. For the upright will live in the land, and the blameless will remain in it; but the wicked will be cut off from the land, and the treacherous will be uprooted from it.

The contrast here involves the metaphor of living or not living in the land. This is a reference to life and salvation. The means of getting to the Promised Land is by walking along The Way and keeping to the path of righteousness. The upright and blameless live and remain, but the wicked are "cut off." Notice how the treacherous are pulled out, roots and all! They are removed both physically and spiritually!

Proverbs 3

3:1 My son, do not forget my teaching, but let your heart keep my commandments;

*V*ery few things we learn fall into the category of "once learned, always learned." We must seek habits that spawn reminders of who we are in God, who we are becoming, what He has done for us, and most of all, who He is. Notice how this was taught in the *Shema,* recorded in Deuteronomy 6:4–9 (compare also 2 Peter 3:1–2). God instructed His people to teach their children about Him and to have many reminders of Him.

To keep commandments *genuinely,* they must first be kept in the heart. In other words, obedience begins internally before it is displayed externally. It begins first in your attitude, will, and motives.

3:2 For length of days and years of life, and peace they will add to you.

This verse tells us of two great promises, long life and peace. These will both be granted to those who meet the conditions, i.e., to those who "keep the commandments." It is interesting to note that there are both an internal reward and an external reward.

> 3:3 Do not let kindness and truth leave you; bind them around your neck, write them on the tablet of your heart.

Notice the union of kindness and truth. Sometimes these concepts are viewed as if they were the antithesis of one another. For example, we sometimes feel that if we are going to be kind, it must be at the expense of truthfulness (note the cliché "the truth hurts"). But this is not so. As we imitate Christ, we can learn to share the truth in kindness. These qualities need to be both external ("around your neck") and internal ("on . . . your heart").

A brief word study here regarding the words translated "kindness" and "truth" may reveal some deeper insights. The word translated as "kindness" is the Hebrew word *checed* (kheh-sed), which can be translated as either kindness, favor, or mercy. This is actually quite similar to the New Testament idea of grace. The word translated as "truth" comes from the Hebrew *emeth*. This word implies stability, certainty, truth, and trustworthiness. The word *emeth* comes from the root word *aman,* which means to build up or support, to foster (as a parent), to be firm or faithful, or to be permanent, true, steadfast, and faithful.

By combining the concepts of kindness and truth, we can see the New Testament idea of edification and the building up of each other. As God grants grace to each of us, we need to show kindness to each other as well. There seems to be a sense of both horizontal (man-to-man) and vertical (man-to-God) awareness that need to be developed when we combine the terms *kindness* and *truth*.

> 3:4 So you will find favor and good repute in the sight of God and man.

Compare this verse to Luke 2:52: "And Jesus kept increasing in wisdom and stature, and in favor with God and men." God sees us spiritually. From Him we seek favor and grace. Men see us more externally. From them we seek to have a good reputation.

3:5 Trust in the LORD with all your heart, and do not lean on your own understanding,

Our society shouts, "Have faith in yourself, and believe in your own abilities!" The Bible tells us to trust in the Lord so completely that we do not depend on our own understanding at all. No matter how arrogant a worldly man becomes, he cannot escape fear and a lack of peace. Those who trust in God find a type of rest and peace that passes understanding.

3:6 In all your ways acknowledge Him, and He will make your paths straight.

In a poetic voice, I offer this commentary:
Every day, in every act and in every choice
Should we openly seek Him, and listen to His voice.
Allowing Him to change and delineate our path
In order that we may avoid all future forms of wrath.
Though the way be narrow and wrought with others' hate
Life and peace He yields, as our path He makes straight.

3:7 Do not be wise in your own eyes; fear the LORD and turn away from evil.

Those who are wise in their own eyes tend to suffer from spiritual blindness. The serpent used "self-wisdom" to deceive Eve (Genesis 3:4–6). The pharaoh of Moses' time also suffered from the blindness of pseudo-wisdom. It was true of the prophets of Baal (1 Kings 18) and the Pharisees of Jesus' time as well. Actually, examples can be found in all eras. Compare Paul's writings about the two different types of wisdom in 1 Corinthians 2:4–16.

Turning away from evil is the natural response of our heart as we cast our gaze upon our Holy Father. See Him as He is. Make this the heartfelt cry of your prayers and His power will be revealed unto you. "Lord, make me to fear You in all Your reverent glory and magnificent holiness!"

3:8 It will be healing to your body, and refreshment to your bones.

Physical benefits are reaped from our spiritual journey. See also Proverbs 4:22.

3:9 Honor the LORD from your wealth, and from the first of all your produce.

How do you honor the Lord? So often this concept seems vague and abstract. Do you praise Him and respect His word? Do you honor Him from your wealth? What a wonderfully tangible way this gives us to show Him honor.

What is the *purpose* of tithing? Read Deuteronomy 14:23 to find a fascinating answer.

3:10 So your barns will be filled with plenty, and your vats will overflow with new wine.

We cannot outgive God. Compare Deuteronomy 28:1–3, 8 and Malachi 3:10.

3:11 My son, do not reject the discipline of the LORD, or loathe His reproof,

Compare the following scriptures: Deuteronomy 8:5; Job 5:17–18; 1 Corinthians 11:32; and Hebrews 12:6–8. These scriptures verify for us that God loves us, and His love is demonstrated to us by both the sacrifice of His Son (Romans 5:8) and by His loving discipline of us, which is designed to draw us closer to Him!

3:12 For whom the LORD loves He reproves, even as a father, the son in whom he delights.

The question is, can you accept His reproof? The voice of wisdom tells us, "Turn to my reproof" (Proverbs 1:23). This is hardly our natural response, but it is the spiritually healthy thing to do. See also Proverbs 13:24.

3:13 How blessed is the man who finds wisdom, and the man who gains understanding.

This marks the beginning of a new motif. Verses 1–12 are statements of advice. Verses 13–26 contain a glorious dialectic about the blessing of the Lord's wisdom. Solomon reminds us again that wisdom must be sought. It is not an automatic, inherent attribute of human nature. To be blessed you must find it, and to find it, you must seek it.

3:14–15 For its profit is better than the profit of silver, and its gain than fine gold. She is more precious than jewels; and nothing you desire compares with her.

Wealth is of little value spiritually. Wisdom is of great value. In fact, when the two are compared, it becomes clear that wealth is *far* less profitable.

Consider the things you desire, and compare them to seeking God and His wisdom. The wisdom spoken of in Proverbs includes, by its very nature, the gift of salvation as well as advice for living.

3:16 Long life is in her right hand; in her left hand are riches and honor.

This verse points out what Solomon himself learned firsthand (see 1 Kings 3:11). When one gains wisdom, the following items are also gained *quid pro quo*: wealth, longevity of life, fullness of life, and honor all come as part of the package deal.

3:17 Her ways are pleasant ways, and all her paths are peace.

Although fools cannot understand how her ways can be pleasant, the man who truly finds wisdom discovers a great pleasure. And how can internal peace be quantified or measured? Obviously, it cannot be measured; it can only be felt and demonstrated.

3:18 She is a tree of life to those who take hold of her, and happy are all who hold her fast.

The book of Genesis mentions another tree of life (Genesis 2:9). After the fall of Adam, God removed man from the garden so that he would not live forever (Genesis 3:22). God sent His Son (the "second Adam"—1 Corinthians 15:45–47) as a second "tree" of life. Wisdom is the path to life and relationship with God is the beginning of wisdom. Men pursue life and happiness, but few find it. The Bible reveals a step-by-step approach to find abundant life, true liberty, and genuine happiness.

To attain happiness, we must get our priorities aligned with God's priorities. Then we must hold on to these priorities, for the world, the evil one, and our own lusts will do everything possible to wrest them from our grasp.

3:19–20 The LORD by wisdom founded the earth; by understanding He established the heavens. By His knowledge the deeps were broken up, and the skies drip with dew.

How was the glory of creation accomplished? Notice how powerful God's wisdom, understanding, and knowledge are. "In the beginning was the *Logos* (word), and the *Logos* was with God, and the *Logos* was God. . . . All things came into being through Him" (John 1:1, 3).

3:21–22 My son, let them not depart from your sight; keep sound wisdom and discretion, so they will be life to your soul, and adornment to your neck.

30

Again we are exhorted to keep wisdom and discretion, both physically (around your neck) and spiritually ("life to your soul").

> 3:23–24 Then you will walk in your way securely, and your foot will not stumble. When you lie down, your sleep will be sweet.

Two metaphors are used here. Solomon refers once again to the "way." When we follow God's way, we will not stumble. We will walk securely. This metaphor seems to refer to our actions and decisions. When we walk God's way, our actions and decisions are done securely.

The second metaphor involves sleep. When we sleep, we can do so peacefully. This metaphor seems to refer to our attitudes, our beliefs, and the state of our minds. When we enter fully into God's "rest" (see Hebrews 4), we experience a sweetness that is truly beautiful. David expressed this idea in the 23rd Psalm when he noted that the Lord "leads me beside quiet waters, He restores my soul . . . I fear no evil." Of course, there is also literal truth to this as well. The person who walks with God and keeps His commandments will literally sleep well. His conscience will be clear, and his worries given over to the Lord. His "sleep will be sweet."

> 3:25–26 Do not be afraid of sudden fear, nor of the onslaught of the wicked when it comes; For the LORD will be your confidence, and will keep your foot from being caught!

Whom should I fear besides the Lord? David, the ultimate man of action, wrote, "The LORD is my light and my salvation; whom shall I fear?" (Psalm 27:1). But Proverbs 3:25 points out that the problem is not just *who* or *what* we fear, but our fear of fear itself. We must take God's promises, mix them with our faith, and rest.

Notice the phrase "when it comes." The onslaught of the wicked *will* come. The issue is twofold: 1) Will we fear it? and 2) Will we continue to trust in the sovereignty of God even after such an onslaught? If we maintain an eternal perspective and our confidence in God, we will not be shaken, and we will overcome! (See Romans 8:28; Revelation 3:21.)

> 3:27 Do not withhold good from those to whom it is due, when it is in your power to do it.

What does the phrase "to whom it is due" really mean? The translation team for the NASB point out that this phrase literally means "its owners." The primary Hebrew word used in this phrase is *ba-al,* which may mean master (or husband), owner, or lord (it is used with other nouns to modify them). When used as a proper noun, this is the same word for Baal, the Phoenician deity.

Here is a principle that can aid us in decision-making. When should you help people out? Ask yourself these two questions: 1) Do they deserve it? 2) Is it in my power to give it to them? If the answer to both of these questions is yes, then we *should* do good to them (e.g., as Boaz did for Ruth).

> 3:28 Do not say to your neighbor, "Go, and come back, and tomorrow I will give it," When you have it with you.

This verse provides a clear example of the principle of verse 27. If they deserve it, and if it is in your power to give it, then do so. Don't try to delay, obstruct, or scheme some bizarre plan. If the two criteria have been met, just help them out.

> 3:29–30 Do not devise harm against your neighbor, while he lives in security beside you. Do not contend with a man without cause, if he has done you no harm.

This is clear advice for dealing with your neighbor. Compare this instruction with that given by Jesus in Luke 10:29–37. In answer to the question "Who is my neighbor?" Jesus told the parable we now call the story of the good Samaritan.

Christians should never be the cause of strife. Because we live in a fallen world, there is plenty of strife without us causing more.

What possible motive could you have for devising harm against your neighbor? A common motive is prejudice. Whatever the motive is, it is not one of seeking glory for God. Put it aside, and seek ways to witness to your neighbor instead.

3:31 Do not envy a man of violence, and do not choose any of his ways.

Compare Psalm 73:1–3, 17–18, 27–28. Coveting is a sin, but it is also fraught with many natural consequences for those consumed by it. Even well-grounded Christians may find themselves influenced by envy. The solution is twofold: give it to God, and don't choose any of the violent man's ways. As Asaph discovered in Psalm 73, the secret is to maintain a perspective on the big picture from God's viewpoint. When you clearly "see" the end of anyone who does not walk with God, you will never have a problem with envying him again.

3:32 For the crooked man is an abomination to the LORD; but He is intimate with the upright.

One of the most evident contrasts between the upright man and the crooked man is that of relationship to Almighty God. God is intimate with the righteous. The word *intimate* refers to closeness and the sharing of secrets. The Hebrew word *cowd* implies a session together with someone. For those who are intimate with the Lord, such sessions may include receiving consultation, counseling, or the conveying of deep insights. The crooked man is not privy to such sessions.

By way of challenge, when was the last time you engaged in such a session with God? Seek intimacy with Him. As Jesus said, "Blessed are the pure in heart, for they shall see God" (Matthew 5:8).

3:33 The curse of the LORD is on the house of the wicked, but He blesses the dwelling of the righteous.

The polarities of blessing and cursing are often seen together throughout scripture. Cursing can come in the form of man cursing man (or things), man cursing God, or of God cursing man. Regarding man versus man, Jesus told us to "bless those who curse you" (Luke 6:28). Scripture also commands us, saying, "You shall not curse God" (Exodus 22:28). The most famous curse of the Bible is that of Genesis 3. Of this curse, Paul writes that we have been "redeemed . . . from the curse" (Galatians 3:13). This is the great tenet of Christianity: that Jesus has removed this curse from us by bearing its penalty in His own body.

By contrast, it is interesting to note that we may bless men, bless God, or be blessed by God. The prerequisite for obtaining the blessing of the Lord illustrated here in Proverbs 3:33 is to be righteous.

3:34 Though He scoffs at the scoffers, yet He gives grace to the afflicted.

Compare James 4:6–8 to this verse. The point James makes is that our goal ought to be that of drawing near to God. Pride is a serious hindrance to this goal.

The contrast of Proverbs 3:34 is between scoffers and the afflicted. According to the spiritual "law of reciprocity," you reap what you sow. Therefore, if you are a scoffer, you will be scoffed at (see also Psalm 2:4). Of the afflicted Jesus said, "Blessed are those who mourn, for they shall be comforted" (Matthew 5:4).

3:35 The wise will inherit honor, but fools display dishonor.

Honor is a very abstract concept. When we look for tangible ways to help us identify who is foolish and who is wise, one of the areas we may look at is genuine honor (although we must be careful to further distinguish between worldly honor and spiritual honor). Just as there exists cheap grace and costly grace (as Bonhoeffer defined them), there exists also cheap honor and costly honor. Any veteran who has lost a close friend in combat knows what costly honor is.

The aspect of contrast stated here involves a worthy inheritance that has been earned versus an inappropriate display. The contrast of the verse is obvious. A mere display is cheap. To live in such a way as to be worthy of an inheritance is often costly. But all this does not diminish the challenge, because which of us can say we have never displayed dishonor?

Failures should not lessen our resolve to stay on the path of God, to obey Him, and to seek His honor alone. One of the major lessons of Proverbs is that those who seek wisdom through relationship with God will indeed become wise, and that wisdom will allow them to eventually inherit honor.

Proverbs 4

4:1 Hear, O sons, the instruction of a father, and give attention that you may gain understanding,

*T*his verse mentions two methods for acquiring wisdom. First, we are directed to hear, and second we are instructed to give attention. To hear, or listen, means that first we must allow input. To give attention implies that we should seek ways to fully understand and apply what we have heard.

Note also that the verse is directed to "sons" in the plural. It may be possible to argue that Solomon intended his advice to be received only by his own biological heirs, but I personally do not believe this to be the case. I believe that Solomon knew he would have a much wider audience (and certainly the Holy Spirit intended it as such). I view his use of the term *sons* here (and the singular "son" elsewhere) as mere literary devices. The advice given is useful for all of us.

4:2–9 For I give you sound teaching; do not abandon my instruction. When I was a son to my father, tender and the only son in the sight of my mother, then he taught me and said to

me, "Let your heart hold fast my words; keep my commandments and live; acquire wisdom! Acquire understanding! Do not
forget, nor turn away from the words of my mouth. Do not forsake her, and she will guard you; love her, and she will watch
over you. The beginning of wisdom is: acquire wisdom; and with
all your acquiring, get understanding. Prize her, and she will
exalt you; she will honor you if you embrace her. She will place
on your head a garland of grace; she will present you with a
crown of beauty."

The advice of a loving, spiritual father is to be honored. For
Solomon it is part of a noble tradition. He received his wisdom
from God (as recorded in 1 Kings 3:11–14) but he received his
desire to acquire wisdom from the lessons and instruction of his
father, David. Now as an older man, he desires to share his wisdom
with others.

The key idea in this passage is "The beginning of wisdom is:
acquire wisdom." This advice is about having a heart open to receive wisdom and actively seeking it. It is about being willing to be
obedient to the requisite commands. In a word, it is about *attitude*.

To the Greeks of later years, education would be summed up
by the phrase "Know thyself." But to the ancient Hebrews, education could be summed up in the phrase "Know God." The first
step is fear of the Lord, and this leads to wisdom with branching
applications to all areas of life.

> 4:10 Hear, my son, and accept my sayings, and the years of your
> life will be many.

The promise of longevity is given if we accept the advice offered. This is similar to Proverbs 3:2, 16. Wisdom is directly concerned with life itself. Wisdom is about improving life, prolong-
ing life, and finding abundant life. At its deepest and most profound levels, wisdom is about leading us on the path that results
in eternal life.

4:11–12 I have directed you in the way of wisdom; I have led you in upright paths. When you walk, your steps will not be impeded; and if you run, you will not stumble.

God's wisdom is glorious and powerful. It is not the same as the world's wisdom. Yet it is *not* unobtainable. It can be acquired, because our loving Father wants to give it to us. Do you want it? "If any of you lack wisdom, let him ask of God . . . and it will be given to him" (James 1:5).

Do you feel your steps have been impeded in recent times? Study again the words of wisdom given in the first twelve verses of Proverbs 3. Heed that instruction, and the promise is given that you will not stumble.

4:13 Take hold of instruction; do not let go. Guard her, for she is your life.

Value instruction as you value your life, because instruction is one of the major conduits of wisdom, which preserves, enhances, and promotes life!

4:14 Do not enter the path of the wicked, and do not proceed in the way of evil men.

Choosing the right path is not a one-time decision. We are faced daily with the possibility of other paths. You can veer off the upright path at any time. The path of the wicked is offered to you frequently. We need to maintain and renew our commitments often. In this way we can walk the upright path. The psalmist has a valuable observation for us to consider as well: "Thy word is a lamp to my feet, and a light to my path" (Psalm 119:105).

To avoid entering the "path of the wicked" there are two necessary things. First we must be able to see clearly. The light of God's word provides such illumination. Second, we must continually choose the right path.

4:15 Avoid it, do not pass by it; turn away from it and pass on.

There is no fatalistic philosophy presented in the book of Proverbs. There are consequences, but there are always choices. We are presented frequently with images that illustrate our free will. Avoid the path of the wicked. You can! Keep the commandments, trust in God, fear Him and honor Him, and do not reject His discipline (see 3:1–12). You can avoid the path of the wicked.

It is a covenant relationship we enter into with God. Our job is to choose His path and then choose to remain on His path. If we do so, then He will be faithful to bring about all that He has promised along that path. Do you hesitate because you recognize your weakness? It is always His strength that enables us. Choose the right path and begin to walk. He will provide the strength to continue.

4:16 For they cannot sleep unless they do evil; and they are robbed of sleep unless they make someone stumble.

Two other verses (Psalm 36:4 and Micah 2:1) describe the premeditating act of planning evil while lying in bed, but this seems to be the only verse in scripture that describes someone who can't get to sleep because of undone evil.

When evil takes complete control of someone, the person surrenders more and more of his own free will. Such a person begins to yield more and more to stimulus, and his response is less and less filtered by thoughts and their innate morality. The man who does so becomes less and less of a man and behaviorally more conditionally controlled, like Pavlov's dogs.

4:17 For they eat the bread of wickedness, and drink the wine of violence.

From the time of Melchizedek, who shared bread and wine with Abram (Genesis 14:18) to the Last Supper and even into our current observation of communion, the metaphor of eating bread and drinking wine has symbolized commitment and unity. Usually it is presented as a positive image. Here it is a negative image, but it is still a picture of commitment and unity. In this instance it reveals commitment to evil and violence and a fellowship of wickedness.

> 4:18–19 But the path of the righteous is like the light of dawn, that shines brighter and brighter until the full day. The way of the wicked is like darkness; they do not know over what they stumble.

A strong contrast is made in this verse between the path of the righteous and that of the wicked. The poetic language makes this passage one of my favorite images to meditate on.

Our path is difficult. But as we tread, the details and potential stumbling blocks become more illuminated. The closer we get to God, the brighter shines the path.

> 4:20–21 My son, give attention to my words; incline your ear to my sayings. Do not let them depart from your sight; keep them in the midst of your heart.

Solomon repeatedly urges us to hear his advice and to incorporate it into the very fabric of our heart and lives.

> 4:22 For they are life to those who find them, and health to all their whole body.

Here Solomon provides an additional rationale for following his advice.

> 4:23–27 Watch over your heart with all diligence, for from it flow the springs of life. Put away from you a deceitful mouth, and put devious lips far from you. Let your eyes look directly ahead, and let your gaze be fixed straight in front of you. Watch

the path of your feet, and all your ways will be established. Do not turn to the right nor to the left; turn your foot from evil.

The chapter ends with several warnings and additional advice. Keep your heart pure (v. 23), your mouth clean (v. 24), and your eyes and feet on the path (vss. 25–27). Our attention must be vigilant and ever focused. The author of Hebrews offered similar advice. He instructed his readers to "lay aside every encumbrance, and the sin which so easily entangles us, and let us run with endurance the race that is set before us, fixing our eyes on Jesus, the author and perfecter of faith" (Hebrews 12:1–2).

This is truly advice for everyone throughout the eons of time.

Proverbs 5

5:1 My son, give attention to my wisdom, incline your ear to my understanding;

*T*he use of the phrase "My son" is a form of repetition. This phrase was used in 4:1, 10, and 20. Through this repetition, the reader is reminded of previous sessions of learning. The phrase "My son" is an endearing term and implies that the author has the reader's best interest at heart. The implication is, "Listen to me, not because I enjoy wagging my finger at you, but because I really do care about you, and I want the best for you."

This chapter contains "father-to-son" advice on sexual conduct. In fact, this chapter is an excellent text to use for sex education if you are a parent or an educator. The sex education training here is not biological, but moral. The three main motifs are 1) make love only to your own spouse (v. 15); 2) be aware that God sees all of your actions (v. 21); and 3) know that sexual sin will trap you (v. 22).

5:2 That you may observe discretion, and your lips may reserve knowledge.

Discretion involves the prudence to make wise decisions. When we behave foolishly, we may throw caution to the wind. The author's advice is that we should be cautious about establishing a relationship with anyone of questionable morals.

> 5:3–5 For the lips of an adulteress drip honey, and smoother than oil is her speech; but in the end she is bitter as wormwood, sharp as a two-edged sword. Her feet go down to death, her steps lay hold of Sheol.

An adulterous person can be both sweet and smooth. In human relationships these two qualities can be extremely powerful emotional and psychological stimuli. It is best to assimilate these words of advice *before* we are placed in a compromising position. When we foresee the end results, it is then easier to resist possible temptations. If we wait until we are in the situation, the sweetness and smoothness may overcome us.

Solomon compares the adulteress to wormwood. What is wormwood? It is an aromatic plant also known as *Artemisia* that yields a bitter extract used to make absinthe, which is a green, bitter, toxic liqueur. Wormwood was regarded as poisonous. The adulterous woman may smell good, but her bite is deadly! In ancient times wormwood may have been considered synonymous with hemlock, which the Greek philosopher Socrates used in his "suicidal" execution. (Of course Solomon wrote these words many years before this event.)

> 5:6 She does not ponder the path of life; her ways are unstable, she does not know it.

Do you ponder the path of your life? This is one of the major differences between fools and those who walk wisely. At the root of sin is self-deception, which is the fuel of pride and selfishness. Decision-making based on self-deceptive beliefs is inherently flawed because of false assumptions. The antithesis of self-deception is the fear of God.

44

The phrase "She does not know it" reveals a great deal about the mind of many sinners. This is a very insightful remark about the mind of a habitual sinner, who has given up his once reasoning mind to his now reactive and depraved mind.

> 5:7–14 Now then, my sons, listen to me, and do not depart from the words of my mouth. Keep your way far from her, and do not go near the door of her house, lest you give your vigor to others, and your years to the cruel one; lest strangers be filled with your strength, and your hard-earned goods go to the house of an alien; and you groan at your latter end, when your flesh and your body are consumed; and you say, "How I have hated instruction! And my heart spurned reproof! And I have not listened to the voice of my teachers, nor inclined my ear to my instructors! I was almost in utter ruin in the midst of the assembly and congregation."

This passage expounds several reasons to avoid an adulterous relationship. Solomon points out that physical energy, financial hardship, health problems (e.g., disease), mental anguish, and social acceptance are some of the areas of life affected by these relationships. His point is simple and clear. If you do not heed the advice, you will definitely regret it someday.

Verses 15–23 use several illustrations about water to describe the proper setting for physical intimacy.

> 5:15 Drink water from your own cistern, and fresh water from your own well.

A cistern is a large tank for storing water. Notice that it is *your* cistern. This ownership is brought about through the shared commitment of marriage. A cistern is large, and all of your needs for intimacy can be provided for through a marriage partner. There is no need to seek sex outside of marriage.

5:16–17 Should your springs be dispersed abroad, streams of water in the streets? Let them be yours alone, and not for strangers with you.

The rhetorical question "Should your streams of water be dispersed abroad?" asks us to ponder the possible action and consequences of physical union with multiple partners. The question is, what can be gained? The answer is, nothing!

5:18 Let your fountain be blessed, and rejoice in the wife of your youth.

Your fountain is where your water is. In this case the metaphor refers to sexual intimacy. Your fountain can be blessed or cursed. Choose blessing by choosing to be faithful to your spouse. But don't just be faithful, *rejoice* also in your love. Let your focus be on the good things in your relationship.

5:19 As a loving hind and a graceful doe, let her breasts satisfy you at all times;

This verse is probably not the one your Sunday school teachers had you memorize as a child, but there are several things we can learn from it. First, we can understand that God invented sex. There is nothing wrong with the beautiful union of a man and a woman. However, the clear position of scripture is that this union should happen only in the context of marriage. Passionate love for your spouse should be maintained and renewed continually. If a man is "intoxicated" by his own wife, why would he even look at another woman longingly? This type of intoxication is very valuable in helping to maintain our marital vows. [Note: The word "hind" is simply a metaphorical reference to a female deer.]

5:20 For why should you, my son, be exhilarated with an adulteress, and embrace the bosom of a foreigner?

46

The question offered by this verse has no good answer. It functions rhetorically to reemphasize a man's need to love only his own spouse.

5:21 For the ways of a man are before the eyes of the LORD, and He watches all his paths.

If you think you can lead a double life and get away with it, you are dead wrong. A life of purity is pleasing to God, and He will know whether or not you are pure.

5:22–23 His own iniquities will capture the wicked, and he will be held with the cords of his sin. He will die for lack of instruction, and in the greatness of his folly he will go astray.

The consequences of sexual immorality are not only spiritual in nature. Some of the natural consequences include disease, unwanted pregnancies, emotional distress, and other "cords" that trap and bind those who are involved.

Proverbs 6

6:1–5 My son, if you have become surety for your neighbor, have given a pledge for a stranger, if you have been snared with the words of your mouth, have been caught with the words of your mouth, do this then, my son, and deliver yourself; since you have come into the hand of your neighbor, go, humble yourself, and importune your neighbor. Do not give sleep to your eyes, nor slumber to your eyelids; deliver yourself like a gazelle from the hunter's hand, and like a bird from the hand of the fowler.

Don't put your financial fate into the hands of others. To "humble yourself" in this context means you should not let pride keep you from rectifying a huge mistake. Solomon's advice to "allow no sleep to your eyes" suggests that you take financial matters seriously and that you should attempt to fix the problem *now*. It also implies that you should not hesitate when you realize in your heart you were wrong. Don't wait and see how things go for a while. The advice to "deliver yourself like a gazelle" suggests that you realize the danger you are in and flee from it.

This advice may seem a bit extreme to some readers. You may ask, "What is wrong with helping friends and family members out

a bit?" Consider, however, this idea: if you become financially ru-
ined, you will cease to be able to help anybody out, and you yourself may become the one begging others to become surety for you.
Search hard and ask yourself, is there a way to help without becoming surety? Usually there is a way. It may not be what the other
person *wants,* but often it is actually what the other person *needs!*
Remember also that helping others has many facets and layers. If
you can help them grow, mature, and develop their own credibility, these intangibles will eventually outweigh the specific tangibles
of the current situation. Helping others to grow spiritually always
trumps helping them on a superficial level.

> 6:6–8 Go to the ant, O sluggard, observe her ways and be
> wise, which, having no chief, officer or ruler, prepares her
> food in the summer, and gathers her provisions in the harvest.

Although these verses are addressed to a sluggard, Solomon is
actually addressing all his readers in the hope that they will learn
vicariously from the mistakes of others and, in fact, avoid ever becoming a sluggard. It is an interesting teaching technique. With a
similar suggestion, the French philosopher Henri Bergson urges us
to "think like a man of action, and act like a man of thought."

What can we learn from observing ants? They work steadily
and they store up food during times of plenty (summer) to help
get them through times of struggle (winter).

Is this idea at odds with Jesus' teaching in the Sermon on the
Mount when He directs us to "not be anxious . . . as to what you
shall eat" (Matthew 6:25)? Do planning and preparation nullify
our faith in God's ability to provide for us? Perhaps the question
should be stated thus: Does faith in God mean that we should not
work hard, plan, and prepare for hard times? A balanced Christian
will make plans, work hard, *and* rely fully on God.

> 6:9–11 How long will you lie down, O sluggard? When will you
> arise from your sleep? "A little sleep, a little slumber, a little

folding of the hands to rest"—And your poverty will come in like a vagabond, and your need like an armed man.

Do you love sleep? Does it control you? Inmates on death row sleep an average of 15–16 hours per day! What is associated here with excessive sleep? Solomon's rationale for us to not be overly enamored with sleep is stated clearly for us, because sleep is associated with laziness. The metaphors about the vagabond and the armed man are quite interesting. The former is sly and sneaky while the latter is violent and forceful. Poverty can sneak up on you, or sometimes take you by force. Solomon's point is that it need not be so if you maintain diligence and a strong work ethic.

6:12 A worthless person, a wicked man, is the one who walks with a false mouth,

In this passage we read of a definition of a worthless and wicked person. What does the phrase about walking with a false mouth mean? Having a false mouth may include bragging, being a false witness, lying, or any form of insincerity. We may apply this verse in two ways. First, by contrast, we ought to strive to live genuinely and with integrity. Second, in the area of discernment as to the worthlessness and wickedness of others, our guidepost is their mouths, for the mouth is a window to the heart.

6:13 Who winks with his eyes, who signals with his feet, who points with his fingers;

Obviously this verse needs to be seen in the context of verses 12 and 14. I have included it here alone because it may be helpful to analyze the "body language" of a worthless person and a wicked man.

First, let's look at the phrase "who winks with his eye." Proverbs 10:10 states that eye winkers cause trouble. Psalm 35:19 refers to a malicious wink. This may also refer to the secretly insincere signal a con man gives you, trying to make you think you're actually getting a great deal. The Hebrew word used here for winking is *qarats* (pronounced kaw-rats'). It may mean to pinch as one would pinch off a piece of clay. It may also mean to bite the lips or to blink an eye in a gesture of malice. To me it implies the typical salesman gimmick: "I shouldn't be letting you have this product for this price, but you seem like a really great person, so . . . (wink, wink)." You are the clay, and you are the one getting pinched!

What does it mean to signal (or literally, "scrape") with one's feet ? While it is speculative hermeneutics, imagine this. Somebody drops a coin. A guy covers it with his foot instead of saying out loud, "Oh look, here it is." Or perhaps you should consider this situation. You're harvesting a crop, and this fellow walks by. He's the one who tries to nonchalantly slide some good food off with his feet so he can get some freebies. Basically, he's a weasel who tries to take whatever he can get without working or paying for it.

Finally we get a third image of this type of fellow. He "points with his fingers." Here he is again, saying, "Look over there!" As soon as you turn to look, he's stealing you blind behind your back.

6:14 Who with perversity in his heart devises evil continually, who spreads strife.

This is a summary of the internal functioning of the "worthless and wicked" person first mentioned in verse 12. He is perverse, which means that he is "obstinately disobedient"[1] and deviates from what is considered right or good. The perversity is in his heart. It is not just a head thing. The heart is the seat of one's beliefs and values as well as the center of one's will. A perverse person is a schemer. He dreams of get-rich-quick schemes and he doesn't care who gets hurt in the process. He devises evil continually. This is not a one-time deal, or even accidental. This is premeditated and planned evil, and the natural consequence of evil is strife.

6:15 Therefore his calamity will come suddenly; instantly he will be broken, and there will be no healing.

Our lesson here is threefold: 1) don't become a worthless and wicked person yourself; 2) learn how to identify others who are worthless and wicked so you can be cautious around them; and 3) don't despair when you see them. Don't stoop to their level by trying to scheme their demise; just realize that their end will come soon and it will be severely calamitous (compare Romans 12:17, 19).

> 6:16–19 There are six things which the LORD hates, yes, seven which are an abomination to Him: haughty eyes, a lying tongue, and hands that shed innocent blood, a heart that devises wicked plans, feet that run rapidly to evil, a false witness who utters lies, and one who spreads strife among brothers.

The consecutive number technique ("six things . . . yes, seven") seems to be a cultural method for stylistically presenting a list in order to make a point. It is similar to a form of poetry not unlike modern cinquains. Agur was also very fond of this technique (for a comparison, see Proverbs 30:7–8, 15–29).

The list of abominable things is universal, meaning it is multicultural and applicable to all generations. If you compare this list to the Ten Commandments, you may observe that the lists are *very* similar. The Ten Commandments are frequently viewed as having two parts: a vertical (man-to-God) part, and a horizontal (man-to-man) part. These things listed here are from the horizontal part.

> 6:20–21 My son, observe the commandment of your father, and do not forsake the teaching of your mother; bind them continually on your heart; tie them around your neck.

At the most basic level, to honor your father and mother means to make them happy. Compare Proverbs 3:1–3. Simply put, remember their lessons.

6:22–23 When you walk about, they will guide you; when you sleep, they will watch over you; and when you awake, they will talk to you. For the commandment is a lamp, and the teaching is light; and reproofs for discipline are the way of life,

These are the key verses of this chapter. We must learn and grow if we are to become wise. No one is without flaw, but we must still understand that bumbling through life, making mistake after mistake, is not the path of wisdom. The answer is to fear God, keep His commandments (which, ideally, were taught to you by your father), and walk a disciplined life. Here is an interesting point of meditation. Can you see any connection between these verses and Jesus' statement that we should be "perfect" in Matthew 5:48?

6:24–29 To keep you from the evil woman, from the smooth tongue of the adulteress. Do not desire her beauty in your heart, nor let her catch you with her eyelids. For on account of a harlot one is reduced to a loaf of bread, and an adulteress hunts for the precious life. Can a man take fire in his bosom, and his clothes not be burned? Or can a man walk on hot coals, and his feet not be scorched? So is the one who goes in to his neighbor's wife; whoever touches her will not go unpunished.

The theme of this passage is summed up in the cliché, "You can't play with fire and not get burned." The commands and teachings and reproofs are for guidance along the paths of life so that we may truly live abundant lives.

Consider the phrase "Do not desire her beauty in your heart." Contrary to pop songs that state things such as "You can't control your heart," the Bible tells us otherwise. In fact, the "heart" *is* the seat of choice and our will.

I love the metaphor Solomon used here: "Reduced to a loaf of bread." If you have ever known anyone in a state of infatuation and puppy lust, you know that this is an apt description. Not only is bread senseless, but it is easily and quickly consumed. Even if it is not completely consumed, the rest of it soon becomes stale, just as adulterous relationships do.

> 6:30–31 Men do not despise a thief if he steals to satisfy himself when he is hungry; but when he is found, he must repay seven-fold; he must give all the substance of his house.

Victor Hugo's *Les Miserables* introduces a desperate man who steals bread for his starving family as a way of introducing the reasons for the French Revolution. Solomon is not saying that it is right, he is simply pointing out that the scenario is understandable. His teaching here is via contrast. If the bread stealer (a relatively minor crime) is caught, he must still repay seven times the value of the bread, even if he must sell all his possessions. His point is, how much more will you lose if you become involved in an adulterous affair?

> 6:32–35 The one who commits adultery with a woman is lacking sense; he who would destroy himself does it. Wounds and disgrace he will find, and his reproach will not be blotted out. For jealousy enrages a man and he will not spare in the day of vengeance. He will not accept any ransom, nor will he be content though you give many gifts.

In the eyes of God, any sin is sin. James says, "Whoever keeps the whole law and yet stumbles in one point, he has become guilty of all" (James 2:10). However, in the eyes of men, there does seem to be a hierarchy of sins. That is, some things do seem to be worse than others. This is a human point of view, but adultery certainly is a very grave sin.

Adultery is sad because it can hurt children by ruining their lives. Adultery is stupid because it will not bring happiness. It will only bring destruction to spousal relationships. Adultery is one of the most dangerous things one can engage in, because a jealous spouse is unpredictable in his or her anger. Money does not and cannot solve all problems, and it is absurd to think that money can in any way solve the problems brought about by adultery. The only solution is to avoid it in the first place.

Proverbs 7

7:1–5 My son, keep my words, and treasure my commandments within you. Keep my commandments and live, and my teaching as the apple of your eye. Bind them on your fingers; write them on the tablet of your heart. Say to wisdom, "You are my sister," and call understanding your intimate friend; that they may keep you from an adulteress, from the foreigner who flatters with her words.

*L*et us look at the phrase "As the apple of your eye." This figure of speech is often used in a context of hope in the Old Testament writings. To be the apple of the Lord's eye is to exist in a state of guarded blessedness—guarded because of His protection and blessed because of His compassion and grace.

Zechariah wrote regarding the people of God, "Whatever touches you, touches the apple of His eye" (Zechariah 2:8). David's Psalm 17 records one of the great testimonies of faith in our resurrection. This is a prayerful psalm that includes several references to the Messiah (the "right hand of God"). In this context David prays for God to keep him as "the apple of His eye" (v. 8).

The main idea to remember here is to value the commandments and wisdom. Compare 6:20–22.

7:6–23 For at the window of my house I looked out through my lattice, and I saw among the naive, I discerned among the youths, a young man lacking sense, passing through the street near her corner; and he takes the way to her house, in the twilight, in the evening, in the middle of the night and in the darkness. And behold, a woman comes to meet him, dressed as a harlot and cunning of heart. She is boisterous and rebellious; her feet do not remain at home; she is now in the streets, now in the squares, and lurks by every corner. So she seizes him and kisses him, and with a brazen face she says to him:

"I was due to offer peace offerings; today I have paid my vows. Therefore I have come out to meet you, to seek your presence earnestly, and I have found you. I have spread my couch with coverings, with colored linens of Egypt. I have sprinkled my bed with myrrh, aloes and cinnamon. Come, let us drink our fill of love until morning; let us delight ourselves with caresses. For the man is not at home, he has gone on a long journey; He has taken a bag of money with him, at full moon he will come home."

With her many persuasions she entices him; with her flattering lips she seduces him. Suddenly he follows her, as an ox goes to the slaughter, or as one in fetters to the discipline of a fool, until an arrow pierces through his liver; as a bird hastens to the snare, so he does not know that it will cost him his life.

It is with a knowing concern that Solomon observed this young man as an ox on his way to the slaughter. While the story may merely be hypothetical, I get the feeling as I read it that Solomon actually observed a real young man, and this observation triggered (through the power of the Holy Spirit) his ruminations regarding the outcomes of such behavior. We all know people who have chosen the wrong path. We often see them on the path, and we intuitively know (or at least suspect) the ultimate outcome. How sorrowful we become. Solomon summarizes the end result in verse 23: "He does not know that it will cost him his life."

The young man is described as "lacking sense" (v. 7). He is confronted with numerous overt warnings, all of which he ignores. When we ignore the call of the voice of wisdom there are severe consequences.

The process of decision-making here is worth consideration. In verse 8 we read, "He takes the way to her home." This is a mental decision with physical consequences. He chooses to allow himself to be tempted. He is still thinking, and he is still able to reason, and he makes a choice. Verse 22 illustrates a different type of decision. It says, "Suddenly he follows her." Here we see the thinking and rational process discontinued. This represents an emotional and physical response. This behavioral decision has spiritual consequences. His will has evaporated. In point of fact, it may be argued as to whether or not such an act is a decision or merely a response to stimulus. B. F. Skinner would claim that this situation proves his determinism and behaviorist ideas. It does not. Skinner attempts to apply behaviorism to all areas of life. But the Bible clearly teaches that man has free will and choice. Nevertheless, one of man's choices is to place himself in poor situations and even to temporarily suspend choice. In such a state of being, a man exists more as an animal and less as a man. Normally a man has reason. Normally man has internal conscience. Paul calls this dissipated state of conscience a "depraved mind" (Romans 1:2).

What shall we say of the adulterous woman? Notice her hypocritical view of religious rituals. She has "paid [her] vows" and this has atoned for her actions (in her mind). She has no true relationship with God. Making the peace offering is her way of maintaining social acceptance.

Solomon's vivid portrait of a young man going as an "ox to the slaughter" serves as a sobering reminder of his earlier advice and the words of Paul that the "wages of sin is death" (Romans 6:23).

7:24–27 Now therefore, my sons, listen to me, and pay attention to the words of my mouth. Do not let your heart turn aside to her ways, do not stray into her paths, for many are the victims she has cast down, and numerous are all her slain. Her house is the way to Sheol, descending to the chambers of death.

Solomon repeats the warning yet again. If you view man as a mere animal, then you view sex as only a natural function with no other implications. But if you view man as Genesis presents him, as the crowning creature of God's creation, then you realize that sex is a precious gift and that it involves bonding in many aspects of life that are beyond the physical alone.

I feel that no further comment I could make here can make Solomon's warning more clear!

Proverbs 8

8:1–7 Does not wisdom call, and understanding lift up her voice? On top of the heights beside the way, where the paths meet, she takes her stand; beside the gates, at the opening to the city, at the entrance of the doors, she cries out: "To you, O men, I call, and my voice is to the sons of men. O naive ones, discern prudence; and, O fools, discern wisdom. Listen, for I shall speak noble things; and the opening of my lips will produce right things. For my mouth will utter truth; and wickedness is an abomination to my lips."

Can you hear the voice of wisdom? In what ways does wisdom call? Wisdom calls and her voice can be heard everywhere. Those who listen will be rewarded with prudence, wisdom, nobility, truth, morality, and knowledge. Wisdom can enhance anyone's life, whether wise or fool. Anyone who listens and heeds will benefit.

8:8–9 "All the utterances of my mouth are in righteousness; there is nothing crooked or perverted in them. They are all straightforward to him who understands, and right to those who find knowledge."

Righteousness is foundational to all true wisdom. There is a huge element of morality contained in the Biblical concept of wisdom. Words of wisdom are straightforward to those who understand. To those who do not understand (meaning that they do not see life from God's perspective), words of wisdom may seem weird or invalid.

> 8:10–11 "Take my instruction, and not silver, and knowledge rather than choicest gold. For wisdom is better than jewels; and all desirable things cannot compare with her."

This is the key verse of this section. I like the way the NIV reads for this verse: "Choose my instruction instead of silver, knowledge rather than choice gold, for wisdom is more precious than rubies, and nothing you desire can compare with her."

How does this passage relate to Jesus' Sermon on the Mount and the directives he gave regarding treasures and worries? If you need to refresh your memory, see Matthew 6:19–34.

> 8:12 "I, wisdom, dwell with prudence, and I find knowledge and discretion."

Wisdom describes herself here by identifying other qualities that she associates with. The ideas of discretion and prudence imply the ability to make fine distinctions and a capacity for judging in advance the likely results of a particular action. These elements are essential for wise decision-making and righteous living.

> 8:13 "The fear of the LORD is to hate evil; pride and arrogance and the evil way, and the perverted mouth, I hate."

There is a reason why "the fear of the LORD is the beginning of wisdom" (Proverbs 9:10). The fear of the Lord comes through being in His presence and realizing His genuine greatness, awesomeness, love, mercy, and holiness. Such an experience can, and in fact must, change us and our perspective on all of life. Only through God's love can we love the way He loves (see I John 4:19). This verse offers a fascinating definition to the concept of fearing the Lord. As we are in His presence we learn also to hate the things He hates. This too is the voice of wisdom.

> 8:14–21 "Counsel is mine and sound wisdom; I am understanding, power is mine. By me kings reign, and rulers decree justice. By me princes rule, and nobles, all who judge rightly. I love those who love me; and those who diligently seek me will find me. Riches and honor are with me, enduring wealth and righteousness. My fruit is better than gold, even pure gold, and my yield than choicest silver. I walk in the way of righteousness, in the midst of the paths of justice, to endow those who love me with wealth, that I may fill their treasuries."

The value and many uses of wisdom are explored in this passage. Wisdom is speaking here, but it is not the wisdom of men (see 1 Corinthians 2:5), it is the wisdom of God. As such it is also the voice of God. When we "hear" the voice of wisdom, it is an opportunity to receive specific revelation from God.

But here is a problem, for throughout history, even evil men have claimed to be listening to the voice of God. How can we discern the difference between the voice of true wisdom and our own thoughts and desires? This passage gives us some of the elements needed to perform such a litmus test. The basic test, as always, is motive. Are we seeking God Himself, righteousness, and justice and then placing wealth, riches, and blessing in His hands? Or are we seeking riches and wealth or fame or whatever on our own, and within our own time frame (i.e., usually *now*)?

Read Matthew 6:33 to see what Jesus said we should be seeking.

> 8:22–31 "The LORD possessed me at the beginning of His way, before His works of old. From everlasting I was established, from the beginning, from the earliest times of the earth. When there were no depths I was brought forth, when there were no

springs abounding with water. Before the mountains were settled, before the hills I was brought forth; while He had not yet made the earth and the fields, nor the first dust of the world. When He established the heavens, I was there, when He inscribed a circle on the face of the deep, when He made firm the skies above, when the springs of the deep became fixed, when He set for the sea its boundary, so that the water should not transgress His command, when He marked out the foundations of the earth; then I was beside Him, as a master workman; and I was daily His delight, rejoicing always before Him, rejoicing in the world, His earth, and having my delight in the sons of men."

The point of this passage is that wisdom was a crucial and integral part of the creation process. God first "brought forth" wisdom, and then wisdom was one of the tools of creation.

As an interesting side, it is worth noting that not all people in ancient times thought the earth was flat! At least one way of looking at Solomon's usage of the Hebrew *chuwg*—which means circle, circuit, or compass—to describe the earth and the oceans is that he understood the earth to be round or circular.

It is also valuable to consider what wisdom rejoices in. Wisdom rejoices in being used by God, being in the presence of God, seeing the world (i.e., nature) as He sees it, and also rejoicing in humanity ("the sons of men"). In these four things we should certainly imitate wisdom.

> 8:32–36 "Now therefore, O sons, listen to me, for blessed are they who keep my ways. Heed instruction and be wise, and do not neglect it. Blessed is the man who listens to me, watching daily at my gates, waiting at my doorposts. For he who finds me finds life, and obtains favor from the LORD. But he who sins against me injures himself; all those who hate me love death."

Solomon closes out this section by restating some of the wonderful blessings to be found by heeding the voice of wisdom.

In this passage, verse 36 contains an interesting statement: "He who sins against me injures himself." Normally we think of the word *sin* in the context of relationship to God. Here it is used in the context of wisdom, as if we can sin directly against wisdom. Biblically, "sin" is not following a command. It is a form of rebellion and disobedience. Sin against God results in death (Genesis 2:17 and Romans 6:23). Death is separation. Thus physical death is separation from physical life as we know it, and spiritual death is separation from the Giver of Life. In this case, when we "sin" against wisdom, the result is self-injury because of our separation from wisdom. This is contrasted with verse 35, which states, "He who finds me finds life."

Proverbs 9

In this chapter Solomon summarizes the key themes of the previous eight chapters. The primary theme remains—"The fear of the LORD is the beginning of wisdom." The rest of the chapter addresses the notable differences between wisdom and folly.

Chapter 9 is the last chapter of Solomon's wisdom speech, and the subsequent chapters change dramatically in style.

9:1 Wisdom has built her house, she has hewn out her seven pillars;

The metaphorical phrase about seven pillars is very enigmatic. What does it actually mean? Perhaps it means that there are seven levels of wisdom. Or perhaps it refers to differing aspects of creation (as the verb *hewn* might be interpreted). We noted in 8:22–30 that wisdom played an integral part in the act of creation and there were seven days in the creation process. Perhaps he is referring to seven pillars in the temple he built. I could find nothing to confirm this idea. In fact, it appears to me that the temple had two main pillars, but I am not a temple scholar.

Another way of looking at it is that perhaps Solomon is just pointing out how foundational wisdom is *in everything*. Wisdom holds up the entire structure of our beliefs. Wisdom operates in the spiritual, psychological, and physical realm of our existence. These pillars have been "hewn" implying they are cut, shaped, and placed in position, and then built upon.

Paul applied a similar metaphor to Jesus Christ when he wrote that He was the "cornerstone" (Ephesians 2:20). Isaiah prophesied: "Thus says the LORD God, 'Behold, I am laying in Zion a stone, a tested stone, a costly cornerstone for the foundation, firmly placed. He who believes in it will not be disturbed'" (Isaiah 28:16).

It is my belief that scripture is intended to be useful to those who seek God, even if it is not always fully understood. However, I also think that God has placed mysterious passages in His word to challenge us perpetually. Ultimately, "His ways are not our ways," and He is bigger, greater, and beyond our ability to fully comprehend.

I may never know what the "seven pillars" really are, but I know that wisdom is invaluable!

> 9:2–6 She has prepared her food, she has mixed her wine; she has also set her table; she has sent out her maidens, she calls from the tops of the heights of the city: "Whoever is naive, let him turn in here!"

> To him who lacks understanding she says, "Come, eat of my food, and drink of the wine I have mixed. Forsake your folly and live, and proceed in the way of understanding."

Wisdom has prepared a feast and a wonderful banquet. A grand party is ready and waiting. The irony is that fools believe wisdom to be dull and the enemy of fun and good times. Nothing could be further from the truth. Many live their entire lives with untrue or half-true assumptions. Wisdom sends out messengers; she calls diligently, loudly, and from the highest points of the city. Even though men will invent numerous reasons, there is simply no valid reason not to heed the call.

9:7–9 He who corrects a scoffer gets dishonor for himself, and he who reproves a wicked man gets insults for himself. Do not reprove a scoffer, lest he hate you; reprove a wise man, and he will love you. Give instruction to a wise man, and he will be still wiser; teach a righteous man, and he will increase his learning.

Correction and reproof are painful but necessary aspects if we are to learn. Do you *want* to *learn?* A scoffer does not. A wise man wants to learn, and herein lies the deepest contrast. What does a wise son do with his father's discipline? What does a scoffing son do with his father's discipline? The scoffing son simply doesn't listen while the wise son "accepts his father's discipline" (Proverbs 13:1).

Proverbs 14:6 points out that "a scoffer seeks wisdom, and finds none." This is because he does not *really* seek wisdom. A scoffer is by definition someone who laughs at wisdom. For him to claim to seek wisdom is an oxymoron. The scoffer may say he wants to learn, but first an internal change must take place in his heart. He needs an attitude adjustment, and he must learn to love the one who is correcting him. There is a huge difference between actually learning and accepting truth and just saying you want to learn. Talk is cheap, especially when change is costly.

The actual warning of this verse is not for scoffers, but for those of us who deal with scoffers.

9:10 The fear of the LORD is the beginning of wisdom, and the knowledge of the Holy One is understanding.

This is the primary theme, the key verse, not only for this chapter but also for the entire first nine chapters of the book of Proverbs. These chapters are labeled by some writers as Solomon's wisdom speech. Solomon began his speech with the theme of fearing God (Proverbs 1:7), and now he concludes his speech with this same motif.

9:11–12 For by me your days will be multiplied, and years of life
will be added to you. If you are wise, you are wise for yourself,
and if you scoff, you alone will bear it.

The principle of reciprocity (reaping what you sow) is hinted
at here via two contrasting ways of living one's life. On one hand,
we may choose to live with wisdom, which brings the acquisition of other rewards. On the other hand, being a mocker is associated with personal suffering that has been brought about by
compounded negative consequences. Because this is a summary
statement of the previous nine chapters, more specific details are
not needed here. We merely need to review the prior eight chapters to see numerous examples.

What are we to make of the phrase "If you are wise, you are
wise for yourself"? What a precious and fascinating commodity
is this thing called wisdom. You may acquire it, you may use it,
you may share it (in a sense), but you cannot just *give* it to someone. A wise father may attempt to teach his wisdom to his son,
but the son may reject it! Wisdom is a very personal possession.
Obviously we may attempt to share it and teach it to others. But
if you are dealing with a scoffer and a fool, by definition, they
will not want to learn it.

Now let us look at the next phrase, "If you scoff, you alone will
bear it." Nowhere is this more evident than in the area of salvation.
In the context of verse 10—"the fear of the LORD is the beginning of
wisdom"—the implication is that this fear of the Lord is a part of
faith. The issue, then, is one of life and death. Again, it is very personal. None of us can pass *our* relationship with God on to another
human being. Whether we are wise or whether we scoff, our relationship with God is our own.

9:13–18 The woman of folly is boisterous, she is naive, and
knows nothing. And she sits at the doorway of her house, on a
seat by the high places of the city, calling to those who pass
by, who are making their paths straight: "Whoever is naive, let

him turn in here," and to him who lacks understanding she says, "Stolen water is sweet; and bread eaten in secret is pleasant."

But he does not know that the dead are there, that her guests are in the depths of Sheol.

Solomon takes one last opportunity to warn us about Mistress Folly. Just as Lady Wisdom beckons to us, so too does Mistress Folly. Who will you heed? The choice is yours.

Some people go into a life of crime, not so much for the money, but more for the thrill of the adrenaline rush. Perhaps they crave the challenge of the test to see if they can "beat the system." For these people, it is sweet. But as verse 18 points out, they are on the path of death (see also Proverbs 10:2).

Proverbs 10

10:1 The proverbs of Solomon. A wise son makes a father glad, but a foolish son is a grief to his mother.

Our goals and decisions bring joy or sorrow to those who love and care for us. Wisdom and foolishness are relational. These characteristics do not demonstrate themselves in a vacuum. They influence our relationships with those around us.

Besides reaping the personal benefits of wisdom for ourselves, this verse points out another beautiful reason for seeking to live according to the path of God's wisdom. It is a wonderful way of honoring your father and mother. Therefore, Solomon begins with the logical beginning point for contrasting the wise and the foolish, by looking at our children as they grow into adulthood. Wisdom and foolishness are not "preprogrammed" into us at birth; we may develop along either path. But as always, we will be able to see both types of individuals around us.

10:2–3 Ill-gotten gains do not profit, but righteousness delivers from death. The LORD will not allow the righteous to hunger, but He will thrust aside the craving of the wicked.

These verses have an interesting syntactic structure. Verse 2 states the general principle while verse 3 gives a precise example. In verse 2 we read of "righteousness" while in verse 3 we read of "the righteous."

The motifs of Proverbs 9:17–18 are continued and expanded upon here. There are three basic ideas: Crime doesn't pay. God will provide for your needs, if you are righteous. If you are wicked, your needs will become increasingly amplified, and they will become addictions, or cravings.

> 10:4–5 Poor is he who works with a negligent hand, but the hand of the diligent makes rich. He who gathers in summer is a son who acts wisely, but he who sleeps in harvest is a son who acts shamefully.

Diligence is a part of good stewardship. These verses echo the theme of honoring one's parents by giving an empirical example. Is the action of sleeping during a harvest an act of irresponsibility or one of laziness? While both of these factors may be at work, the implication is that it is actually an act of defiance. This is an excellent example of how wisdom often is actually a simple choice between selfishness and being other-centered.

When contrasted with the son who gathers, we understand that the shameful son *could* have acted wisely but that he *chose* to act shamefully.

> 10:6 Blessings are on the head of the righteous, but the mouth of the wicked conceals violence.

This presents an unusual contrast between the blessings of the righteous and the concealing words of the wicked. Perhaps we can simplify it this way: The wicked are attempting to cover their tracks. To do this, they must lie frequently. But during this process, they do not grow, they do not help others in any way, and in fact, they do not help themselves in any way. There is nothing constructive going on because all they can do is attempt to cover their violence. Meanwhile, the righteous continue to do their righteous deeds, not to gain something, but just because it is who they *are,* and the blessings continue to stack up. Once again, we can see the familiar principle of reciprocity at work.

10:7 The memory of the righteous is blessed, but the name of the wicked will rot.

If you were composing the words you would want engraved on your own tombstone, what would you write? To think about your life, its value and meaning, and what you would like to remain after you're gone is a process that bears its own innate value. This is what good existential thinking is about.

Decide what you want your life to stand for, and begin to pray now that God will use you and work in and through you to be a blessing to Him and others, even after you have become "just a memory." This is what the book of Ecclesiastes is really about.

10:8 The wise of heart will receive commands, but a babbling fool will be thrown down.

This verse suggests numerous images. Think of a soldier who follows directions versus one who chooses to ignore an order. Imagine a businessman who accepts the directive of the factory who manufactures the products he sells versus the businessman who insists upon his own way, and thus loses the future contract. This verse compares the *doer* to the *talker.*

Talk is cheap, but the chattering fool may not realize it until he is brought to ruin. Sadly, most of these chattering fools do not realize it even then. They prefer to rant and rave about karma, bad luck, lousy workers or partners, etc. Some people choose to live a pattern of blame, and they may never truly analyze their own shortcomings.

10:9 He who walks in integrity walks securely, but he who perverts his ways will be found out.

The principle of this verse is important for all of us to keep in mind at all times. Integrity cannot be bought. It must be a daily commitment. Keep it like a precious gem, for once it is tarnished it is all but impossible to erase it from the memories of others.

10:10 He who winks the eye causes trouble, and a babbling fool will be thrown down.

Remember Proverbs 6:13 and Psalm 35:19? This time, the winking imagery seems to be a warning to us to be careful around people who try to talk us into things. Those get-rich-quick or immoral ideas that seemed so good at the time just cause trouble, and the "babbling fool" who championed these ideas will be "thrown down." Don't get caught up. Instead, look for the warning signs.

10:11 The mouth of the righteous is a fountain of life, but the mouth of the wicked conceals violence.

Here the contrast is between two types of mouths. The mouth of the wicked "conceals violence." This same phrase was used in verse 6. If one is concealing violence, then logically we assume that person has previously *committed* violence. As we have previously commented, covering or concealing one's past is really a waste of time because nothing constructive comes of it. Don't commit such acts in the first place. But if you do, confess and repent so that forgiveness and renewal may be yours.

Those of us who desire to be righteous have a higher calling upon which to focus. The words which come out of our mouths should be a fountain of life. That is quite a commission! Perhaps it would be beneficial to make a list of things that would qualify as "fountain of life" utterances. Valuable insights can be found in Psalm 37:30, Proverbs 13:14, Proverbs 10 and Matthew 15. Notice how these passages combine the concept of obeying God and how this leads to what comes out of one's mouth.

10:12 Hatred stirs up strife, but love covers all transgressions.

Peter liked this latter idea so much he used it in his book: "Above all, keep fervent in your love for one another, because love covers a multitude of sins" (1 Peter 4:8). James likewise employed this idea in his writings: "Let him know that he who turns a sinner from the error of his way will save his soul from death, and will cover a multitude of sins" (James 5:20).

Despite the free will of all individuals, love is an incredibly powerful force. With it, we do not control, but we may influence. We cannot predict when we will play a key part in transforming the lives of others.

10:13 On the lips of the discerning, wisdom is found, but a rod is for the back of him who lacks understanding.

This is the first of several "rod" texts in the book of Proverbs (see also Proverbs 13:24; 14:3; 22:8; 22:15; 23:13–14; 26:3; and 29:15). Several "rod" passages refer to corporal punishment as one aspect of discipline in parenting. This verse, however, is not commenting on parenting at all. The contrast between "the discerning" and the person who "lacks understanding" is the most interesting aspect of this verse. Wisdom benefits both the individual who applies and uses it as well as all those within the sphere of influence of "the discerning" one. There is a sense of universal usefulness. But the one who "lacks understanding" benefits no one, including himself.

The rod is appropriate for such an individual so that learning may take place. We should never settle for lack of understanding. We should always seek to understand, especially God and His ways. The purpose of the rod in this sense, then, is to drive away complacency.

10:14 Wise men store up knowledge, but with the mouth of the foolish, ruin is at hand.

The question we must ask ourselves is this: Do we value knowledge? The idea that we can store it up, like food supplies, is an interesting comparison. It begs the questions of how we can store knowledge and where we should store it. The psalmist wrote, "Thy word have I hid in my heart" (Psalm 119:11).

The second part of the verse reflects a familiar theme regarding how much damage the mouth can do.

10:15 The rich man's wealth is his fortress, the ruin of the poor is their poverty.

This is one of those dangerous verses that can be misleading if it is taken out of context. One should not build an entire philosophy of stewardship and the acquisition of wealth and label it as "biblically based" because of Proverbs 10:15. This verse represents an observational analysis based on the principle of the work ethic, as Solomon illustrated in verse 5. Our *modus operandi* regarding the interpretation of scripture should consider the principle of Psalm 119:160: "The sum of Thy word is truth." One verse by itself may be a support for speculative reasoning. However, doctrines and dogma should be supported with numerous passages.

Having said this word of caution, how are we to understand verse 15? We should simply take it to mean that it is wise to store up what we can, as was pointed out in Proverbs 10:5. We must always and ever remember that our trust is in God, who has promised to supply our needs. However, many chapters of the book of Genesis were devoted to the story of Joseph, and this is one the lessons of his story.

10:16 The wages of the righteous is life, the income of the wicked, punishment.

This is a wonderful summary of the theme of the entire chapter. Notice how Paul picked up on this idea in Romans 6:23—from the opposite perspective. No other contrast speaks as loudly to us as that of the end result of something, and no end result is more important and more final than death.

10:17 He is on the path of life who heeds instruction, but he who forsakes reproof goes astray.

Many proverbs deal with being on the right path. This proverb addresses two different causes and two different effects. Are there any overt tests we may conduct to determine if we are going "astray" or if indeed we are on the "path of life"? Yes, such a test does exist. How do we handle criticism, instruction, and reproof? This simple test reveals a great deal about our overall walk.

10:18 He who conceals hatred has lying lips, and he who spreads slander is a fool.

Rather than a contrast, here we are presented with a parallel. A cursory look at the phrase "He who conceals hatred" would suggest that hatred should be openly expressed rather than hidden. But notice the latter portion of the verse. Basically, slander *is* a form of hatred openly expressed! The truth is that neither is appropriate. The *real* solution is to absolve the hate by giving it to God, asking Him for forgiveness, and then asking the offended party for forgiveness also. Hide it and you're a liar. Express it and you're a fool. Do something to change your heart, and you're a wise man.

10:19–21 When there are many words, transgression is unavoidable, but he who restrains his lips is wise. The tongue of the righteous is as choice silver, the heart of the wicked is worth little. The lips of the righteous feed many, but fools die for lack of understanding.

James wrote, "Be quick to hear, slow to speak" (James 1:19). The Hebrew uses three words for the phrase "transgression is unavoidable": *chadal lo pesha'*. *Chadal* can mean to desist, cease, end, or forsake something. Figuratively it may mean to be idle or lacking. *Loh* is a term of negation. It may mean no, not, neither, or never, depending on the context. In this case it is represented by the prefix *un*—in the word *unavoidable*. *Pesha'* refers to a revolt (e.g., national, moral, or religious). It may also refer to a rebellion, sin, trespass, or transgression. So there are numerous possible renditions of this phrase in English. However, the general gist of it is this: wherever there is a lot of talk, there will also be problems. Those problems may be in the form of sin, revolt, or transgressions, but they will be there.

The positive word images associated with the righteous versus the negative images of the wicked serve to help us realize the intrinsic value of righteous words as well as righteous actions.

> 10:22 It is the blessing of the LORD that makes rich, and He adds no sorrow to it.

What *is* being "rich"? Notice how this verse defines the concept of being rich. Simply stated, being rich means being blessed by God. So you may ask, what does it mean to be blessed? The following is gleaned from Matthew 5:3–12: To be a part of the kingdom of heaven, to be comforted, to inherit the earth, to be satisfied with righteousness, to receive mercy, to see God, to be a son of God, and to have a reward in heaven—this is what it means to be blessed, for this is true wealth.

> 10:23 Doing wickedness is like sport to a fool; and so is wisdom to a man of understanding.

Why does a wicked man do a wicked deed? Because he thinks it will be fun and amusing. The human mind is an amazing thing, craving constant stimulus and input. Our mind desires something to think about. Have you ever tried not thinking? A whole school of religious thought (Zen Buddhism) has been developed around this idea. Apart from existing in a state of trance, it is impossible to *not* think.

This phenomenon creates a secondary phenomenon that we label boredom. Boredom cannot occur when our minds are focused on something. Boredom always occurs during an "in-between" state of focus when we allow our mind to wander. Boredom occurs during "stream-of-consciousness" thinking. It is our *will* that controls what we focus on and indeed if we will focus at all. We may choose to focus on wickedness or on God and wisdom. One of the best methods for identifying and classifying people is to observe what gives them pleasure. What's your "sport"?

> 10:24 What the wicked fears will come upon him, and the desire of the righteous will be granted.

This is the great antithesis of Christianity. Read Psalm 37:1–5 for a more detailed look at this covenant of blessing and cursing.

> 10:25 When the whirlwind passes, the wicked is no more, but the righteous has an everlasting foundation.

The wise man builds his house upon the rock. What a blessing it is to realize we have an everlasting foundation. Tests and trials prove the depth of our anchor. What is it that you are anchored to right now?

> 10:26 Like vinegar to the teeth and smoke to the eyes, so is the lazy one to those who send him.

Vinegar is an acid that can eat away the enamel of your teeth. Smoke, of course, irritates your eyes. A sluggard is a major irritant to anyone who attempts to utilize his services. This is especially true if you're in a situation where you're really counting on this irresponsible individual to come through for you!

10:27 The fear of the LORD prolongs life, but the years of the wicked will be shortened.

This time the subject of the contrast is life. To be more specific, it is the length of life. Thus we infer that the subject is physical life rather than spiritual life. (Our resurrected bodies will live forever and thus have no length to measure or contrast.) While being wicked is general, we are given a very specific statute in order to acquire the blessing.

10:28 The hope of the righteous is gladness, but the expectation of the wicked perishes.

Hope is a beautiful and powerful thing. It is a cognitive attribute that mystically connects to our emotions as it changes the internal manner in which we perceive the realities and events around us. No wonder Paul called the gospel our "blessed hope." Our hope makes us happy, but notice what happens to the hope (if you can call it that) of the wicked. Even their puny hopes and expectations and dreams for the future perish as they slowly realize the vanity of their existence.

10:29 The way of the LORD is a stronghold to the upright, but ruin to the workers of iniquity.

This is all the eschatology we actually need. One man said after reading the entire book of Revelation that he didn't understand everything, but the good guys won in the end.

The Lord's "way" is not our way. The prophet Isaiah and the Psalmist remind us that His path is narrow. But it leads to life. The early Christians in the book of Acts were first known not by the title of "Christians" but as members of the "Way."

It is a fascinating paradox that His way leads to both life and destruction (life to the righteous and destruction to the wicked). Can we imagine any more uncomfortable feeling than being in the glorious presence of Almighty God while realizing we are unclean and uncovered by the proffered blood? Let us always seek His way!

10:30 The righteous will never be shaken, but the wicked will not dwell in the land.

The righteous have a security the wicked can only envy, for how can a man whose rightful place is in heaven be uprooted? Of course, he cannot be.

10:31–32 The mouth of the righteous flows with wisdom, but the perverted tongue will be cut out. The lips of the righteous bring forth what is acceptable, but the mouth of the wicked, what is perverted.

Compare the following ideas from scripture to these two verses. If you think you're religious, but you don't control your tongue, then you're not as religious as you think you are (see James 1:26). Guarding your mouth should be an especially careful concern for you while the wicked are in your presence (Psalm 39:1). We do not want to give the devil any opportunity at all.

Proverbs 11

11:1 A false balance is an abomination to the LORD, but a just weight is His delight.

*I*f you are ever tempted to cheat, remember that God is aware and He abhors it. If you want His delight, then obey His commands.

11:2 When pride comes, then comes dishonor, but with the humble is wisdom.

This verse helps the person who is questing after wisdom to take another step along the path of righteousness. It is as we walk along this path that the acquisition of true wisdom occurs. Each step toward God contains new insights, new transformations, and new wisdom.

We have learned that we should fear God; now we see that we should walk with humility as well (see Philippians 2:3–7 for a scriptural definition of humility). The enemy of humility has a name: *pride*. When we choose to focus on ourselves, the source of pride is fed and becomes stronger. It is in this manner that we discover what it means to become our own worst enemy.

11:3 The integrity of the upright will guide them, but the falseness of the treacherous will destroy them.

What is integrity? Let us first define what it is *used* for according to this verse. Integrity serves as our guide to keep us on the right path. Often we think of integrity as a sociological function in the sense of one man's integrity (or lack thereof) influencing those around him. But Solomon points out that the real value of being a man of integrity is how it affects us internally. To pronounce to myself, "I am a man of true integrity, because God is at work in my life," is a very powerful assertion.

The English word *integrity* comes from the Latin word *integritas,* from which we also get our mathematical word *integer,* which means a whole number. It is this function which integrity performs for us, providing us with a sense of wholeness. Integrity brings with it a sense of righteousness, for true integrity comes from the Giver of life.

11:4 Riches do not profit in the day of wrath, but righteousness delivers from death.

As you live your life, you have opportunities to make your life count. You may even achieve something that lasts beyond your years here, something that still benefits and influences others even after you are gone. Some examples are the lives you have touched (especially children); something you have built, such as a house; or a creation of yours, such as a work of art or writing that others still read or listen to after your death. However, for you personally, there is only *one* thing of value that you take with you upon your death: *righteousness.*

The word *riches* implies something of value. Upon our death, wealth cannot be used for anything. In other words, it will have absolutely no value. With this in mind, it is amazing that so many of us strive so diligently for it throughout our lives. Jesus dealt with this very same issue in His parable of the rich fool in Luke 12:15–21.

11:5–6 The righteousness of the blameless will smooth his way, but the wicked will fall by his own wickedness. The righteousness of the upright will deliver them, but the treacherous will be caught by their own greed.

You *get* what you *are*. That is the theme of these verses. Evil desires are more than just thoughts, they are always a trap.

Solomon observes that righteousness smooths your way. Walking on a smooth way is the opposite of having to deal with traps. The Hebrew verb *yashar* means to be straight or even, but it can also be used figuratively in a cause-and-effect manner. It is this latter sense that seems to describe the role of righteousness in our walk with the Lord. The cause is righteousness and the effect is a smooth way.

11:7 When a wicked man dies, his expectation will perish, and the hope of strong men perishes.

A similar idea is found in Proverbs 10:28: "All he expected of his power comes to nothing." Shortly after the exile, Zechariah wrote that righteous things are accomplished "'not by might nor by power, but by My Spirit,' says the Lord of hosts" (Zechariah 4:6).

No matter how strong and powerful a man is, his strength is futile for righteousness. Scripture directs us to be God-reliant rather than self-reliant.

11:8 The righteous is delivered from trouble, but the wicked takes his place.

This familiar contrast underscores our understanding of salvation. We know the value of righteousness, but what is intriguing about this verse is how it connects salvation and judgment with righteousness. God is righteous and as such cannot tolerate sin. But the wicked are still subject to spiritual "trouble" and, in fact, take the place of the righteous in receiving this trouble. The wages of sin must be paid for. Goliath (1 Samuel 17) and Haman (Esther 7) are examples of this idea.

> 11:9 With his mouth the godless man destroys his neighbor, but through knowledge the righteous will be delivered.

If you ever decide to write that ill-advised article on how to destroy your neighbor in one easy lesson, it should start off with this advice:

Step 1. Just open your mouth.

This verse talks about destroying others with our mouths while Proverbs 13:3 points out how our mouths can easily bring destruction upon ourselves. Don't forget how the boomerang effect of our actions often comes back to us. [Note: Articles on how to destroy others are not really a necessary commodity. People seem to be able to do it without any help at all!]

Now let us look at the phrase "Through knowledge the righteous escape" (NIV). This is more than just a contrast between wicked and righteous people. What is *really* being contrasted are the *results* of the godless man's words. The normal result is destruction, but the righteous are able to escape because of their knowledge.

> 11:10 When it goes well with the righteous, the city rejoices, and when the wicked perish, there is glad shouting.

Here are two different situations that result in similar responses—glad shouting and rejoicing. When society realizes that someone who is truly righteous has triumphed, it invokes great rejoicing. Likewise, when someone who is truly evil has been brought down and is no longer a threat, this too brings rejoicing. When both situations have occurred simultaneously (e.g., the end of World War II), then the rejoicing is even more widespread. It's human nature to cheer for the good guys. People love to see the bad guys lose and the good guys win. This is the reason so many stories conclude with this type of ending.

> 11:11 By the blessing of the upright a city is exalted, but by the mouth of the wicked it is torn down.

This is a basic sociology lesson. Your city will be helped by righteous people, but messed up by wicked people. When you think about it, "the mouth" and other forms of communication greatly contribute to the problems of many cities. Graffiti and the mouths of those who threaten and demean others produce fear. Fear leads those who *can* flee to do so. Businesses fail and the infrastructure of the community becomes weaker, unattractive, and often crime ridden. All these issues are due in large part to the "mouth" of evildoers.

The opposite occurs when a community is filled with and run by many upright citizens.

> 11:12 He who despises his neighbor lacks sense, but a man of understanding keeps silent.

Here we see what the deciding factor is in a man who mocks, laughs at, and derides those around him compared to one who does not. The difference is understanding and judgment. Think before you make that derogatory remark. Chances are you'll realize you should not make it at all.

We have discussed the behavioral issue here, but the attitudinal issue is that of pride. How can you be filled with godly humility and despise your neighbor?

> 11:13 He who goes about as a talebearer reveals secrets, but he who is trustworthy conceals a matter.

Proverbs tells us many things we should not want and many things we should want. Most of the things we should want involve our character, such as integrity (11:3), humility (11:2), righteousness (11:4–6), and here in this verse, trustworthiness. Make it your desire for people to be able to say you are a trustworthy individual. It is a matter of character and personal integrity.

> 11:14 Where there is no guidance, the people fall, but in abundance of counselors there is victory.

What is it that provides guidance? Guidance can be provided by a personal guide, a map, a compass, sighting off of a star, or a light on a dark night. We have pastors and teachers to guide us. We have the Bible to serve as our spiritual map. The cross is our compass, directing us ever to follow in the footsteps of our Savior. Sighting off of a star is a process of looking at something far away in the distance to see where we are at the moment. For this the Christian has hope. Jesus Himself is the light of the world. But if a nation does not avail itself of these types of guidance, its people will "fall."

Let's look at the second part of the verse: "Many advisors make victory sure" (NIV). To follow this advice is not as easy as it sounds. To utilize many advisors we must first be willing to listen, which is often a rare condition. Furthermore, we must have a balance between open-mindedness and conviction. To seek a wide degree of opinions and viewpoints is wise, but only a fool is swayed by every clever argument that comes along. To have an open mind means to truly listen and observe. To have conviction means to filter that information through the worldview grid of your beliefs and then to act in accordance with your beliefs, which have been based on the firm foundation of the Bible. As a cautionary note, be aware that often these beliefs will not be the majority opinion.

> 11:15 He who is surety for a stranger will surely suffer for it, but he who hates going surety is safe.

In the area of business, if you must err, then err on the side of caution. An overly cautious businessman may lose out on some opportunities and may not reap quite as much profit as possible. But an incautious man may lose everything. The primary issue here is trust. You should trust in the Lord, knowing that people may often fail you. The secondary issues are personal responsibility and deferred gratification. Surety issues are almost always for wants rather than needs.

Another factor to be considered is how well you know the person you are thinking of helping. The verse mentions providing surety for a "stranger."

Occasionally you may still feel great confusion. Perhaps you feel a strong sense of obligation to help someone. Are you not merely being helpful and nice when you co-sign? The person asking for help may imply that if you do not help him, a tragedy will occur and an opportunity will be lost. The only reason he can see for you to refuse is because *you* are greedy and uncaring.

But is this the truth?

If greediness is a part of the situation, it is almost certainly to be found on the part of the asker. If he could *truly* afford whatever the item is, then he would not need a co-signer. Perhaps such people need to build credit, be patient, live within their means, and experience deferred gratification. To "help" such a person avoid the growth of this experience may actually hurt him in the long run.

I don't want readers misunderstanding this point. The Bible is full of examples of people helping others. Abraham helped the kings and rescued Lot. The Good Samaritan really did help the wounded man. Jesus cast out demons and healed many people. And there are many other stories. But we should always look for deep and lasting ways of helping others. Remember Peter and John and the lame man? He asked for money, but instead they offered him the power of Jesus Christ!

11:16 A gracious woman attains honor, and violent men attain riches.

Everyone wants respect, but how should we go about getting it? This verse points out that we may get it by being gracious. Violence will never get us the true respect we crave. It will only get us temporal things, such as the fear of others and unstable riches. For some, this is precisely what they want. But the Bible looks much deeper and illustrates the genuine vanity of this. The biblical principle is that "whoever exalts himself shall be humbled, and whoever humbles himself shall be exalted" (Matthew 23:12).

> 11:17 The merciful man does himself good, but the cruel man does himself harm.

This is another poignant illustration of the kingdom principle of reciprocity. In Proverbs 11:5–6 we noted that you *get* what you *are*. Here we see the idea again, but this time more from the perspective of receiving what you give.

> 11:18 The wicked earns deceptive wages, but he who sows righteousness gets a true reward.

This is a key concept throughout all of Proverbs. Paul says it another way: "Do not be deceived, God is not mocked; for whatever a man sows, this he will reap . . . . Let us not lose heart in doing good, for in due time we shall reap if we do not grow weary" (Galatians 6:6, 8). It takes great vision to look deep into the future and analyze the difference between true rewards and deceptive wages.

> 11:19 He who is steadfast in righteousness will attain to life, and he who pursues evil will bring about his own death.

Make no mistake about it, righteousness is a matter of life and death. What will it take for us to become truly steadfast? David prayed diligently for it: "Create in me a clean heart, O God, and renew a steadfast spirit within me" (Psalm 51:10). Paul gave this benediction to the Thessalonians: "May the Lord direct your hearts into the love of God and into the *steadfastness* of Christ" (2 Thessalonians 3:5). In John's vision in Revelation 3, his theme is: "He who overcomes, I will grant to him to sit down with Me on My throne" (v. 21).

Don't confuse steadfastness with other static behaviors, such as passivity or laziness. To be steadfast is hard work. It does not mean you are merely static, it means you are committed to continual growth in the Lord and in this you refuse to be distracted or swayed.

> 11:20 The perverse in heart are an abomination to the LORD, but the blameless in their walk are His delight.

The perverse in heart seek their own delights. The "blameless" simply want to delight the Lord. The blameless find their desires through the process of their "walk." "Delight yourself in the LORD; and He will give you the desires of your heart" (Psalm 37:4).

Ask yourself what you have done lately to delight God. Is there something you can add to your daily walk that will delight Him? Possibly you could engage in more prayer time, or more time in the word of God. Or how about a definitive act of edifying some other believer, or some obedient act involving your witness to someone? Is there something you can delete from your life that would also bring delight to Him?

> 11:21 Assuredly [literally, "hand to hand"], the evil man will not go unpunished, but the descendants of the righteous will be delivered.

The Hebrew text uses a word picture here ("hand to hand" is a literal translation) of certainty as in the sealing of an arrangement with a handshake. The NASB uses the term "assuredly" and the NIV uses the phrase "Be sure of this" in place of the metaphor. This verse implies that our righteousness benefits not only ourselves but also our descendants. What a wonderful thought for parents to meditate upon.

11:22 As a ring of gold in a swine's snout, so is a beautiful woman who lacks discretion.

What is beauty? When it comes to personal human beauty, true beauty is more than external trappings. I define beauty as having or maintaining some connection to the concepts of wholeness and *unity* (we will explore this more in Proverbs 30:18–19 and 31:30). A sunset is beautiful not because of only one thing, such as the sun itself, but because of the sun's relationship to other objects (ourselves, as witnesses, included). The wondrous shades of color result from the refraction of light that is bent by our atmosphere, and we see not just sun, but the entire sky. In this example the sensation of beauty comes from the unity of the entire sky and horizon and the sensation of wholeness between our planet, a distant object (the sun), and our whole universe.

The opposite of beauty is ugliness. When we perceive something to be ugly, invariably there is something that seems to be broken, "wrong," or out of place. When this occurs, in essence, we intuitively perceive a lack of unity or wholeness.

In the absurd example of this verse, indiscretion destroys the unity of an implied relationship, and what is left is merely potential beauty that has been corrupted.

11:23 The desire of the righteous is only good, but the expectation of the wicked is wrath.

The author of Hebrews speaks of those who "desire a better country." Paul writes that we should "desire spiritual gifts." Asaph declares in Psalm 73, "Besides Thee I desire nothing on earth." Jesus' admonition is for us to "seek first the kingdom of God" (Matthew 6:33). The more righteously transformed we have become, the more we desire what is good.

Another observation of interest in regard to this verse is to consider the concept of hope. The righteous have hope, but the wicked have only dread.

11:24–25 There is one who scatters, yet increases all the more, and there is one who withholds what is justly due, but it results only in want. The generous man will be prosperous, and he who waters will himself be watered.

One of the best ways to understand this principle is from an agricultural perspective. If I hold a handful of seeds and stingily hoard them, they will never reproduce. But if I freely scatter them, then each will have an opportunity to bear fruit. Give and you shall receive.

11:26 He who withholds grain, the people will curse him, but blessing will be on the head of him who sells it.

It is wise to save, but it is foolish to hoard. There is a time to be frugal and a time to give, but never a time to be stingy. It is the wise man who seeks to comprehend the difference.

Notice also, that the latter part of the verse is not saying you must always *give* everything away. You can sell it, but you should make an honest profit. The contrasting former part of the verse implies that the main principle is that we should think of the needs of others. Do unto others as you would have them do unto you.

11:27 He who diligently seeks good seeks favor, but he who searches after evil, it will come to him.

This verse not only provides a contrast between the acquisition of grace and evil, but it reveals an interesting method for spiritual growth. Whereas evil *can* be found by pursuing evil, only in general terms do we find righteousness by pursuing righteousness. There is a surface level where this is true. But as we grow and plumb the depths of spiritual growth, we discover certain antithetical polarities ("opposites") at work that seem to defy human wisdom.

To get down to the actual specifics of *how* righteousness is acquired, we must first get away from the way the world views the acquisition of things. Indeed, we must be active in our pursuit, but the specific area of growth we attain is not always exactly what we *do*.

Here are some examples of what I mean. To receive honor, humble yourself. To become rich, learn to give things away. To walk in God's way, learn to *rest* in Him. To become truly free, follow His commandments. To save your life you must lose your life. To attain favor, seek to do good.

> 11:28 He who trusts in his riches will fall, but the righteous will flourish like the green leaf.

Do not trust in riches, but trust rather in God. As a point of interest, there is another fascinating connection between the phrase "The righteous will flourish" and Psalm 72, which was also written by Solomon.

Psalm 72 is a messianic psalm that speaks of "the king's son" as a righteous instrument of salvation. In verse 7 we read, "In his [the Messiah's] days the righteous will flourish." Verses 10 and 11 of Psalm 72 ("The kings of Sheba . . . offer gifts . . . let all kings bow down before him") are possible foreshadowings of the magi in the Christmas story. Verse 14 is a key verse regarding the purpose of the Messiah, and verse 16 states, "Those from the city flourish like vegetation of the earth."

> 11:29 He who troubles his own house will inherit wind, and the foolish will be servant to the wisehearted.

This verse offers advice in two areas of life. Concerning your family (i.e., your "house"), don't cause numerous problems and then expect an inheritance from the will. Furthermore, you cannot be a fool and expect to be given the opportunity for leadership to rule over others. The fact of the matter is, if you are the fool, it is you who will be ruled over.

11:30 The fruit of the righteous is a tree of life, and he who is wise wins souls.

Usually we think of a tree producing fruit. Here it is the fruit that produces a tree, and of course, this makes perfect sense as well. But notice what kind of tree it is—a tree of life! Biblically, this is the symbolic representation of eternal life (see Genesis 2:9 and 3:22).

What does it mean to "win a soul"? It means we should attempt to bring others into a closer walk with God. We must focus on spiritual needs above physical needs, for physical concerns are temporal while spiritual needs bear eternal results. This does not mean we ignore the physical aspect of helping others. It means we see the whole person and that when we use physical things to help others, we have the ultimate goal of winning their souls and seeing them brought into the kingdom of God.

At all times we should be intensely aware of this need in all men, and we should be willing to discuss spiritual things with people. If we seek to convince them of their need and of God's *soul-u-tion,* we are wise.

11:31 If the righteous will be rewarded in the earth, how much more the wicked and the sinner!

The "if" here is not suggesting a question of whether or not the righteous will be rewarded; the underlying assumption is that they will be. Ultimately, everyone gets a "reward." The Apostle John put it this way: "Those who did the good deeds, to a resurrection of life, those who committed the evil deeds to a resurrection of judgment" (John 5:29). The theme of reaping what you sow has been woven throughout this chapter, and this verse reiterates this once more. The "reward" (wages) for being wicked is death.

Proverbs 12

12:1 Whoever loves discipline loves knowledge, but he who hates reproof is stupid.

Do you love discipline? Most people would say, "Not really." But what is the purpose of discipline? The word comes from the same root as the word "disciple," which means to be a learner. Change, growth, learning, new skills, new insights, and many achievements can all come from discipline. Perhaps we need to change our view of reproof and look upon it as an opportunity for growth.

Pride cannot tolerate reproof, but humility can. Our fragile egos will actually benefit in the long run if we heed reproof. Keep in mind that the alternative may mean we have unknowingly chosen to "wander" in a wilderness for many years! Any coach can relate stories of players who were "coachable" and also stories of players who refused to be coached.

Consider also these passages: "Blessed is the man whom Thou dost chasten, O Lord" (Psalm 94:12). "My son, do not reject the discipline of the Lord, or loathe His reproof, for whom the Lord loves He reproves, even as a father, the son in whom he delights" (Proverbs 3:11–12). Compare also Hebrews 12:5–11.

> 12:2 A good man will obtain favor from the LORD, but He will condemn a man who devises evil.

Basically, this verse demonstrates that there are two types of people. There are those who obtain the Lord's favor and those who receive His condemnation. Luke 2:52 states that "Jesus kept increasing in wisdom and stature, and in favor with God and men." We too can obtain favor. The New Testament uses the word *grace* to convey the concept of receiving the favor of God.

Do not confuse being a "good man" with being a man who achieves favor only by good works. Some Christians seem to have the notion that the New Testament teaches that salvation is by grace while the Old Testament and its law emphasized works. (Dispensationalism appears to reach this conclusion.) This latter idea about the Old Testament is absolutely not true. While the Jewish people eventually evolved into a works-oriented system, it does not mean that it was biblical. In fact, it was the system of the Pharisees and the Sadducees that Jesus spoke against!

In the Old Testament, salvation was through faith, both before and after the Law was given. Abraham "believed in the LORD; and He reckoned it to him as righteousness" (Genesis 15:6). Spiritually speaking, no man is "good" apart from righteousness, and righteousness comes only as a gift from God to those who believe.

Notice that the latter part of the verse says that God will condemn a man who devises evil. Condemnation *is* a part of God's plan. Negative consequences would not be necessary in a realm that did not allow for free will and that maintained no standards. But God chose to create a system that allows free will. In such a system evil must be a possibility. If there is only one "choice," then choice is a misnomer, and not a true reality. But man does have true and legitimate choices. Additionally, once the idea of "standards" is also introduced into a system, consequences become a necessity. There can be no standard if there is no consequence for not maintaining the standard.

12:3 A man will not be established by wickedness, but the root of the righteous will not be moved.

Our root is Jesus. Isaiah wrote concerning the Messiah, "A shoot will spring from the stem of Jesse, and a branch from his roots will bear fruit. And the Spirit of the LORD will rest on Him, the spirit of wisdom and understanding, the spirit of counsel and strength, the spirit of knowledge and the fear of the LORD" (Isaiah 11:1–2).

Allow Him to be the vine into which you are grafted as a living branch that bears fruit (see also John 15). While the wicked are attempting to get the booty of others, they fail to realize that it will never "establish" them. The wealth, peace, joy, and security of this type of booty are just an illusion. You are established only by developing roots. Roots anchor you and provide you with nutrients and life-giving water, allowing you to grow even further (compare Proverbs 12:12 to this verse). Jesus is our root and He is also our living water!

12:4 An excellent wife is the crown of her husband, but she who shames him is as rottenness in his bones.

The marriage relationship is important not only for one's personal happiness (unless you have the gift of celibacy), but also because it can make or break you in many areas of life. A marriage can be healthy and beautiful or unhealthy and ugly. In a healthy marriage, both partners are motivated to achieve more than they might otherwise achieve. This is because commitment and love forces us to look beyond ourselves and see the needs of those around us. While this begins in the family, it often extends to the world around as well.

Conversely, selfishness is the primary root of most unhealthy marriages (and I might add, most forms of poor parenting as well). King Lemuel begins his passage on the virtuous wife in Proverbs 31 with this question: "A wife of noble character, who can find her?" (NIV). A lifetime partner of character is to be cherished and treasured.

> 12:5 The thoughts of the righteous are just, but the counsels of the wicked are deceitful.

Here is a short poem to sum up this idea:
Righteous and godly plans are just,
But wicked advice will often deceive.
God's hand is a must,
To avoid being dust,
So, in devilish counsel do not heed or believe.

> 12:6 The words of the wicked lie in wait for blood, but the mouth of the upright will deliver them.

Once again we see here a contrast between the words of the wicked and the words of the upright. The *purpose* of the words of the wicked is to pull others down. Their beliefs seem to contain an attitude of self-superiority couched subtly in humanistic language. Hang around a devout humanist long enough and you will hear him seek to destroy someone (often a Christian) in the name of lifting up someone else. The phrase "lie in wait for blood" presents both the idea of ambush and of murderous intent. It is reminiscent of Proverbs 1:10–12, 18. Notice how the purpose of the upright person's mouth differs from the wicked's purpose. The goal of the upright is the bring salvation to others rather than to destroy them.

> 12:7 The wicked are overthrown and are no more, but the house of the righteous will stand.

This verse shows again the unassured and perilous position of the wicked as the antithesis of the position of the righteous. The righteous are secure. This verse also implies something of the eternal consequences of the wicked. The phrase "are no more" implies annihilation while "the house of the righteous will stand" implies an eternal state of rest and bliss.

12:8 A man will be praised according to his insight, but one of perverse mind will be despised.

The path of wisdom is a path that leads to honor. But it is honor that has been earned without having been sought. The contrast developed in this verse is between a mind that has insight and a perverse mind. Paul writes in Romans 12:2 that we should "be transformed by the renewing of [our] mind." With a renewed mind, insights can be made that were not previously possible.

12:9 Better is he who is lightly esteemed and has a servant, than he who honors himself and lacks bread.

Are fame and honor worthy of our pursuit? To answer this, let us first analyze what fame is. Fame is the acknowledgment of others. According to the Bible, our aim should be to receive acknowledgment from God. There are two issues involved in this verse. One is fame and the other is pretension (or the act of pretending). The former is fleeting while the latter is false.

The lesson is to live within your means, and not worry about the opinions of others. Both you and your "servant" will be better off.

12:10 A righteous man has regard for the life of his beast, but the compassion of the wicked is cruel.

One of the most obvious contrasts between righteous and wicked people can be found in the realm of stewardship. Our attitudes about animals and personal property allow us to demonstrate stewardship and godly ideals in very practical and overt ways.

12:11 He who tills his land will have plenty of bread, but he who pursues vain things lacks sense.

What is the difference between pursuing a dream (or goal) and chasing a fantasy? This verse points out that one of the key differences is the work ethic involved. A second difference highlighted in this verse is that of possessing "sense," or literally, "heart."

It is OK to pursue a dream if you have goals and take the necessary steps to get to those goals (such as tilling the land, in this example). The third element this verse points out is discernment. To understand the difference between something vain and something worthwhile requires discernment.

12:12 The wicked desires the booty of evil men, but the root of the righteous yields fruit.

When a wicked man sees a wealthy man who acquired his wealth through some means other than hard, honest work, his observation turns quickly to envy. "That could be me," he reasons. He feels a natural covetousness and a deep sense of longing for the things he could buy through similar "get-rich-quick" schemes.

There are two additional things to note from this verse. First, notice that wicked people will *never* be satisfied. They will always want something else. Second, note that righteous people flourish (NIV) and yield fruit. God's way is best in every aspect of our lives. We are commanded to avoid covetousness, not so much to simply avoid materialism, but because envious people are seldom happy, never satisfied, and never joyful. God wants us to experience a more joyful and spiritually deep life. When we concentrate on living lives that bear spiritual fruit, we are truly blessed. As David wrote, "Trust in the LORD, and do good; dwell in the land and cultivate faithfulness. Delight yourself in the LORD; and He will give you the desires of your heart" (Psalm 37:3–4).

12:13 An evil man is ensnared by the transgression of his lips, but the righteous will escape from trouble.

The implication of this verse is that the righteous man escapes trouble because he controls his mouth and does not utter sinful talk. The righteous man avoids the snares and traps that come with sinful talk. Rain falls on both the righteous and the unrighteous, illustrating that the natural system allows both "good" and "bad" things to happen to all people. Theologically we know that righteous people will not escape all forms of trouble. But there is much trouble that is generated from various causes. Sin, as well as runaway "lips," will cause no end of trouble. There are natural and spiritual consequences. It is these avoidable forms of trouble that the righteous easily escape.

12:14 A man will be satisfied with good by the fruit of his words, and the deeds of a man's hands will return to him.

There are two ways to receive rewards presented in this verse. You can work for them, and you can use your mouth wisely. Both methods will net you positive results. Why not use both methods!

While salvation is not a result of good works, as children of God we ought always to strive to show our faith through our good works (see James 2:18).

12:15 The way of a fool is right in his own eyes, but a wise man is he who listens to counsel.

Do you listen to advice? More importantly, do you accept advice? How sure are you of your opinions? Are you certain of your perspective, even before you've gotten all the facts? Do you distinguish between your opinions and your beliefs?

There is a realm of truth, and a realm of personal taste. Beliefs belong only in the realm of truth. Opinions exist along the sliding scale from personal taste to the boundaries of the realm of truth.

Beliefs are those things for which you are willing to die before you would truly change your perspective. Beliefs are those things that are foundational to your entire worldview. Opinions are things that you hold, but in which you also admit to the possibility of error.

Most people think they possess a great deal of beliefs and a few opinions. The reality is the reverse. When you realize that most of the things you hold to are actually only opinions, then you are more likely to receive counsel. He is a fool who believes that in all things and at all times his "way" is right.

Of our beliefs, we should be rock-solid, certain, and unwavering. Of our opinions, we should be flexible, open, and equally willing to reflect or adapt. It is the wise man who knows the difference between his beliefs and his opinions.

12:16 A fool's vexation is known at once, but a prudent man conceals dishonor.

Do you wear your negative emotions on your sleeve? How do others see you and characterize you? Are you the one who always complains? Do even little things annoy you? Perhaps you take yourself too seriously and your Lord not seriously enough.

12:17 He who speaks truth tells what is right, but a false witness, deceit.

In case you had any doubt about what the ninth commandment meant (see Exodus 20:16), this section of verses (Proverbs 12:17–20) should help clarify its meaning.

12:18 There is one who speaks rashly like the thrusts of a sword, but the tongue of the wise brings healing.

Analyze the motive of your heart as you observe the purpose of your words. Jesus said, "But the things that proceed out of the mouth come from the heart and those defile the man" (Matthew 15:18).

Is your purpose to wound or to heal?

12:19 Truthful lips will be established forever, but a lying tongue is only for a moment.

How important is the truth to you? You may think to yourself, *It is only a little white lie.* You may rationalize, *I only said it because I didn't want to upset her.* Stop and consider if there is another way to avoid upsetting or hurting others without lying. Remember to take it seriously, and don't mess with lying.

12:20 Deceit is in the heart of those who devise evil, but counselors of peace have joy.

Peace leads to joy. Deceit leads to evil. Deceit is foundational to nearly all sins. Deceit is the primary strategy used by the devil to corrupt the minds of believers and nonbelievers alike. Let's analyze the role of deceit in several areas.

Pride is at the root of many other sins, but deceit is at the root of pride. The sin of pride always involves a false belief about oneself, such as one's own superiority. The desire to acquire great wealth is another area where deceit is often readily at work. Those who believe that wealth will bring joy are deceived.

There are also many other areas of sin that involve deceit. Try to think of a sin that does not involve some form of deceit or self-deceit. I could not think of a single one.

12:21 No harm befalls the righteous, but the wicked are filled with trouble.

This verse should be understood not as a promise but as a generalization. As Jesus pointed out, "In the world you have tribulation, but have courage, I have overcome the world" (John 16:33). Of course, just prior to this statement, He said, "In Me you may have peace." These two ideas help us to look at "harm" and "trouble" differently from those with worldly perspectives.

107

Generally speaking, righteous people avoid troubles while wicked people amplify their problems. Wicked people create problems where problems shouldn't even exist. However, even the concept of "harm" is redefined for the Christian. Some things that appear to the world to be harm (such as death) are really not "harm" to the true believer. The death of Stephen is only one example.

12:22 Lying lips are an abomination to the LORD, but those who deal faithfully are His delight.

Lying lips offend God far more than we usually give them credit. Most of chapter 12 has contrasted evil men with righteous men, but this verse shows us a very different kind of contrast. It shows us how God feels *emotionally* toward different types of men. When we are new in the faith we often focus on what God has done for us and on what He is currently doing in our lives, and of course, we should never lose sight of this. But as we mature, we begin to ask the question, "What can I do for God?" This verse reveals one answer to this question. By dealing faithfully with integrity we will bring Him delight.

12:23 A prudent man conceals knowledge, but the heart of fools proclaims folly.

Here is a little mystery: Why would a prudent man conceal knowledge? Perhaps the answer can be found in Matthew 7:6, "Do not give what is holy to dogs, and do not throw your pearls before swine, lest they trample them under their feet, and turn and tear you to pieces."

This verse contrasts three things: 1) prudent men with fools, 2) talking versus silence or concealment, and 3) knowledge versus folly. Part of being prudent is knowing when to impart knowledge and when to simply hold your tongue.

12:24 The hand of the diligent will rule, but the slack hand will be put to forced labor.

There is an irony concerning the work ethic. Those who work hard will eventually not need to work as hard because they will rule over others and oversee the work. Those who attempt to avoid work will ultimately have to work very hard, and then without reward, for in their effort to avoid work and responsibility, they will become slaves to others. In our society, we would probably refer to them as slaves of the system.

12:25 Anxiety in the heart of a man weighs it down, but a good word makes it glad.

This verse is one of several verses in Proverbs dealing with the motif of how anxiety and fear (of anything except God) can bring negative effects. The contrast presented in this verse shows how powerful our words are. When used correctly we can influence the attitude and demeanor of others in a very positive way.

12:26 The righteous is a guide to his neighbor, but the way of the wicked leads them astray.

Time and again throughout the book of Proverbs Solomon points out the value of righteousness. It is of truly *infinite* value to those who possess it. Righteousness, through God's grace, brings the gift of eternal life. But it is also of *great* value to society. The righteous provide guidance to those around them. (Of course, whether they follow this guidance or not is still a matter of free will.)

12:27 A slothful man does not roast his prey, but the precious possession of a man is diligence.

A lazy man is so slothful that he has many unsavory and un-healthful habits. In this comical illustration, he is so lazy that he refuses to spend the time to cook. Instead, the implication is that he just eats the meat raw. Rather than provide a contrasting illustration, Solomon simply contrasts it with a statement of principle. One of the most valuable things you can possess is diligence. Diligence may be defined as a willingness to work hard and not give up easily, even when a task is difficult. This is an admirable trait in any profession.

12:28 In the way of righteousness is life, and in its pathway there is no death.

This is a beautiful proverb that reiterates the importance of walking in "the way of righteousness." In this pathway there is salvation and life, both now and forever. Notice the lack of contrast in this verse. This is a stylistic change from most of the chapter. Such a change helps to emphasize the ideas within this verse.

Proverbs 13

13:1 A wise son accepts his father's discipline, but a scoffer does not listen to rebuke.

 wise son is contrasted here with a scoffer. A scoffer tends to proclaim himself to be wise and in charge of his own life. He despises learning because he does not see the need to learn.

While we may be more willing to apply this verse to our earthly fathers, we must also accept our heavenly Father's discipline. The problem of evil haunts all of us at many times in our lives. If God is loving and faithful and He promises to protect us, why does His "protection" seem to be lacking or inadequate at times? Why does He allow evil to befall those whom He loves and claims as His children? Is He never satisfied with our growth and the depth of our faith? We have all seen people who have been driven back into relationship with God because of adversity—but if God is omniscient, why does He allow the evil to occur to those whom it seems to drive away from Him? Some people seem to lose faith and to become angry with God.

Perhaps wrestling with such issues is beneficial, so that we may avoid complacency and also avoid becoming flabby and spiritually weakened. Romans 5:12 addresses the cause of evil: "Through one man sin entered into the world, and death through sin, and so death spread to all men." God does not cause evil, but He does allow evil. Evil *must* be allowed if free choice is a part of the equation.

But not all forms of suffering are "evil." To further understand this, we need to understand the difference between trials and tribulations, as the Bible refers to these things. "The problem of evil" is a philosophical label that refers to all suffering, sin, and evil, etc. God does allow, and in fact, often "cause" trials. This is not synonymous with causing evil, although at times, from a human perspective, trials and evil may appear to be synonymous. *Real evil* is never caused by God, because evil is the antithesis of God Himself.

Tribulations occur because of the curse of living in a fallen system. Tribulations may be natural or designed. A natural tribulation may be the result of a storm, famine, or some other natural event. Tribulation may be self-generated or other-generated. The problems caused by the consequences of sinful behavior, as well as the actions and workings of other intelligent evil beings (i.e., Satan, evil spirits, and even evil men), may all bring about tribulations. If a tribulation is designed (meaning an intelligent being is involved), its purpose is to see us fall.

If a trial is involved, the purpose is to see us grow. The author of Hebrews wrote, "All discipline for the moment seems not to be joyful, but sorrowful . . . [but] afterwards it yields the peaceful fruit of righteousness" (Heb. 12:11). For more on this, see 1 Thessalonians 3:3–11 and James 1:2–4.

Having looked at a spiritual application of this verse, it is important to realize how truly profound this statement is when applied to our physical fathers as well. The whole idea of *discipline* is to learn. If we do not accept it, then clearly we have not learned. Mistakes will be repeated and people will be needlessly hurt once again.

13:2–3 From the fruit of a man's mouth he enjoys good, but the desire of the treacherous is violence. The one who guards his mouth preserves his life; the one who opens wide his lips comes to ruin.

Your mouth is one of your most powerful tools, especially when it is coupled with nonhypocritical actions. Solomon's advice to us is this: Use your mouth wisely and you will receive [literally, "eat"] good.

Guarding our mouths represents an area of self-discipline. We have a great deal of control over certain areas of our lives. But there is a great deal of difference between possessing control and utilizing control. Do *you* control your mouth? Yes, of course you do. But do you *control* your mouth?

13:4 The soul of the sluggard craves and gets nothing, but the soul of the diligent is made fat.

This verse provides a great insight into the nature of man. The combination of craving and laziness seems to create selfish, demanding, and blaming behavior. This leads to a view that psychologically dehumanizes others. Notice also, that winning the lottery will *not* make your soul fat. *Diligence* is what brings about a "fat" soul, and this illustrates the value of work. Not only does work feed our mouths, but it also feeds our souls.

Diligence includes the ideas of steadfastness, a strong work ethic, and responsible behavior. A sense of genuine appreciation often accompanies that for which we have toiled and waited.

13:5 A righteous man hates falsehood, but a wicked man acts disgustingly and shamefully.

What do you hate? To hate what destroys the relationship of people with their Creator, and to hate what God hates, is both right and proper for Christians. The psalmist wrote, "Hate evil, you who love the L ORD" (Psalm 97:10). Proverbs 6:16–19 includes a list of seven things the Lord Himself hates.

> 13:6 Righteousness guards the one whose way is blameless, but wickedness subverts the sinner.

If we do not keep ourselves blameless, we will eventually suffer a consequence. When we think about putting on the whole armor of God, as Paul mentions in Ephesians 6, then we must diligently include righteousness and blamelessness. Righteousness is our internal and eternal protection, protecting us from God's wrath and providing us with the means to eternal life. Blamelessness is our external and temporal protection as we live honorable lives with our fellow man and in the sight of God. The righteous man shall live by faith, but his faith is demonstrated through blameless living.

> 13:7 There is one who pretends to be rich, but has nothing; another pretends to be poor, but has great wealth.

What lifestyle are you pursuing? Jesus said that no one can serve two masters (Matthew 6:24) and it is hard for a rich man to enter heaven (Matthew 19:23). When you compare this verse to the beatitude of Matthew 5:3, "Blessed are the poor in spirit, for theirs is the kingdom of heaven," you may see the richness of this proverb in a new light.

> 13:8 The ransom of a man's life is his riches, but the poor hears no rebuke.

Without spiritual riches one can ransom only material things. A man with only physical wealth has forfeited control over his spiritual future. Can you save your soul by giving up all of your riches? No, reply the scriptures. No possession you possess is more valuable than your life, yet you cannot redeem it yourself with riches, or through any other means. Only he who gives up his life can save his life.

The NIV records the latter part of this verse this way: "A poor man hears no threat." While it is true that a wealthy man may be able to buy his way out of a ransom situation, a poor man can live in peace knowing that he will never be placed in such a situation.

13:9 The light of the righteous rejoices, but the lamp of the wicked goes out.

Is Solomon really talking about oil lamps here? Actually, he seems to be referring to life through the analogy of lamps. The light of the righteous goes on and on.

13:10 Through presumption comes nothing but strife, but with those who receive counsel is wisdom.

Daily we make decisions and categorize people according to our perceptions and assumptions. When we presume that we know something, we may distance ourselves from the truth. Gossip, false perceptions, distortions of reality, and heresies may all arise through presumption.

13:11 Wealth obtained by fraud dwindles, but the one who gathers by labor increases it.

The principle set forth in this verse is easily understood and applied. Be a good steward of your income, and slowly but steadily your wealth will increase. The verse does not suggest that we seek first the kingdom of wealth, it is merely stating the value of a good work ethic.

A thief does not have a steady income. If he steals thousands of dollars, in a few weeks or months it is gone and he must steal again and so on. The wealth he seeks is far more elusive than he first assumed upon beginning this "vocation." Be thankful for the job you have.

13:12 Hope deferred makes the heart sick, but desire fulfilled is
a tree of life.

Viktor Frankl wrote in *Man's Search for Meaning* that hope is
the most important element of psychology. When he was in the
Nazi concentration camps, those who maintained hope were the
survivors. Without hope, men fell into despair because they had
nothing to live for. Frankl believed they had no meaning in their
lives.[2]

Hope is foundational to faith (Hebrews 11:1). No matter what
trial we may pass through, Jesus remains our "blessed Hope."

13:13 The one who despises the word will be in debt to it, but
the one who fears the commandment will be rewarded.

How true this verse is concerning the entire word of God! Jesus
said, "He who is of God hears the words of God" (John 8:47). The
world does not heed the words of God because they do not truly
hear the word of God. Thus will they be in debt to it. In John 12:47–
48 Jesus also gave the following warning: "If any one hears My
sayings, and does not keep them, I do not judge him . . . . He who
rejects Me, and does not receive My sayings, has one who judges
him; the word I spoke is what will judge him at the last day." When
we fear God, we live in awe of His greatness and desire to be obedient to His commands. This does not make our lives either boring or
stilted in any way as some may presume. Instead, our lives are
blessed and enriched in many ways.

13:14 The teaching of the wise is a fountain of life, to turn
aside from the snares of death.

This verse directs our attention to a beautiful gift we ought to
strive to impart to others. It is the gift of wise teaching. It is a fountain of life. Because it bubbles up, a fountain implies clear and pure
water coming from a source that is so full and overflowing that it

must release its pressure by bubbling over. So it is when we are full of truth and God's word and wisdom. In this state we feel as though we must share with those around us. Ponce de Leon should have read this passage and spent more time reading the Bible instead of searching for the elusive fountain of youth in Florida!

13:15–16 Good understanding produces favor, but the way of the treacherous is hard. Every prudent man acts with knowledge, but a fool displays folly.

One of the major benefits of studying the book of Proverbs and applying the truths contained therein is that in so doing we may attain favor from both God and man. It will also increase the quality of our lives. Notice the contrast, however, between the fool and the prudent man. The fool (by definition, of course) acts foolishly and his *way* is hard. While many Christians may point out that living a life for Christ is also *hard,* by way of contrast, the fool's life is much harder, in ways it does not need to be.

13:17 A wicked messenger falls into adversity, but a faithful envoy brings healing.

Simply do what you are supposed to do. This is the cornerstone of stewardship. Are you reliable? Are you trustworthy? The implication of this verse is that a wicked messenger may get into trouble, complications, or adversity because he does wicked things. By contrast, when we are faithful, healing may begin.

13:18 Poverty and shame will come to him who neglects discipline, but he who regards reproof will be honored.

We've heard it before, but Solomon understood that learning comes through repetition. Is it possible to have too much discipline? Solomon didn't think so. Perhaps he realized all too well his own weaknesses in this area. Learn to value reproof rather than feeling defeated by it.

13:19 Desire realized is sweet to the soul, but it is an abomination to fools to depart from evil.

The fool cannot understand why a person would quit being evil. In our society, gang members greatly resent any fellow gang member who attempts to leave the gang. Rehabilitation in regard to criminal behavior has an extremely small success rate. This is because one must both *want* to change and see the *need* to change. This is actually the first aspect to understanding the gospel. All have sinned and fall short of the glory of God. We all need His gift of salvation, but not all realize or accept this reality.

To see a promise fulfilled and to experience "desire realized" is to be truly blessed. David wrote, "Cultivate faithfulness, delight yourself in the LORD; and He will give you the desires of your heart" (Psalm 37:3–4). How sweet it is!

13:20 He who walks with wise men will be wise, but the companion of fools will suffer harm.

What a responsibility we possess on our part. We must seek out wise men, and if we in turn have become wise ourselves, it behooves us to share our wealth with others. Ask yourself this question: When others walk with me, what is the end result? Do they become more wise or more foolish? Perhaps we fool ourselves when we rationalize that they have their own free will and they are virtually unchanged by being around us. Consider Proverbs 27:17. Iron does sharpen iron, but you must truly prove your metal. This verse presents a challenge; will you rise to it?

13:21 Adversity pursues sinners, but the righteous will be rewarded with prosperity.

Sometimes adversity comes slowly to those who deserve it, and sometimes it comes it at breakneck speed—but it always comes. The end of the wicked is coming, and they *will* be paid their wages.

Every time a sinner turns his head and looks behind him, he will notice that he is still being chased. Insecurity is the watchword of his existence. Not so for the righteous. Those who are righteous, by the blood of Christ, understand that their reward is great.

13:22 A good man leaves an inheritance to his children's children, and the wealth of the sinner is stored up for the righteous.

Were you wondering what to do with any material wealth in your estate upon your death? Perhaps your grandchildren should receive first consideration. The theme of this verse is about the contrast between good men and sinful men and the amount of control and influence they have *after* they die. Evil men forfeit all after-death control. Compare Solomon's insights into this subject from the philosophical book of Ecclesiastes (2:26): "For to a person who is good in His sight He has given wisdom and knowledge and joy, while to the sinner He has given the task of gathering and collecting so that He may give to one who is good in God's sight."

13:23 Abundant food is in the fallow ground of the poor, but it is swept away by injustice.

This verse addresses two elements needed for those who are poor to prosper. Those two elements are opportunity and justice. Fallow ground implies latent possibilities and opportunity. It is land that can be developed into productive crops. Combined with intelligent labor, it will yield abundance. But Solomon identifies a distinct sociological need that *must* accompany any situation that has these same possibilities and opportunities. That need is *justice!* Without justice, no amount of labor will bring about the desired abundance.

13:24 He who spares his rod hates his son, but he who loves him disciplines him diligently.

119

This politically incorrect idea is essential to understand if we are going to parent biblically. This verse is not saying that we should be overly authoritarian. It is saying that we should not be overly permissive. Children should not run the household. The love of a child for his parents requires respect if it is to be healthy. The love of a parent for his children requires diligent discipline. We must demonstrate our love by insisting that they learn and practice moral behavior. The focus should be on morality. We do not discipline because the child got a math problem wrong. We may discipline because the child chose not to do or attempt an assignment. When you use the "rod," be sure to identify the area of morality that is involved.

13:25 The righteous has enough to satisfy his appetite, but the stomach of the wicked is in want.

Paul penned the idea this way, "And my God shall supply all your needs according to His riches in glory" (Philippians 4:19).

Proverbs 14

14:1 The wise woman builds her house, but the foolish tears it down with her own hands.

*S*olomon and King Lemuel (see also Proverbs 31) both had a very high view of women. This is a rather extraordinary view considering the era and the general culture of the times. However, in order to achieve this place of honor, the prerequisite consideration was that a woman must be wise.

How many men and women have contributed to the breakdown of their own families? Modern man has become quite foolish in so many areas of endeavor. Can you think of several ways in which you could help build *your* house?

14:2 He who walks in his uprightness fears the LORD, but he who is crooked in his ways despises Him.

What path are you on? Where does the path you're on end? How can we walk in uprightness? Solomon wrote in Proverbs 4:11, "I have directed you in the way of wisdom; I have led you in the upright path."

This verse gives us a clue for discovering what path we are on. It involves the thematic motif regarding the fear of the Lord. The fear of the Lord is the beginning point in the development of wisdom. Those who are upright maintain a proper perspective of who God is. Read Proverbs 4:12–19 for more on this subject.

14:3 In the mouth of the foolish is a rod for his back, but the lips of the wise will preserve them.

Once again we see the power of the mouth. It can destroy or save us.

14:4 Where no oxen are, the manger is clean, but much increase comes by the strength of the ox.

This is another one of my personal favorites from the book of Proverbs. I once heard a sermon by Charles Swindoll in which he pointed out that a creative mess is better than tidy idleness. If you want to eat, you may have to shovel some manure. The point is, what are your priorities?

Are you the type of person who would get rid of the ox so you would be able to quit cleaning its stable? This may work during the winter, but what happens in spring and harvest when you need to plant and reap? It seems to me that there are two types of people who would get rid of the ox. A lazy person might get rid of it just to avoid the daily grind of feeding and cleaning. Or a control-oriented person might get rid of it because the mess is simply disgusting.

We live in an orderly universe, for God created it as such. Therefore, as we emulate our Father there is certainly a place for us to be orderly and neat. More than neatness, what the verse is really getting at is finding balance in the way we approach decisions. Martha was a type of controlling person. But as Jesus told Martha in Luke 10:38–41, "You are worried and upset about many things, but only one thing is needed."

Keep the ox. Accept the discipline necessary to keep it fed and clean. Certainly there is an "ox" in your life somewhere. Thank God for providing for your needs, even if you have to do some work for it. And when your harvest is abundant, praise God as you use His blessings to further His kingdom.

14:5 A faithful witness will not lie, but a false witness speaks lies.

What is a faithful witness? Clearly, based on this verse, it is one who does not lie. If we consider the totality of scripture we will note that it is much more. In the book of Revelation, John referred to Jesus Christ as "the faithful witness, the firstborn of the dead, and the ruler of the kings of the earth" (Revelation 1:5). Jesus is the ultimate faithful witness, for it is He who bears witness to our relationship with Him.

Quiz question: Which of the Ten Commandments states, "Thou shalt not lie"? Is it number 7 or number 9?

Actually, neither Exodus 20 nor Deuteronomy 5 says "Thou shalt not lie." The command is, "You shall not bear false witness against your neighbor." It is simply summarized frequently as "Do not lie."

14:6 A scoffer seeks wisdom, and finds none, but knowledge is easy to him who has understanding.

What are the prerequisites to wisdom? One is listed here in this verse—don't be a mocker or scoffer. What is the nature of a scoffer? What does a scoffer believe in? What motivates a mocker to mock?

There is a relationship between seeking truth and wisdom, just as there is a relationship between those who do not believe in truth and those who find no wisdom. Postmodern thinkers who believe we all create our own truth and that there is no real "truth" cannot find wisdom because they do not believe it exists.

How would you connect this verse in Proverbs with Jesus' statement—"Seek and ye shall find"—or James' encouragement—

"If any of you lack wisdom, let him ask of God who gives to all men liberally" (James 1:5)? Does God give to all men "liberally" except scoffers?

As Thomas discovered, our Father *does* completely tolerate a certain degree of uncertainty and questioning. But when we are on our quest for truth, we must genuinely remain open. When we cross over from questioning to scoffing, we have indeed stepped off of one path and onto another.

The idea of a mocker seeking wisdom is simply a spiritual oxymoron. It is painful for me to remember the many times that I have shared the gospel with someone who has said something like "Oh, I read the Bible once" or "I tried that for a while; it just didn't work for me."

On the other hand, the latter part of the verse is very comforting: "Knowledge comes easily to the discerning." A wise man gains increasing amounts of wisdom easily. A proper daily walk should be yielding steady, continual growth in your knowledge as well.

> Proverbs 14:7 Leave the presence of a fool, or you will not discern words of knowledge.

The Apostle Paul wrote the idea this way: "You . . . who teach another, do you not teach yourself?" (Romans 1:21). Why shouldn't you hang around with fools? Because you won't learn wisdom, and also because you may lapse into a fool's way of thinking (and thus become a fool yourself). In addition to this, if you hang around fools, you will not *discern* words of knowledge. Don't confuse the difference between ministering to fools and hanging out with fools. Do the former; avoid the latter.

> 14:8 The wisdom of the prudent is to understand his way, but the folly of fools is deceit.

Metacognition is the term educators give to thinking about your thinking. The NIV version points out that "the wisdom of the prudent is to give thought to their ways."

Do you understand the way you are going? Do you understand your path and its end? We ought to meditate as did the psalmist, "Who is the man who fears the LORD? He will instruct him in the way he should choose" (Psalm 25:12). We should also pray as David did, "Make me know Thy ways, O LORD; Teach me Thy paths. Lead me in Thy truth and teach me" (Psalm 25:4–5).

14:9 Fools mock at sin, but among the upright there is good will.

Fools take sin lightly (review Proverbs 13:19). It's a way of life. Everybody's doin' it, and "the fool has said in his heart, 'There is no God'" (Psalm 14:1). If there is no God, then there is no such thing as sin. Look out for number one. This is a fool's mentality.

Isaiah wrote, "Woe to those who call evil good, and good evil" (Isaiah 5:20). The man of God ought to maintain his eyes on God as Isaiah did: "Woe is me . . . for I am a man of unclean lips" (Isaiah 6:5).

Even Christians need to be very cautious regarding this point. If you even utter the following sentence, ask yourself what you actually mean by it: "Well, everybody sins." Are you making a theological statement of truth, or are you justifying your own past shortcomings? Are you planning on future sins?

Is sin real? For the Christian, this strikes at the heart of the gospel. Not only is it real, but it has wrought a chasm between man and God, and its wages are death. The fool who mocks sin has a depraved mind that cannot comprehend true reality.

14:10 The heart knows its own bitterness, and a stranger does not share its joy.

Intimacy is something most of us long for, yet often it eludes many of us. Life is filled with both bitterness and joy. Bitterness is decreased when it is shared in intimacy, just as joy is increased when it is shared. Bitterness shared sometimes allows us to see meaning in our sorrow. It allows us to see a larger picture, and this increased perspective often allows us to forgive. Bitterness, once sown and allowed to grow, reaps blame. This blame may be directed toward others, ourselves, and even toward God. How intimate are you with your spouse, with yourself, and with the Creator of your heart? The answer may also reveal something about the level of joy in your life.

Solomon noted in Ecclesiastes 4:9–10: "Two are better than one because they have a good reward for their labor. For if either of them falls, the one will lift up his companion. But woe to the one who falls when there is not another to lift him up."

Job knew the sharp pain of loss and bitterness:

Naked I came from my mother's womb, and naked I shall return there. The LORD gave and the LORD has taken away. (Job 1:21)

Shall we indeed accept good from God and not accept adversity? (Job 2:10)

Job opened his mouth and cursed the day of his birth. (Job 3:1)

However, Job had no true intimacy with his friends.

Then Job answered, . . . "Sorry comforters are you all. Is there no limit to windy words?" (Job 16:1–3)

But his intimacy with God slowly grew stronger.

As for me, I know that my Redeemer lives, and at the last He will take His stand on the earth. Even after my skin is flayed, yet without my flesh I shall see God; whom I myself shall behold, and whom my eyes shall see and not another. (Job 19:25–27)

At the end, because of the growth through pain and loss *and* because of Job's increased faith, he was able to declare, "I have heard of Thee by the hearing of the ear; but now my eye sees Thee" (Job 42:5).

14:11 The house of the wicked will be destroyed, but the tent of the upright will flourish.

This verse contrasts three areas: 1) a house with a tent, 2) the wicked with the upright, and 3) destruction with flourishing. This verse forces us to examine our priorities. A house in danger of destruction is of little value. Notice how similar this idea is to the words of Jesus about a wise man who built his house on rock and a foolish man who built on sand. This story can be found in Matthew 7:24–27. The contrast here in Proverbs is that a tent can be better than a house because protection and safety are the real issues.

14:12 There is a way which seems right to a man, but its end is the way of death.

We ought to examine our *way* daily (see also Proverbs 16:25). Keep the present in perspective by glancing always into the future, while you use the past to learn and to grow from. Above all, walk God's way rather than your way!

14:13 Even in laughter the heart may be in pain, and the end of joy may be grief.

Solomon had some interesting ideas concerning laughter and sorrow: "It is better to go to a house of mourning than to go to a house of feasting, because that is the end of every man . . . . Sorrow is better than laughter, for when a face is sad a heart may be happy. The mind of the wise is in the house of mourning, while the mind of fools is in the house of pleasure" (Ecclesiastes 7:2–4).

127

In my opinion, God wants us to be partial Christian existentialists. An existentialist realizes what a gift life is, for as we consider death, we come to grips with the temporality of our flesh. This gives value to our existence, and it means that we realize that we ought to make our lives count for God in the here and now. What legacy will you leave with your children or to those you have led to the Lord? This line of thinking brings a healthy sense of urgency to live our lives "fully."

However, the reason Christians can never be full-fledged existentialists is because we know we will be resurrected and exist in another place that Jesus has prepared for us. We know we will enter God's rest and through His grace live in peace. We know, beyond a shadow of a doubt, that this life is *not* all there is.

Remember that the external features of an individual may be a facade. Attempt to look at your own heart, as our Lord does.

Keep time in perspective as well. Solomon wrote, "The *end* of joy may be grief." By maintaining an eternal worldview, we see the importance of living our lives here and now as we heed the advice of James[3] by showing our faith through our works.

> 14:14 The backslider in heart will have his fill of his own ways, but a good man will be satisfied with his.

Today we might paraphrase this verse as "What comes around goes around." Don't grow weary in doing good. You will be rewarded. Someday you will hear the blessed words, "Well done, thou good and faithful servant," if you persevere and are obedient. As for the backslider, don't worry about him; he will get his just reward.

> 14:15 The naive believes everything, but the prudent man considers his steps.

Christians talk a great deal about belief. So does the world. The world says you should believe in yourself. The Bible says, "Believe in the Lord Jesus and you shall be saved" (Acts 16:31).

Don't believe everything, believe in the truth—Jesus Christ. Some people believe in UFOs, others in a politician, still others in "nothing" (this is called *nihilism* by philosophers).

What do you believe in? As we seek to understand God's word we must take the scriptures as a whole. Psalm 119:160 enlightens us that "the sum of Thy word is Truth." Let us be prudent, giving thought to our steps. God created us with the ability to be rational creatures (at least to some degree!). Our faith is not a blind faith. In fact, the more clearly we "see" our majestic Father, the greater our faith becomes.

14:16 A wise man is cautious and turns away from evil, but a fool is arrogant and careless.

Why do you shun evil? Genuine fear of the Lord is enough to reinforce in our hearts and minds the necessity to shun evil. Why is the fool careless? Because of his arrogance, he does not perceive his mortality nor discern his vulnerability.

14:17 A quick-tempered man acts foolishly, and a man of evil devices is hated.

Self-control is crucial to living wisely. If we do not control our tempers, we will often participate in foolish behavior.

14:18 The naive inherit folly, but the prudent are crowned with knowledge.

This typical contrast between a naive person and a prudent person ought to reinforce within us a desire to be men and women of God who will be crowned with knowledge. Knowledge is a tool, and by it we may glorify God and help those around us. God wants us to be knowledgeable rather than filled with folly.

14:19 The evil will bow down before the good, and the wicked at the gates of the righteous.

This principle has been clearly shown through the story of Joseph. John also wrote about the great white throne judgment in Revelation. In this world there will always be evil, but our hope is in an eternal God who is always there and will always be there. We know who wins the final battle!

> 14:20–21 The poor is hated even by his neighbor, but those who love the rich are many. He who despises his neighbor sins, but happy is he who is gracious to the poor.

These two verses should be read together. Verse 20 contains an observation. The poor have it tough. It is implied by both verses that a wise man should strive to not be poor. Solomon has stressed hard work, planning, asking many "counselors" for advice, and trusting in the Lord to supply your needs. "All hard work brings a profit" (Proverbs 14:23).

Being poor is a relative term in each society. We are not to condemn or hate the poor, and we must understand, as Jesus pointed out, that "the poor you have with you always" (Matthew 26:11). But it is to be our goal to be able to *give* to the poor. God may choose to bless us with wealth, but regardless of the world's standards, we are to be good and faithful stewards of what the Lord allows us to use. We use it because we do not possess it. That which a man possesses may in the end possess him. (See also Matthew 5:3.)

Let's summarize the application this way. Don't worry about defining whether people are poor or rich (including yourself, and perhaps especially yourself). Don't despise anyone, and always have a ready attitude to give to those in need.

Having gone through this concept, another Christian asked me if this means we must give to every beggar we come across. He lived in a city where he is constantly running into beggars. I can't answer this for everyone in every situation, but I can only say I have never helped someone out and later had a regret for it. There have been several times when I chose not to help someone and my conscience did bother me. The principle is to be "gracious to the poor." How *you* define that is between you and God.

14:22 Will they not go astray who devise evil? But kindness and truth will be to those who devise good.

This verse begins with a rhetorical question, "Will they not go astray . . .?" We possess the ability and opportunity for devising good or evil. However, the cause-and-effect results of our choices will influence many aspects of our lives. What does it mean to "go astray"? Solomon again thematically refers to the "way." Going astray is veering from the path that leads to God and righteousness and life.

How can this verse be applied to our daily lives? Why not devise something good right now? Begin with a list of several things you could do this week or month.

14:23 In all labor there is profit, but mere talk leads only to poverty.

Talk is cheap (although the results of the tongue can be very expensive indeed!). You can talk all day, but unless you begin to *do,* nothing will come of it. There is no substitute for a strong work ethic.

14:24 The crown of the wise is their riches, but the folly of fools is foolishness.

When do we acquire our crown? When do we earn our crown? Consider the following passages:

Bless the LORD . . . who crowns you with lovingkindness and compassion. (Psalm 103:4)

The prudent are crowned with knowledge. (Proverbs 14:18)

A gray head is a crown of glory. (Proverbs 16:31)

Grandchildren are the crown of old men. (Proverbs 17:6)

131

What do you hope to be crowned with?

On a light note, it is intriguing to observe the alliteration of the English translation: "The folly of fools is foolishness." How true it is and how easily observed.

14:25 A truthful witness saves lives, but he who speaks lies is treacherous.

Keep in mind that the telling of lies is often a matter of life and death! Be truthful. God is in the business of saving lives, and we can be too! To save a life brings great joy in heaven (see Luke 15:7). Think of this also in your witness to others concerning the Lord. You can be a spiritual lifesaver!

14:26 In the fear of the LORD there is strong confidence, and his children will have refuge.

Most fear brings terror, but fear of the Lord brings peace rather than terror. We have refuge in him. To have a place of refuge— what a blessed thought. As my Biblical Foundations teacher, Dr. Morris, used to say, "Take God's promises, mix them with your faith, and rest."

Notice the thematic difference here in this portion of the book of Proverbs as compared to the first nine chapters. In chapters 1– 9, the fear of the Lord was the beginning of wisdom. Now in this portion of scripture, it is seen as much more. It is the means of "strong confidence" (v. 26) and a "fountain of life" (v. 27). Proverbs 16:6 states, "By the fear of the LORD one keeps away from evil" and Proverbs 19:23 points out that it "leads to life."

.What a blessed privilege it is to realize that we are God's children. John 1:12 points out that those who believe are children of God. In Galatians 3:26, Paul reminds us we are "sons of God through faith in Christ Jesus." As children of God we not only have a refuge, we are also heirs. See also Romans 8:17; Galatians 4:7; and James 2:5.

14:27 The fear of the LORD is a fountain of life, that one may avoid the snares of death.

Do you want the fountain of life? Then fear the Lord! How do you avoid the snares of death? Again, fear the Lord.

"Who is the man who fears the LORD? He will instruct him in the way he should choose. His soul will abide in prosperity, and his descendants will inherit the land. The secret of the LORD is for those who fear Him, and He will make them know His covenant" (Psalm 25:12–14).

14:28 In a multitude of people is a king's glory, but in the dearth of people is a prince's ruin.

What is a king without people to rule? Not much.

The NASB uses the term *dearth* in this verse. *Dearth* is a Middle English word meaning lack or scarcity. The Hebrew word used here is *'ephec* (eh-fes). This word can indicate want, cessation, or even the idea of "less than nothing."

Can a leader without followers still call himself a leader? Clearly, a leader without followers is like a dog chasing its own tail. He may be keeping himself entertained, but he is accomplishing very little for others.

14:29 He who is slow to anger has great understanding, but he who is quick-tempered exalts folly.

Be slow to anger. Whenever you get angry swiftly, you are exalting folly. Seek always to exalt the Lord. Analyze your anger. Is it righteous? A fool becomes angry easily, at the drop of a hat. The wise man *may* become angry, but he does so in a measured fashion.

14:30 A tranquil heart is life to the body, but passion is rottenness to the bones.

Our mental state of being influences our physical state of being. Having a "tranquil heart" means having internal peace. Looking simply at the contrast that declares, "Passion is rottenness to the bones," we can see that Solomon is telling us to be in control of our emotions. The Hebrew word used here is *qin'ah,* which may be translated as jealousy or envy. It is derived from the root word *qana'* (kaw-naw') meaning to be zealous in a bad way. "Thou shalt not covet" was issued as a command not because our Father wanted to tease us or make life more difficult. This command (as are all of them) is given to us to improve the quality of our life. Coveting is a combination of desiring something (or someone) and craving it. When *want* is allowed to reign in our minds until a metamorphosis transforms it into a *need,* coveting has taken place. In such a state of mind, God is no longer first in our thoughts or in our lives. This is the danger of passions that rot us from the inside out. May all of your passions flow from the passion of a heart panting after God.

> 14:31 He who oppresses the poor reproaches his Maker, but he who is gracious to the needy honors Him.

This is a powerful statement. It demonstrates that how we treat others is in effect a direct correlation reflecting our relationship with Almighty God. This verse gives us a practical way in which we may seek to honor God. See how Jesus expanded upon this idea in Matthew 25:34–40.

> 14:32 The wicked is thrust down by his wrongdoing, but the righteous has a refuge when he dies.

One of the most profound thoughts of Christianity is that there is much more to life than life itself. There is life beyond life as we currently experience it. Just as the resurrection of Christ is a reality, no less a reality is our own coming resurrection (John 5:28–29). Keep in mind this beautiful truth: "Precious in the sight of the LORD is the death of His godly ones" (Psalm 116:15).

14:33 Wisdom rests in the heart of one who has understanding, but in the bosom of fools it is made known.

Understanding is a precursor of wisdom. All people have access to wisdom. Psalm 19:1 states that the heavens declare the glory of God. The wise man looks for this wisdom. He grasps it and utilizes it and makes it a part of his being, and thus a part of his heart. But a fool ignores it, even if it rests within the same proximity. Notice the contrast given in the verse: the fool has it within his "bosom." This is a part of his chest, but the wisdom here may be exhaled as easily as it was inhaled. By contrast, the wise man allows it to "rest in [his] heart."

Possibly the verse should be interpreted another way. The man of understanding has wisdom, and he thus avoids certain unwise choices and behaviors. These things he observes others doing, and these others experience the results of their folly. This merely confirms to the man of understanding the truth of what he already knew.

14:34 Righteousness exalts a nation, but sin is a disgrace to any people.

Morality and a desire for truth and justice are all part of a nation that is righteous. It is these facets of character that enable a nation to rise up. These characteristics enable a people to see beyond themselves. Where righteousness is diminished, egocentrism sets in. People become "me"-centered, and begin to look out only for their own personal interests. Crime rises, the quality of life is lessened, bribery increases, and people turn increasingly to vices as a way of escaping either responsibility or pain.

Tolerance of evil is also a byproduct as sin becomes increasingly prevalent. In becoming more tolerant as a nation, we may view ourselves as more enlightened, more advanced, less barbaric, etc., but the rest of the world looks on us with more and more disgrace.

14:35 The king's favor is toward a servant who acts wisely, but his anger is toward him who acts shamefully.

Wise acts and shameful acts have consequences not only in eternity, but also in the here and now.

If you are interested in seeing how this proverb has been illustrated elsewhere in scripture, consider the following passages: Nehemiah 2:1–8; Daniel 6:3–24; Luke 12:40–48, 19:12–26.

Proverbs 15

15:1 A gentle answer turns away wrath, but a harsh word stirs up anger.

To have the ability to turn away wrath is a truly wonderful skill. Knowing the principle of this verse has helped me out numerous times personally. The following story is true.

One day I was visiting Santa Barbara, California, and I went into a public restroom. There was no one in the facility except a large, muscular man and myself. Suddenly I felt myself being pushed against the wall and I was punched twice in the abdominal area. However, I could tell the man was drunk, and his punches were surprisingly soft. I looked at his bloodshot eyes and said, "It looks to me like you've had a hard day."

Just as suddenly as the attack had begun, it dissipated. The man relaxed and announced that, in fact, he was having a bad day. We talked a few minutes before I left. I know nothing about where he is now, but I do know that on that day, I was able to avert wrath because I was able to utter a gentle answer.

15:2 The tongue of the wise makes knowledge acceptable, but the mouth of fools spouts folly.

Teachers should attempt to make knowledge acceptable. This includes making it meaningful, clear, and applicable. In Acts 8:30–35 Philip asked the Ethiopian court official if he understood Isaiah. He then explained it to him. In Luke 24:25–27 Jesus explained the meaning of the Old Testament messianic scriptures to two men on the road to Emmaus. These are powerful examples for us to follow as we seek to make knowledge acceptable (see also Proverbs 15:7).

15:3 The eyes of the LORD are in every place, watching the evil and the good.

God sees all and He knows what we do! The author of Hebrews noted, "There is no creature hidden from His sight, but all things are open and laid bare to the eyes of Him" (Hebrews 4:13).

15:4 A soothing tongue is a tree of life, but perversion in it crushes the spirit.

Our tongues are amazingly powerful, and they can be used for either good or evil. We can encourage and build up others, or we can tear down and seek to destroy others.

15:5 A fool rejects his father's discipline, but he who regards reproof is prudent.

How do you handle reproof? Do you blame, make excuses, and reject suggestions out of hand? Or do you consider the reproof, ponder your options, act upon the information, and thank the reprover? Fools hate discipline, but a disciple is a learner. Fools hate to learn, but a wise man demonstrates his prudence by regarding reproof.

15:6 Much wealth is in the house of the righteous, but trouble is in the income of the wicked.

The contrast between the righteous and the wicked is very common in the book of Proverbs. What makes this verse so interesting are the differing outcomes associated with being either righteous or wicked. In this example, both the righteous and the wicked have wealth. But the wealth of the wicked has strings attached to it. When Solomon contrasts a sluggard with a prudent man (elsewhere in Proverbs), the contrast focuses on what the sluggard does not have, such as food in the winter. The sluggard has no wealth. The wicked here has wealth, but at an additional price of trouble.

15:7 The lips of the wise spread knowledge, but the hearts of fools are not so.

To spread knowledge, you must first possess it. If you possess it, you may then choose to spread it. It is very much like sowing seeds. This verse suggests that you will *want* to spread knowledge if you are wise. By contrast, fools don't want to help others, because they are self-centered.

15:8 The sacrifice of the wicked is an abomination to the LORD, but the prayer of the upright is His delight.

Cain's sacrifice (Genesis 3:3) made a mockery of the word *sacrifice* to the Lord. It was unacceptable. As followers of Christ we are to be living sacrifices to the Lord. Matthew 12:7, 33–37 offers additional insights into what God desires of us. We are to bear good fruit and have compassion rather than offering pseudo-sacrifices. In Matthew 23:14, 28 Jesus points out that pharisaical hypocrisy is a deadly disease. He warns, "How shall you escape the sentence of hell?" (Matthew 23:33). How can a warning be stated any more emphatically?

The later portion of verse 8 offers us a joyous insight. Our prayers are not in vain, nor do they fall on deaf ears. In fact, God delights greatly in them. Revelation 5:8 points out that our prayers are like incense to God!

15:9 The way of the wicked is an abomination to the LORD, but He loves him who pursues righteousness.

God hates the sin but He loves the sinner (see Romans 5:8). It is the *way* of the sinner that He finds to be an abomination.

Do you want to be righteous? Abraham "believed in the LORD; and He reckoned it to him as righteousness" (Genesis 15:6). Many Christians bemoan the fact that they are constant sinners. To this, I ask how they define sin. Are they living each day in rebellion to God, or do they simply slip on occasion? To live a victorious Christian life *is* possible. Review Romans 6 and 8 for Paul's insights into how to pursue righteousness. We must understand Romans 7 within the context of chapters 6 and 8.

15:10 Stern discipline is for him who forsakes the way; he who hates reproof will die.

Don't be arrogant. We need to be men and women of God who accept reproof.

15:11 Sheol and Abaddon lie open before the LORD, how much more the hearts of men!

Sheol is defined in Strong's dictionary[4] as the world of the dead. We have no exact synonym in English, although the figurative usage of the word *grave* might do as well as any.

Abaddon is somewhat similar to the Greek term *Hades*. Basically it means destruction. It comes from the root *abad,* which means to lose oneself, or to break or destroy.

While they are both used as nouns, *Sheol* is used more as a reference to a place, rather like the Norse idea of the Netherworld. *Abaddon* is used more to express the result of the act of destruction.

David wrote, "Where can I go from Thy Spirit? Or where can I flee from Thy Presence? If I ascend to heaven, Thou art there; If I make my bed in Sheol, behold, Thou art there" (Psalm 139: 7–8).

One concept is clear from this verse, and it is repeated in other scriptures as well. The realm of death is not off limits to God. He is the author of life, so therefore He is also the inventor of death.

The comparison of the verse is fascinating, as Solomon compares death with our hearts. You cannot hide your heart from God's omniscient gaze. For a more in-depth look at the concepts of Sheol and Abaddon, see Appendix B at the back of the book.

15:12 A scoffer does not love one who reproves him, he will not go to the wise.

It is amazing how many of those who ask the question "How can you believe the Bible?" refuse to give it a truly thorough reading. I have known many foolish people who claim to be looking for *truth,* yet refuse to believe it may be found in the Bible. Because of their assumption they refuse to ask any Christian for information about truth. Fools do not want to learn. They may say that they do, but actually they really just want their ears tickled and their egos fed.

15:13 A joyful heart makes a cheerful face, but when the heart is sad, the spirit is broken.

The *heart* influences us physically, psychologically, and spiritually. "A joyful heart is good medicine, but a broken spirit dries up the bones" (Proverbs 17:22).

15:14 The mind of the intelligent seeks knowledge, but the mouth of fools feeds on folly.

You are what you eat—but not only physically! The Bible clearly points out that fools become increasingly depraved in a downward spiral (see Romans 1). The opposite is equally true. No one becomes a spiritual giant overnight. We are all in process, and that process involves growth and change toward an ever deeper relationship with God and thus ever greater spiritual maturity.

"If any of you lacks wisdom, let him ask of God" (James 1:5). The intelligence spoken of by Solomon has nothing to do with IQ or the internal "smarts" you were born with. It has everything to do with the choices you make and your moral intelligence. According to the Bible, you choose whether to be a fool or a wise man. You were not born a fool or a sage. Remember, when Solomon penned these words, he was very much aware that his personal wisdom was not possessed at birth, or through his childhood. It was acquired as a gift from God because of his choices and desires.

> 15:15 All the days of the afflicted are bad, but a cheerful heart has a continual feast.

Solomon points out the basic difference between the optimist and the pessimist. Optimism and pessimism both have to do with attitude and outlook. How important are attitude and outlook in developing a grateful and thankful perspective? How important are gratefulness and thankfulness in maintaining praise and a proper prayer life? These last two questions help us to see how attitude bleeds over into every area of relationships. To a great extent, we create our perceptions of reality. While the actual situations may be identical, the opportunities perceived and the way we react to each situation may be greatly different, depending on whether we are "cheerful" or not!

> 15:16–17 Better is a little with the fear of the LORD, than great treasure and turmoil with it. Better is a dish of vegetables where love is, than a fattened ox and hatred with it.

We should strive to be rich toward God (in the sense of laying up treasures in heaven) rather than materially rich (see Luke 12:16–22).

But these verses get at the issue of marriage as well. What was the original "American dream"? Was it a house with a white picket fence with wealth and affluence? No, the original American dream of those who landed at Plymouth Rock was to worship God in a political climate of freedom. Our desire ought to be one of ever drawing nearer to our Lord. Value love, and treasure your relationships, but never value wealth at the expense of your relationships.

15:18 A hot-tempered man stirs up strife, but the slow to anger pacifies contention.

People with bad tempers get into a habit of utilizing their ill temper. It provides an adrenaline rush that may be very addictive. It also may give them a sense of power (if those around them are cowed by their outbursts). It is a cyclical phenomenon, because as Solomon points out, the hot-tempered man stirs up strife. This strife feeds his own temper, and it also creates more strife, which will soon give him more reason to complain.

15:19 The way of the sluggard is as a hedge of thorns, but the path of the upright is a highway.

A sluggard is a person who is habitually lazy and idle.

We are all on a path and a journey. There is only one path, one "way," that leads to the Father. The path of the upright is a highway. It is narrow, but the Lord goes before and clears the path, thus making it a highway. But it is also a high and lofty way. It is a way of righteousness that leads to heaven. It is morally a *high* way.

The sluggard has difficulty moving forward because of the thorns that block his path. This is a part of the curse spoken of in Genesis 3.

It is also of interest to note how Isaiah used this concept of a highway. Isaiah wrote: "And a highway will be there, a roadway, and it will be called the highway of holiness. The unclean will not travel on it, but it will be for him who walks that way, and fools will not wander on it, no lion will be there . . . but the redeemed will walk there . . . they will find gladness and joy, and sorrow and sighing will flee away" (Isaiah 35:8ff.).

This highway must be chosen, and you cannot simply wander onto it! Isaiah implies that this highway leads to a place like heaven. See also Isaiah 62:10–12; Proverbs 16:17; Psalm 84:5; and Jeremiah 31:21–34 for further study.

15:20 A wise son makes a father glad, but a foolish man despises his mother.

Have you made your earthly father glad? What about your heavenly Father? There are many things in life that may motivate our choices and decisions. Choosing to do something you believe will make your father and mother glad is an honorable motive. Remember, "Honor your father and mother" is a command with a promise (see Ephesians 6:2). Utilizing God's statutes will also make us positive, influential examples for others.

15:21 Folly is joy to him who lacks sense, but a man of understanding walks straight.

"I love to be a jerk." Thus saith the fool. Compare the fools in Proverbs 1:10–18, who said, "Let us lie in wait for innocent blood, let us ambush the innocent without cause."

Fools don't need a reason to do stupid things. The act alone is cause enough. The habitual fool possesses a seared conscience. The fool is self-centered. The Golden Rule, "Do unto others as you would have them do unto you," is translated and simplified by a fool's mind as just "Do unto others." He laughs at the pain of others.

The observation "Folly is joy . . ." may be understood by thinking about so-called "get-rich-quick" schemes. Such a scheme is a real source of joy to the fool. A fool may be a dreamer who never perspires. He may be a man of many dreams who brings few to fruition. Notice the contrasted teaching in verse 21. The man of understanding walks straight. He is goal oriented, and he proceeds straight on target. By contrast, the fool wanders here and there. The fool does not "count the cost," as Jesus demonstrated in Luke 14:28–32.

144

15:22 Without consultation, plans are frustrated, but with many counselors they succeed.

Counselor role models include Samuel, Nathan, Daniel, Barnabas, and Jesus, whom Isaiah identified as our "wonderful counselor."

What is the biblical role of counselors? Biblical counselors seek the Lord first, ask God Himself for advice, and recognize the role of the Holy Spirit. To be biblical, they must steep themselves in the word of God continually. Their role is to act as advisors and encouragers. To the believer, a biblical counselor offers helpful reminders of biblical principles and insights into how those principles may be applied to a current situation. To the unbeliever the biblical counselor offers bold and truthful advice regarding the unbeliever's need for repentance and relationship with God.

15:23 A man has joy in an apt answer, and how delightful is a timely word!

How important is timing? To edify others should be a goal of all Christians. We can do this through encouragement. Paul issued the following advice to Timothy, but it is valuable for each of us as well: "Be diligent to present yourself approved to God as a workman who does not need to be ashamed, handling accurately the word of truth" (2 Timothy 2:15). By studying and preparing, we can be ready to offer an apt answer and a timely word.

15:24 The path of life leads upward for the wise, that he may keep away from Sheol below.

Here Sheol is seen as a place that the wise man may avoid. A key thing to remember from this verse is that the path of life leads upward. The wise man evaluates his position daily. Is he still on that path? With his eyes on the glories of heaven and the Bible as his sextant, he sights and plots and continues to journey on that sweet path. Did Old Testament believers understand the concept of resurrection? Yes! David wrote, "I will be satisfied with Thy likeness when I awake" (Psalm 17:15). There are many other references, but my personal favorite is Job's statement in Job 19:25–27. Appendix B has more information for those readers who are interested.

> 15:25 The LORD will tear down the house of the proud, but He will establish the boundary of the widow.

The house of the foolish man, built on the sand, will fall down on its own. God will allow nature to take its own course. Not so the house of the proud. His house will literally be torn down by God's own hands. Woe to the man who both is proud and attempts to mess with the property of a widow.

> 15:26 Evil plans are an abomination to the LORD, but pleasant words are pure.

God looks at our hearts. He sees our plans. He knows the thoughts and intents of our hearts. Evil plans are internal and covert to all but the Lord. Pleasant words are external and overt. "Whatever is true, whatever is noble, whatever is right, whatever is pure, whatever is lovely, whatever is admirable . . . think about such things" (Philippians 4:8).

> 15:27 He who profits illicitly troubles his own house, but he who hates bribes will live.

In some countries bribery is an acceptable cultural practice. This does not mean that it is biblically correct. The problem is that bribery leads to corruption and injustice. Bribery is rooted in greed. When those in a position of authority accept bribes, they cease to be public servants and become a leech on the lifeblood of society. As always, we ought to seek to lay up for ourselves treasures in heaven. Embezzlement is a direct affront to God's command, "Thou shalt not steal." Solomon points out that illicit gain will destroy the peace of one's own household. In the end it will bring only trouble. See also 1 Timothy 6:6–10 for additional insights into godly contentment versus a love of money.

> 15:28 The heart of the righteous ponders how to answer, but the mouth of the wicked pours out evil things.

Paul directed Timothy to "be ready in season and out of season" (2 Timothy 4:2). Compare 1 Timothy 4:11–16 and 2 Timothy 2:15 as well.

What proceeds out of the mouth is directly related to what is in the heart.

> 15:29 The LORD is far from the wicked, but He hears the prayer of the righteous.

Proximity, meaning how close we are to the Lord, is always an important issue. When we think of how far the wicked are from the Lord, the next question we may ask is who moved, God or the individual? Scripture states that God is unwilling that any should perish and He is always ready to accept any prodigal back into the fold. Therefore, it must be that the wicked has moved away from the Lord.

The next question that comes to my mind is how near to the Lord am I? And how vibrant is my prayer life? Remember John's warning in which God said, "I will spit you out of My mouth" (Revelation 3:16) because you are lukewarm!

> 15:30 Bright eyes gladden the heart; good news puts fat on the bones.

Your attitude and outlook on life can greatly affect you.

> 15:31 He whose ear listens to the life-giving reproof will dwell among the wise.

Good listening never goes out of style. But listening to reproof is never easy. However, for the man who does listen to reproof, his feet will remain on the path of life. Solomon no doubt learned this truth firsthand, as he was told the stories of Saul and his father. King David, despite his position as monarch, never became so proud that he lost his ability to heed advice.

15:32 He who neglects discipline despises himself, but he who listens to reproof acquires understanding.

How disciplined are you? Are you willing and able to accept reproof? Self-discipline is seen by the world primarily in the physical realm. For example, we often describe great athletes as being very self-disciplined. But self-discipline, as it is expressed in the Bible, deals with the *will* of man.

If you take an undisciplined approach to your prayer life, your devotional life, and your personal witness, then you may not realize it, but you demonstrate by your actions that spiritually you despise yourself. Also, if the Lord Himself chastises you, and you ignore or neglect that discipline, this demonstrates that you despise yourself as well.

Accepting reproof demonstrates a willful commitment to humility. It maintains you in the presence of the wise, and it allows you to acquire understanding.

15:33 The fear of the LORD is the instruction for wisdom, and before honor comes humility.

One of the most profound statements in the entire chapter is "Before honor comes humility." James and John wanted to be at the right hand of Jesus in His glory. This position was for God the Father to decide upon. Seek the kingdom of God with humility. Meditate upon God, fear Him, and live humbly in His presence. These actions you will never regret.

Proverbs 16

16:1 The plans of the heart belong to man, but the answer of the tongue is from the LORD.

*D*o you believe you are acting according the will of God? Remember Solomon's advice from chapter 3, "Trust in the LORD with all your heart, and do not lean on your own understanding. In all your ways acknowledge Him and He will make your paths straight."

Make your plans, but listen to the voice of the Lord. Don't become paralyzed by an irrational fear of being out of the will of God to the point that you can't do anything. There is a seemingly antithetical contrast between the sovereignty of God and the free will of man, but the reality is that both exist. In the big picture, God is in full control. But as a part of that control, He allows what He has created to make choices and to act freely. Thus, in the small picture it may appear that He is not in control. Such an appearance is a perceptual illusion, as the Creator will never be out of control of His creation. God created man with free will, and He expects us to utilize that free will. The "plans of the heart belong to man." Our actions should be done with an attitude that demonstrates our awareness of God and our desire to please Him (see also Proverbs 16:9 and 19:21).

16:2 All the ways of a man are clean in his own sight, but the LORD weighs the motives.

The rich young ruler[5] came before Jesus feeling pretty good about himself. His ways were clean in his own eyes. But as always, Jesus looked deeper into his soul. "All we like sheep have gone astray, each of us has turned to his own way" (Isaiah 53:6). How can we avoid turning to our own way? Solomon's advice is to commit your works to the Lord (see verse 3 also)!

16:3 Commit your works to the LORD, and your plans will be established.

This is a key verse to aid our understanding of the relationship between our plans and the will of God. To "commit" your works to God means to acknowledge Him and dedicate all that you do to Him. Paul wrote, "Whatever you do, do all to the glory of God" (1 Corinthians 10:31).

If you believe in determinism, then Proverbs is not the book for you. Proverbs assumes free will; in fact, Proverbs proves it with numerous examples.

Make plans, but listen to the Lord. Evaluate your motives. Weigh them. Then commit your works to the Lord, and the promise is made that then your plans will succeed. They will be "established," meaning they will be set up and recognized by God. David wrote, "Commit your way to the LORD, trust also in Him, and He will do it" (Psalm 37:5).

16:4 The LORD has made everything for its own purpose, even the wicked for the day of evil.

Everything has a purpose! From Ecclesiastes 3 we learn that there is a time and a place for all things (see also Romans 8:28). What is your purpose? Why are you here? Are you fulfilling your purpose?

Sometimes we wonder why the wicked appear to prosper. This verse reminds us that justice is coming.

16:5 Everyone who is proud in heart is an abomination to the LORD; assuredly, he will not be unpunished.

This verse offers a stiff warning. There are different types of pride. Perhaps the worst type of pride is to be "proud in heart." Man, as a created being, can take no credit for the condition of his heart. We have either a heart full of sin, which is nothing to boast of, or a heart saved by the mercy and lovingkindness of God, which is also nothing to boast of, because it is merely a result of God's grace. It is interesting to note that Solomon chose to use the double negative words "will not go unpunished," rather than the words "will be punished." The use of the double negative in Hebrew adds emphasis. When threatened with punishment, many people in their minds may say, "Maybe, *if* I get caught . . . and maybe I can get away with it." Stated with the double negative, it is clear that a consequence will definitely be forthcoming.

16:6 By lovingkindness and truth iniquity is atoned for, and by the fear of the LORD one keeps away from evil.

This is an important thematic verse. John wrote in his gospel, "The *Word* became flesh and dwelt among us . . . full of grace and truth" (John 1:14). The atonement spoken of in the Old Testament is synonymous with the salvation spoken of in the New Testament. "All of us like sheep have gone astray . . . but the LORD has caused the iniquity of us all to fall on Him . . . He Himself bore the sin of many and interceded for the transgressors" (Isaiah 53:6, 12).

How important is the fear of the Lord? It is crucial to our daily walk. If our mind is not on God it is most likely on ourselves and our desires, our wants, etc. Our fear of God helps us to maintain a proper perspective on reality. It allows us a "reality check."

> 16:7 When a man's ways are pleasing to the LORD, he makes even his enemies to be at peace with him.

A good example of this appears in Genesis 26:12–22. Isaac dug a well in Gerar, and when it was completed the former inhabitants of the land claimed the water as theirs. What would you have done? Would you do what Isaac did? Jesus also discussed this topic in Luke 6:27–28, 33–36. We are called to look for the greater good, the possible eternal consequences, the "bigger picture" if you will. Isaac had a "right" to the well, but he chose another course of action.

Having looked at these passages, how do you think Matthew 10:34 should be understood? "Do not think that I came to bring peace on the earth; I did not come to bring peace, but a sword."

This is one of those concepts that must be viewed in juxtaposition to other scripture verses. Jesus had enemies, and so too shall we. However, we should not readily seek enemies (as some almost gleefully do). We should be characterized as people of peace and good hardworking citizens. As the Sermon on the Mount reminds us, we should love our enemies. God loved us and sent His Son to die for us, even while we were yet His "enemies."

How would others describe you—as a bitter, harsh, self-righteous individual, or as a gentle, loving, and humble peacemaker? This verse reveals a direct application of how we should witness to others. The path of wisdom is not always easy, but when we find it, it is always truly best. As Paul advised us, "Do not be overcome by evil, but overcome evil with good" (Romans 12:21).

> 16:8 Better is a little with righteousness than great income with injustice.

What is better than righteousness? In the spiritual realm there are causes and effects, and righteousness yields blessings both now and forever.

Make a list of the benefits of righteousness! By doing so, surely you will see that nothing is of greater value.

16:9 The mind of man plans his way, but the LORD directs his steps.

To the Christian attuned to God, both God and the individual have a part in the decision-making process (see also 16:1–3). You may and should plan, but be sure to allow God to direct your steps. There is no simple formula for this. However, "Fear God and keep His commandments" (Ecclesiastes 12:13) is a good beginning point. God wants us to live in this type of relaxed tension (between the human and the divine) in our decision-making.

16:10 A divine decision is in the lips of the king; his mouth should not err in judgment.

This verse and the next few verses deal with spiritual leadership. Have you ever made a "divine decision"? When you are in a position of leadership, your decisions may be viewed by others as "God's will." It is a serious event. Don't be unfaithful or flippant in your decisions. Use your mind, but allow the Lord to direct your steps. According to Romans 13:1, "there is no authority except by God, and those which exist are established by God." If leadership has been granted to you, take care to use it well and wisely.

16:11 A just balance and scales belong to the LORD; all the weights of the bag are His concern.

Remember the commandment, "Thou shalt not steal" (Exodus 20:15). When the Lord sets us on the scale of judgment, His balance will be just. If we have the redemption of Jesus on our side, the balance will come out in our favor! He expects no less from us

153

in our dealings with others. As a matter of integrity, we must deal faithfully and justly with those around us. If we maintain a proper perspective on wealth, this will not be an area of strong temptation. If we focus on ourselves and our wants, we may experience a great deal of temptation.

> 16:12 It is an abomination for kings to commit wickedness, for a throne is established on righteousness.

Leaders have a higher, greater responsibility because they have a greater sphere of influence. Historians Will and Ariel Durant observed that governments endured where there was a sense of religion and morality. But corrupt governments soon resulted in the downfall of that particular nation. It is the obligation of a leader to live by the highest of standards. Failure to do so affects not just the leader himself, but also the entire nation.

> 16:13 Righteous lips are the delight of kings, and he who speaks right is loved.

Leaders need counselors. When you are in a position of leadership, surround yourself with righteous people so that you may receive righteous advice. Solomon's advice may be understood in two ways: 1) as a leader, make sure that your lips are righteous, so that those under you will love you; or 2) as a leader, surround yourself with other "righteous lips" to assist you in decision-making so those you are leading may prosper. In this sense the one "loved" is the counselor. This latter view seems more consistent with the first part of the verse.

> 16:14 The wrath of a king is as messengers of death, but a wise man will appease it.

Leaders have great power (at some level, we all find ourselves in the role of leader). Beware; do not misuse your power and authority. Listen to the wise men around you. Here Solomon demonstrates another practical value of wisdom. Wisdom is able to avert unnecessary wrath and death.

16:15 In the light of a king's face is life, and his favor is like a cloud with the spring rain.

As a leader, you have the power to *really* make someone's day special. A smile and a word of cheerful encouragement can go a long way and be a great blessing to someone else! Consider refreshing someone today!

16:16 How much better it is to get wisdom than gold! And to get understanding is to be chosen above silver.

Verses 10–16 have all dealt with aspects of wisdom in leadership. As a final word of advice in this section, a leader should realize that wisdom is better than wealth. Solomon learned this personally (see 1 Kings 3:3–13). Leaders who focus on personal wealth bring corruption and tear down their nation rather than building it up. Why is wisdom better to acquire than gold and silver? Make a list of your own personal reasons.

16:17 The highway of the upright is to depart from evil; he who watches his way preserves his life.

Do you actively "depart from evil," or is evil something you simply "avoid if possible"? Stay on the right path, the highway of the righteous, and "watch your way," for doing so will preserve your life. If you value your life, do not adopt a passive, *laissez-faire* approach to avoiding evil.

16:18 Pride goes before destruction, and a haughty spirit before stumbling.

Could this concept be stated any more clearly? How does this process of destruction come about? The destruction seems to be first internal and then external. Pride brings spiritual destruction. It begins in the form of self-deceit. This inner spiritual corruption then begins to overflow into emotional, psychological, and physical aspects of our being. Jeremiah 49:16 points out, "The arrogance of your heart has deceived you." It is interesting to note that Paul was also quoting from Jeremiah when he advised the Corinthians, "Let him who boasts, boast in the LORD" (1 Corinthians 1:31).

> 16:19 It is better to be of a humble spirit with the lowly, than to divide the spoil with the proud.

You have free will, and you may choose whom to associate with. (How often have we told this to our children?) Will you choose to be with prideful people or those who are humble? Don't be misled by the call of riches and/or fame.

> 16:20 He who gives attention to the word shall find good, and blessed is he who trusts in the LORD.

According to John Calvin, it is necessary to study the word of God if we are to know God: "We must go to the word, in which God is clearly and vividly mirrored for us in His Works, and where the Works of God are appraised not by our perverse judgments but by the criterion of eternal truth."[6]

Martin Luther pointed out in his *95 Theses*: "Injury is done the word of God when, in the same sermon, an equal or larger amount of time is devoted to indulgences than to the word."[7]

The author of Hebrews reminds us that "the word of God is living and active and sharper than any two-edged sword" (Hebrews 4:12).

Psalm 119 has some truly great teaching about the word of God in verses 9, 18, 50, 89, 130, 147, 160, 165.

Teaching via parallels in this verse, Solomon directs us to apply what we learn from the word with trust in the Lord. All men trust something. Some trust in Wall Street. Some trust in the government. Some trust in science. Some trust themselves. A few trust in God.

16:21 The wise in heart will be called discerning, and sweetness of speech increases persuasiveness.

The wisdom of the heart is God's wisdom and it involves the will and morality. If you find that you must choose between different types of wisdom, choose the wisdom of the heart. God's wisdom is far superior to man's wisdom. God's wisdom leads to life. Man's futile wisdom brings vanity.

The prophet Hosea advises us in this manner: "Whoever is wise, let him understand these things; whoever is discerning, let him know them. For the ways of the LORD are right, and the righteous will walk in them, but transgressors will stumble in them" (Hosea 14:9).

16:22 Understanding is a fountain of life to him who has it, but the discipline of fools is folly.

The elusive "fountain of life" is available to all men, if we simply seek understanding. Some commentators believe Solomon uses this word translated here as "understanding" as another synonym for wisdom.

Self-discipline usually involves habits—most often habits that help us to grow and learn. But Solomon points out here the truth of the modern cliché "garbage in, garbage out." If you habitually practice folly, by definition, you will become a fool.

The NIV has a different slant on the latter phrase of this verse. It states that "folly brings punishment to fools." Seen in this way, fools are punished by their own foolishness and the results of their own actions.

16:23 The heart of the wise teaches his mouth, and adds persuasiveness to his lips.

The mouth must be tamed. James reminds us that "the tongue is a small part of the body, and yet it boasts of great things. Behold, how great a forest is set aflame by such a small fire! . . . For every species of beasts and birds, of reptiles and creatures of the sea, is tamed, and has been tamed by the human race. But no one can tame the tongue, it is a restless evil and full of deadly poison. With it we bless our Lord Father, and with it we curse men, who have been made in the likeness of God" (James 3:5–9).

Do you ever find yourself in a position in which you wish you could convince someone of your own sincerity? Solomon's advice is that when the heart teaches the mouth, the mouth becomes far more persuasive. We love to hear great speakers speak from the heart. Therefore, when you witness, be sure your words come from your heart.

Moses complained to the Lord that he didn't know what to say and that he was a poor speaker. The Lord said He would give him the words to say.[8] When our hearts are attuned to the voice and desires of our Father, then our hearts can teach our mouths.

16:24 Pleasant words are a honeycomb, sweet to the soul and healing to the bones.

Give encouragement to someone today. This week, see if you can offer pleasant words to someone every day! You can help them emotionally, physically, and even spiritually.

16:25 There is a way which seems right to a man, but its end is the way of death.

Look down at your feet. Now look at the path you're standing on. Now let your eyes gaze out into the distance to where the path you're on ends. Where does it end? If it seems as though you can't quite make out the end of the path you're on, then check your guidebook (the Bible). We ought to examine our "way" daily. Keep the present in perspective by glancing always into the future, while you use the past to learn and grow from (compare Proverbs 14:12).

16:26 A worker's appetite works for him, for his hunger urges him on.

Our need for food reminds us of our need for work. In Genesis, God told Adam, "Because you have listened to the voice of your wife, and have eaten from the tree about which I commanded you, saying, 'You shall not eat from it'; Cursed is the ground because of you; In toil you shall eat of it all the days of your life" (Genesis 3:17).

Choosing to work so that you can avoid going hungry may not seem like a high moral standard, but it definitely beats the alternative. It is interesting to observe that a great deal of crime in our society is a direct result of people attempting to avoid this directive from God (by seeking to avoid hard work). People often cheat or steal because they want an easier way.

16:27 A worthless man digs up evil, while his words are as a scorching fire.

A worthless man looks for evil. He digs it up. His motto is "You can never cause enough trouble." Being self-centered, he enjoys scorching others with his words. (This partially explains the motivation of some of our modern-day graffiti vandals!) Being worthless has its advantages—one does not need to achieve anything of worth, and all one's time can be usefully focused on digging up that evil!

16:28 A perverse man spreads strife, and a slanderer separates intimate friends.

That which is perverse is directed away from what is right or good. Being perverse can also mean obstinately persisting in an error or fault, or being wrongly self-willed or stubborn.[9]

We need to be peacemakers. Do you spread complaints or encouragement? Think for a minute about what it is that you spread!

A slanderer separates intimate friends. Let's analyze why. Is slander based on truth? (Remember, "Thou shalt not lie" is a Christian imperative). While the truth may hurt, it is usually lies that separate bosom buddies and intimate friends. How then can you avoid these types of separations when a slanderer attacks you or someone you love? The first step is to discern truth. Remember, Satan himself is an expert slanderer. Jesus made note that in Jewish law, "the testimony of two men is true" (John 8:17). Before you accept scandalous gossip as fact, seek corroboration.

Secondly, seek patience. "Do not go on passing judgment before the time, but wait until the Lord comes who will both bring to light the things hidden in the darkness and disclose the motives of men's hearts; and then each man's praise will come to him from God" (1 Corinthians 4:5).

Furthermore, the New Testament stresses unity and commands us to "love one another"(1 John 4:7). Therefore, we need to seek unity. Do not allow yourself to become a member of the group listed in Romans 1:28–32!

> 16:29 A man of violence entices his neighbor, and leads him in a way that is not good.

Discern who is violent and who is not. Do not follow those who are violent. Follow the path of God rather than the path of violence.

> 16:30 He who winks his eyes does so to devise perverse things;
> he who compresses his lips brings evil to pass.

All of us have the ability to discern right from wrong. Solomon's advice to us is to look for outward, external indicators of the inward, spiritual condition of those around us. One aspect of wisdom is being able to discern people's beliefs, motives, and desires. Jesus was an expert at this! We need to beware of perverse men who seek evil. Pay attention to body language. Careful observation can reveal a great deal.

16:31 A gray head is a crown of glory; it is found in the way of righteousness.

It is good to live to a "ripe old age." But this verse should be taken as a generalization rather than as doctrinal dogma. Never assume that a young person who died was not following the way of righteousness. The principle of the verse is that those who pursue righteousness are far more likely to find old age than those who live unrighteously.

16:32 He who is slow to anger is better than the mighty, and he who rules his spirit, than he who captures a city.

Here's a similar verse: "Like a city that is broken into and without walls is a man who has no control over his spirit" (Proverbs 25:28).

The 1960s "Star Trek" TV series popularized the phrase "Space: the final frontier." But in many ways, the Bible points out that exploring the depth of your relationship with God is the actual "final frontier." Solomon offers us a very powerful metaphor concerning self-control.

16:33 The lot is cast into the lap, but its every decision is from the LORD.

Voltaire blundered in his thinking when he declared in 1767, "His Sacred Majesty, Chance, decides everything."[10] Our world is controlled not by chance, but by God Almighty.

Making decisions is often very difficult. This verse offers us a reminder of God's sovereignty. Lot-casting should not be used for

161

all of our decision-making. Don't forget how the first three verses of this chapter began. We need to think, plan, and commit our ways to the Lord. Solomon is merely pointing out that our Lord reigns and is in control. But perhaps there are times when the use of lots is appropriate.

Scripture does offer us a few positive examples of lot-casting for decision-making purposes. In Leviticus 16:8–10 we read, "Aaron shall cast lots for the two goats, one lot for the LORD and the other lot for the scapegoat. Then Aaron shall offer the goat on which the lot for the LORD fell, and make it a sin offering. But the goat on which the lot for the scapegoat fell, shall be presented alive before the LORD to make atonement upon it, to send it into the wilderness as the scapegoat."

At Shiloh, Joshua used lots to help divide the land (Joshua 18:6). Saul used lots to discern who had eaten the honey. (It was Jonathan— see 1 Samuel 14:40–43.) In 1 Chronicles 25:8 "they cast lots for their duties." In Nehemiah they cast lots to determine who would bring the firewood to the priests and Levites and at what appointed time. They also used lots to establish the rebuilt city (nine-tenths were to remain in their cities, and one-tenth were to resettle Jerusalem). The sailors of a ship headed for Tarshish cast lots to discover that Jonah was the cause of their near-calamity (Jonah 1:7).

In the New Testament the apostles chose a twelfth apostle, but using lots was the third step, not the first. First, they consulted scripture (Acts 1:16). Then they prayed (Acts 1:24). Finally, they drew lots (Acts 1:26). Other examples in scripture imply that we are to be active and open, instead of being simply open, yet passive. What I mean is this: read scripture, pray, and proceed with a plan. Keep your heart sensitive to the Holy Spirit's promptings, and keep your mind alert to all that is going on around you.

Think of an upcoming decision you must soon make. Apply these principles to this decision, and remember to praise God for His sovereignty and His guidance. You may be directed as Paul was in Acts 16:6–10!

Proverbs 17

17:1 Better is a dry morsel and quietness with it than a house full of feasting with strife.

What is it that you count when you count your blessings? If you have peace and a dry crust, give thanks to God for providing for your needs. This verse also sets up a contrast that demonstrates a polarity between types of people and lifestyle choices.

There are always those of us who are never satisfied with what we have. We may have to deal with the sin of coveting, for often we wish we had what we see others possessing. The point of this verse is to be satisfied. This includes giving thanks to God for our many blessings. To enjoy peace is better than to have a feast. As the old hymn reminds us, we should count our blessings and "name them one by one."[11]

"Be on your guard against every form of greed, for not even when one has an abundance does his life consist of his possessions" (Luke 12:15).

17:2 A servant who acts wisely will rule over a son who acts shamefully, and will share in the inheritance among brothers.

The theme of the "faithful servant" is borne throughout scripture. Scripture reminds us not to take our inheritance for granted. Such an attitude displays a type of arrogance that God does not approve of. Esau sold his inheritance for a pittance. John the Baptist informed the Pharisees and Sadducees that God could raise up "sons of Abraham" from stones (Matthew 3:9).

God has chosen specific people for specific tasks throughout history, yet always maintained a universality within His grace. Faithful servants are rewarded by God and are readily grafted into the "vine." But unfaithful servants will be "cut off" from the vine (John 15:2–6).

17:3 The refining pot is for silver and the furnace for gold, but the LORD tests hearts.

Things of value must often be refined. Your heart is worth refining to God because of its great value. Often this process requires the heat of God's fire to bring about the refinement of the heart that the Lord desires. 1 Corinthians 3:13 says, "Fire itself will test the quality of each man's work." Proverbs 17:3 is a good summary of the book of Job.

An additional point of consideration is that testing and temptation are not synonymous. James points out that "the testing of your faith produces endurance" (James 1:3). Testing often comes from God. However, James also points out that temptation is different and *not* from God: "Let no one say when he is tempted, 'I am being tempted by God'; for . . . He Himself does not tempt any one. But each one is tempted when he is carried away and enticed by his own lust" (James 1:13–14). Is it possible that God is testing you right now?

17:4 An evildoer listens to wicked lips, a liar pays attention to a destructive tongue.

What is it that tickles your ears? What do you pay attention to and listen to? The answers to these questions reveal a great deal

164

about the condition of your heart. There is a difference between hearing and listening. It is the observable difference between being aware of auditory input and understanding fully. We may hear the wicked man's words, but we should not listen to his words and incorporate them into our worldview. Rather, we ought to listen intently to the voice of our heavenly Father.

This verse reveals another parallel. We like what is similar to us. The example given here is that a liar likes a destructive tongue, apparently because he can relate to it.

> 17:5 He who mocks the poor reproaches his Maker; he who rejoices at calamity will not go unpunished.

Jesus was intimately aware of the teachings of Proverbs. He proclaimed, "Blessed are the poor, for yours is the kingdom of heaven" (Luke 6:20) and "The poor you have with you always" (Matthew 26:11). Much of our Christian walk involves our attitude.

"He who rejoices at calamity will not go unpunished" reminds us that often we see bad things happen to others and we respond by thinking out loud, "I told you so," or "Good! That person really deserved what he got." But Jesus told us, "Love your enemies" and "Pray for those who mistreat you" (Luke 6:26, 28). One of our daily tasks is to do an attitude check!

This verse also implies that we should not use the calamity of others for our own profit. Even in business our approach is to be that of servants rather than predators.

> 17:6 Grandchildren are the crown of old men, and the glory of sons is their fathers.

Some things haven't changed much in 3,000 years. Jesse shared David's glory. Jacob shared Joseph's glory. We do not live in a vacuum. Our family members share our achievements as well as our defeats. This should be another motivation to live well.

17:7 Excellent speech is not fitting for a fool; much less are lying lips to a prince.

How do you expect a fool to talk? What types of things do fools say? You expect fools to say foolish things, not to proclaim wisdom. Just as it is impossible or improper for a fool to have "excellent speech," so it is even far more improper for a prince (i.e., leader) to lie. How far from God's principles we have come in American politics. We not only accept lying from our leaders, we expect it.

17:8 A bribe is a charm in the sight of its owner; wherever he turns, he prospers.

Is scripture condoning bribery here? At first reading it may seem so, however, the prosperity of the owner of the bribe may be short-lived. It may seem like a "charm" because he gets results whenever he offers the bribe. Other verses of scripture imply that additional results may come to the briber, such as the corrupted results he did not anticipate. Before we make our conclusion, let us look at some other scriptural statements that use the Hebrew word *shachad,* translated here as "bribe":

You shall not take a bribe, for a bribe blinds the clear-sighted and subverts the cause of the just. (Exodus 23:8)

The LORD your God is the God of gods and the Lord of lords, the great, the mighty, and the awesome God who does not show partiality, nor take a bribe. (Deuteronomy 10:17)

Cursed is he who accepts a bribe to strike down an innocent person. (Deuteronomy 27:25)

When Samuel was old . . . he appointed his sons judges over Israel . . . . His sons, however, did not walk in his, but turned aside after dishonest gain and took bribes and perverted justice. (1 Samuel 8:1–3)

O LORD, I love the habitation of Thy house . . . . Do not take my soul away along with sinners . . . in whose hands is a wicked scheme, and whose right hand is full of bribes. (Psalm 26:8–10)

Your rulers are rebels and companions of thieves; everyone loves a bribe, and chases after reward. They do not defend the orphan, nor does the widow's plea come before them. (Isaiah 1:23)

He who walks righteously, and speaks with sincerity, He who rejects unjust gain, and shakes his hands so that they hold no bribe . . . he will dwell on the heights. (Isaiah 33:15–16)

Scripture clearly points out that God himself cannot be bribed, accepting a bribe is a sin, and it is not done by a man of integrity.

However, from here we reach a somewhat gray area regarding the difference between gift-giving, bribery, and offering a ransom. Most of the verses cited above deal with the principle of not taking a bribe. The reasons given involve the perversion of justice and the avoidance of doing the right thing, such as helping out widows and orphans.

Logically, we conclude that if we are not to take a bribe, then we are not to offer a bribe as well. However, while this is a logical assumption, these verses do not specifically say not to offer a bribe. If a Christian used a bribe to help smuggle out a Jew from Nazi Germany, or if he paid a ransom (or tribute) to save another or to avert bloodshed, are we to assume these examples should be taken as sins? These areas are not as clear-cut.

Motivation is a crucial aspect to analyze in each situation (whether real or hypothetical). Additional verses to consider include the following:

A gift in secret subdues anger, and a bribe in the bosom, strong wrath. (Proverbs 21:14)

A man's gift makes room for him, and brings him before great men. (Proverbs 18:16)

Many will entreat the favor of a generous man, and every man is
a friend to him who gives gifts. (Proverbs 19:6)

Shachad in Hebrew can also be translated as "gift," "present,"
or "reward." "Bribe" is only one of the possible interpretations of it.
Therefore, if we insert one of these more positive terms here in
verse 8, rather than the term *bribe,* we get quite a different feel.

Gift giving is done out of love, with no other expectation attached. A ransom is perhaps a type of bribe, but it is a special category done not for personal gain, but out of the motivation of love.
Paying tribute is a type of bribe done at a national level for the
purpose of gaining peace. What do you think about these issues?

17:9 He who covers a transgression seeks love, but he who
repeats a matter separates intimate friends.

Don't gossip. If you know some dirt on someone else, then
"cover" it. This shows that you seek love. Peter expressed the concept this way: "Love covers a multitude of sins" (1 Peter 4:8).

How can we cover a transgression and still beckon others to a
higher standard? Our model for dealing with nonbelievers is found
in John 8, where Jesus confronted the woman caught in adultery.

The scribes and Pharisees wanted to make her sin a public matter, but Jesus revealed to all present that her sin was actually a private matter. He did this by getting all of them to analyze their own
lives. Jesus demonstrated grace to the woman, but then He admon-
ished her to "sin no more."

We must follow a different process to cover the sin of a fellow
believer. First we must understand that "covering" it *does not mean
ignoring it!* This is not what scripture teaches. Covering it means
you initially keep it private, between you and the sinful fellow believer. First confront the individual privately *in love* (Galatians 6:1
and Matthew 18:15). Confronting in love does not mean to be-
little, it means to seek the individual's genuine renewal into God's
grace and unity with Him. This is the stage of renewal where the

offense may remain completely hidden. Second, if the individual is still sinning and unrepentant, then go back and confront him with two or three other Christians (Matthew 18:16). At this stage, you should still maintain confidentiality, except for these few close believers. Finally, if this does not work, then you may "shun" this person (Matthew 18:17). The point of Proverbs 17:9 is that your responsibility as a Christian who is aware of another's transgression is to not write an exposé for a national tabloid.

At any stage, as soon as a person apologizes and repents, "covering" the transgression means that we should let it go and work to renew our relationship. As much as possible, forget it and move on.

> 17:10 A rebuke goes deeper into one who has understanding than a hundred blows into a fool.

Are you a mirror or a transparent prism? When light strikes a mirror, it is not absorbed, but reflected. The light does not penetrate; it merely bounces off. But a prism allows the light to penetrate into its heart. Further, it refracts the light, bringing about change in the form of a spectrum. Does a rebuke bounce off you like light off a mirror, or does it penetrate and change you? Willingness to change (which itself is painful) is an indication of understanding and maturity.

> 17:11 A rebellious man seeks only evil, so a cruel messenger will be sent against him.

According to The American Heritage Dictionary,[12] *rebellion* is "an act or show of defiance toward an authority." God is our authority. Therefore, "a rebellious man seeks only evil" because he seeks his own way, rather than God's way.

The strange punishment of "a cruel messenger" is a bit vague. Angels are, literally, messengers, but the cruel messenger spoken of here may be a human. Regardless of the actual identity of the cruel messenger, a consequence for rebellious behavior is definitely forthcoming.

> 17:12 Let a man meet a bear robbed of her cubs, rather than a fool in his folly.

Avoid fools whenever you can. They are dangerous! Metaphors can be a powerful tool for learning, and for remembering what you have learned. This type of metaphor easily paints a picture in our minds. It is easy for us to become arrogant, to simply laugh at fools and not take them seriously. This verse reminds us how hazardous fools can be.

> 17:13 He who returns evil for good, evil will not depart from his house.

Do not return evil for good, and do not return evil for evil either! "Just as you want men to treat you, treat them in the same way . . . . If you love those who love you, what credit is that to you? For even sinners do the same thing . . . . But love your enemies, and do good, and lend expecting nothing in return, and your reward will be great, and you will be sons of the Most High; for He Himself is kind to ungrateful and evil men. Be merciful, just as your Father is merciful" (Luke 6:31–36). This is a part of the kingdom principle of reciprocity and harvest, which states that you will reap what you sow. Paul included this idea in Romans 12:17–21. His conclusion was, "Do not be overcome by evil, but overcome evil with good."

> 17:14 The beginning of strife is like letting out water, so abandon the quarrel before it breaks out.

A dam, once broken, becomes more and more damaged as the speed and pressure of the water break it down further. Any relationship is a dam, holding and building greater and greater depths of intimacy. Your experiences are like the water. But once the dam of trust has been broken—watch out!

Another point is that timing is critical. If you patch up a relationship quickly, before the other person has had time to allow bitterness to grow and fester, you can allow forgiveness to heal the relationship quickly.

Do you love a "good" argument? How important is *your* opinion? Pride does not want you to abandon the quarrel. List several reasons why you personally quarrel. Which of your reasons are scripturally valid?

> 17:15 He who justifies the wicked, and he who condemns the righteous, both of them alike are an abomination to the LORD.

Don't call sin something other than what it is! Who can justify the wicked? God alone can provide justification.

Likewise, do not condemn the righteous. The question must arise then, how do we discern which is which? Sure, most of the time it is obvious, but sometimes it is not always so clear.

The *law* was given so that sin would be revealed. God reveals sin to us so that we will discern our *need:*

> The righteous will live by his faith. (Habakkuk 2:4)

> Therefore, having been justified by faith, we have peace with God. (Romans 5: 1)

> The law has become our tutor. (Galatians 3:24)

In addition to this, scripture teaches us: "The Holy Spirit, whom the Father will send in My name, He will teach you all things, and bring to your remembrance all that I said to you" (John 14:26).

What happens when you tolerate something that is clearly a sin? One example of this is given to us in Exodus 32:1–35. Aaron accepted the people's sin of unbelief (v. 1). He then tolerated an idol (v. 4). He then tried to justify the evil (v. 5). Then he lied about the whole event (v. 24), and finally God punished the Hebrews (vss. 33–35). Clearly Aaron was one of the sorriest priests you can imagine—until you think of Caiaphas (Matthew 26:57). In Matthew 26 we read of the ultimate example of a man condemning something that is righteous.

Solomon has more to say on this subject: "He who says to the wicked, 'You are righteous,' Peoples will curse him, nations will abhor him" (Proverbs 24:24).

Solomon's own life is a powerful reminder of how much danger is latent in the attitude of a man who justifies evil or who condemns righteousness. "Now King Solomon loved many foreign women along with the daughter of Pharaoh: Moabite, Ammonite, Edomite, Sidonian, and Hittite women, from the nations concerning which the LORD had said to the sons of Israel, 'You shall not associate with them, neither shall they associate with you, for they will surely turn your heart away after their gods.' So Solomon held fast to these in love . . . . For it came about when Solomon was old, his wives turned his heart away after other gods; and his heart was not wholly devoted to the LORD his God, as the heart of David his father had been . . . . Solomon did what was evil in the sight of the LORD" (1 Kings 11:1–6).

17:16 Why is there a price in the hand of a fool to buy wisdom, when he has no sense?

You can buy a master's degree (sort of), but you can't buy wisdom! Some things just can't be bought. Simon the sorcerer tried to buy God's power, but Peter quickly put him in his place! (See Acts 8:9, 18, 20.)

Actually, Solomon points out that it is nonsense for a fool to want "sense."

17:17 A friend loves at all times, and a brother is born for adversity.

Whom can you count on? Perhaps more important, who can count on you?

> 17:18 A man lacking in sense pledges, and becomes surety in the presence of his neighbor.

Surety is a pledge or formal promise made to secure against loss, damage, or default. It is a guarantee. Surety involves a person who has contracted to be responsible for another person. Enter into such an arrangement with extreme caution. Actually, Solomon advises us to avoid such arrangements altogether.

> 17:19 He who loves transgression loves strife; He who raises his door seeks destruction.

Basically this verse points out that you can't love sin without loving trouble. This is a sarcastic oxymoron, for no one really "loves" strife. However, Solomon is demonstrating the interconnectedness of sin and trouble. Although most people want to do the sin without the problems it creates, it doesn't work that way. Take, for example, the sin of adultery. If one loves the transgression, he'd better be prepared to "love" the heartache, strife, scandal, financial problems, and possible births such an action may bring.

If you live your life in a carefree, devil-may-care manner, then destruction may soon come. Do not confuse the biblical concept of "do not worry" with an incautious attitude toward sin.

> 17:20 He who has a crooked mind finds no good, and he who is perverted in his language falls into evil.

Can you "find" good? When God finished His creation He saw that it was "good" (Genesis 1: 25). When He finished creating man, He saw it was "very good" (Genesis 1:31).

While we were yet sinners, God saw good (or worth) in us. Even when we were unlovely—He loved us and sent His Son to die for us. Contrast this with Satan. When Satan looked at Job, he could not see good. With a crooked heart and mind, he is blinded to anything that is good. Let us strive to see the way God sees. Paul reminds us, "Be imitators of God, as beloved children" (Ephesians 5:1).

Solomon tells us, "He who is perverted in his language falls into evil." James reminds us of how much danger is in the tongue (James 3:8). Paul wrote, "Let no unwholesome word proceed from your mouth" (Ephesians 4:29).

Matthew 12:34; 37 also illustrates the power of *words!* "The mouth speaks out of that which fills the heart . . . For by your words you shall be justified, and by your words you shall be condemned."

> 17:21 He who begets a fool does so to his sorrow, and the father
> of a fool has no joy.

Our folly affects others, not just ourselves. The expression "It's *my* life, I'll do what I want as long as I don't hurt anyone else," is a fool's statement. It shortsightedly ignores the fact that if something ill befalls me, those who also love me suffer as well. The example given here is of a father who is deeply pained by the actions of his son, but this truth extends to all relationships. When John Donne penned the words, "No man is an island,"[13] this idea is a part of what he was addressing.

> 17:22 A joyful heart is good medicine, but a broken spirit dries
> up the bones.

Have you laughed today? Remember, there is much more to joy than just laughter (see also Proverbs 14:30 and 15:13).

Some will read this and say it's a crazy idea, you can't laugh for no reason! But that is the point, *you must find a reason!* Often it is simply just looking at a situation from a different perspective.

17:23 A wicked man receives a bribe from the bosom to pervert the ways of justice.

Bribery contaminates—both individuals and entire societies in which bribery is commonly practiced. It leads to the perversion of justice. With a bribe a wicked and guilty man may "buy" his innocence. With a bribe false witnesses may be bought to testify of the guilt of an innocent person (see also notes regarding 17:8).

The word used in the NASB translation as "bribe" is the Hebrew *shachad* (pronounced shakh'-ad). My Hebrew dictionary gives five possible English words for this: a donation, bribe, gift, present, or reward. But however you translate it, if it perverts justice, it is intolerable.

17:24 Wisdom is in the presence of the one who has understanding, but the eyes of a fool are on the ends of the earth.

"The beginning of wisdom is: Acquire wisdom; and with all your acquiring, get understanding" (Proverbs 4:7). Is wisdom in your presence, or are your eyes on the ends of the earth?

Consider this: Is wisdom something you possess? Perhaps wisdom has a quality akin to that of time. Time is not something we possess; we have only opportunities. As we gain cognitive understanding, we enter into the presence of wisdom. When in our hearts, our attitudes and choices are directed by this knowledge and our actions and behaviors are transformed by this understanding, then this gift becomes wisdom.

There is a cliché, "You can't lose what you never had!" This is not true in the spiritual realm, for any gift of God may be lost if one chooses to ignore or abuse it. Solomon lost his wisdom when it became mere knowledge. Ironically, through his own wives his eyes became cast upon "the ends of the earth."

17:25 A foolish son is a grief to his father, and bitterness to her who bore him.

Your foolishness grieves those who love you most. The command to honor your father and mother means you must avoid the foolishness that brings them bitterness. If young men and women ask themselves, "Will this bring honor to God and honor to my father and mother?" before they engage in any questionable activity, it will be a great aid to their personal wisdom.

> 17:26 It is also not good to fine the righteous, nor to strike the noble for their uprightness.

Righteousness should be admired, praised, and rewarded. This verse speaks to us corporately as a society more than just as individuals. The advice is that if we value and desire character qualities such as integrity, uprightness, and righteousness, then we must reward these qualities in our society. When the wicked are rewarded and when our leaders and politicians are encouraged to be unrighteous, then a disease of anemic morality quickly permeates all of our society. (See the entire book of Judges—or this week's newspaper! See also Proverbs 18:5.)

> 17:27–28 He who restrains his words has knowledge, and he who has a cool spirit is a man of understanding. Even a fool, when he keeps silent, is considered wise; when he closes his lips, he is counted prudent.

These verses should be taken together. Think before you talk. Then think again. Restrain your words and maintain a cool spirit. People can't tell if you're a fool unless you show them you are. (Note: This does not apply to God—He knows, no matter what you do with your mouth!) "The fool has said in his heart, 'There is no God'" (Psalm 14:1). This is the beginning of folly, just as the beginning of wisdom is to fear the Lord (see Proverbs 1:7).

Proverbs 18

18:1 He who separates himself seeks his own desire, he quarrels against all sound wisdom.

*B*eware of seeking your "own desire." As children of God, we ought to be seeking the desire of God. A wise man seeks the counsel of others (especially others who are also seeking the desire of God). A foolish man avoids the counsel of others or ignores it when he does hear it.

Many other verses allude to this precept as well:

Where there is no guidance, the people fall, but in abundance of counselors there is victory. (Proverbs 11:14)

Through presumption comes nothing but strife, but with those who receive counsel is wisdom. (Proverbs 13:10)

Listen to counsel and accept discipline, that you may be wise the rest of your days. (Proverbs 19:20)

The way of a fool is right in his own eyes, but a wise man is he who listens to counsel. (Proverbs 12:15)

See also Proverbs 2:2, 8:33, and 21:2–3.

Psalm 32:8 reminds us that "I [the Lord] will instruct you and teach you in the way which you should go; I will counsel you with my eye upon you." Beware of separating yourself from God. Separation from God is the theological definition of spiritual death!

Listen to the counsel of the Lord. Then seek the counsel of others (remembering that the counsel of humans may be fallible).

18:2 A fool does not delight in understanding, but only in revealing his own mind.

What is your attitude toward understanding? Do you delight in it? Or do you only desire to reveal your own thoughts to those around you? Consider the motive of the individual within this latter category. He is filled with pride, selfishness, and foolishness. All these terms describe one who only wishes to reveal his own mind.

18:3 When a wicked man comes, contempt also comes, and with dishonor comes reproach.

Wickedness will always bring contempt. Wicked people have contempt for the law and for righteous people. In fact, wicked individuals have contempt for others whom they perceive to be wicked as well. Basically, this is because wicked people are self-centered. Being self-centered leads to pride, and pride leads to contempt.

The latter portion of this verse deals with the concepts of dishonor and reproach. What is the difference between dishonor and reproach? Dishonor is the cause, while reproach is the effect. Dishonor is, of course, the opposite of honor, and it is similar to the concept of shame. Dishonor is generally associated with a specific incident. Reproach deals more with the attitudes of others. It is a part of the labeling process of members of a society.

18:4 The words of a man's mouth are deep waters; the fountain of wisdom is a bubbling brook.

Wisdom truly is a bubbling brook. It keeps flowing, it has an eternal source, and it is refreshing. Solomon may be implying here by the phrase "The words of a man's mouth are deep waters" that words can be dangerous. You can figuratively drown in your own words, and your words can also literally be the cause of your death.

18:5 To show partiality to the wicked is not good, nor to thrust aside the righteous in judgment.

Don't esteem the wicked. Wicked people will merely use you! Don't honor them or place them on a pedestal.

Samson showed partiality to Delilah, who at heart was wicked (Judges 16), and it cost him his sight (maybe in some ways he was already blind).

The latter part of the verse contrasts the opposite extreme of wrongly judging the righteous. This is demonstrated when someone who is truly good and righteous is accused of evil that in fact he has *not* committed. Justice and truth are trampled on when we paint the wicked as good or the righteous as bad. Solomon already warned us about this in 17:26 (see also the warning in James 2:1–10).

18:6–7 A fool's lips bring strife, and his mouth calls for blows. A fool's mouth is his ruin, and his lips are the snare of his soul.

The mouth is a window to the heart. We see into a man's heart via the words of his mouth. Solomon points out here an interesting relationship between what is internal and what is external. Compare also the following: "The one who guards his mouth preserves his life" (Proverbs 13:3) and "I will guard my ways, that I may not sin with my tongue; I will guard my mouth as with a muzzle, while the wicked are in my presence" (Psalm 39:1).

18:8 The words of a whisperer are like dainty morsels, and they go down into the innermost parts of the body.

Gossip, like many sins, seems sweet for the moment, but it is dangerous for our own spiritual health. It is a cumulative poison rather than good nutrition.

18:9 He also who is slack in his work is brother to him who destroys.

When a person works for someone else and is lazy, he is actually stealing from his employer. Therefore, being slack in your work is akin to robbing your employer, just as someone who destroys his property also robs him of some of his assets.

18:10 The name of the LORD is a strong tower; the righteous runs into it and is safe.

God's name is powerful. When David faced Goliath he announced, "You come to me with a sword, a spear, and a javelin, but I come to you in the name of the LORD of hosts, the God of the armies of Israel" (1 Samuel 17:45). The ancient Hebrews revered the official name of the Lord so much that they would not pronounce YHWH aloud.

18:11 A rich man's wealth is his strong city, and like a high wall in his own imagination.

Safety and salvation can be found only in the Lord. Any safety perceived because of one's personal wealth is an illusion. In Psalm 73 Asaph confessed, "My feet came close to stumbling; my steps had almost slipped. For I was envious of the arrogant, as I saw the prosperity of the wicked . . . . They are not in trouble as other men . . . . The garment of violence covers them . . . . Their eye bulges from fatness; the imaginations of their heart run riot . . . . They mock, and wickedly speak of oppression . . . . They have set their mouth against the heavens . . . . They say, 'How does God know?' Behold, these are the wicked; and always at ease, they have increased in wealth. Surely in vain I have kept my heart pure, and washed my hands in innocence; For I have been stricken all day long . . . . Until I came into the sanctuary of God; Then I perceived their end. Surely Thou dost set them in slippery places; Thou dost cast them down to destruction" (Psalm 73:2–18).

18:12 Before destruction the heart of man is haughty, but humility goes before honor.

In the kingdom of God humility brings honor and haughty pride brings destruction.

Hear the words of David: "O LORD, my heart is not proud, or my eyes haughty; nor do I involve myself in great matters . . . surely I have composed and quieted my soul . . . O Israel, hope in the LORD from this time forth and forever" (Psalm 131:1–3).

The prophets also warn us not to be proud: "In that day you will feel no shame because of the deeds by which you have rebelled against Me; For then I will remove from your midst your proud, exulting ones, and you will never again be haughty on My holy mountain" (Zephaniah 3:11).

Paul directed us to "be of the same mind toward one another; do not be haughty in mind, but associate with the lowly. Do not be wise in your own estimation" (Romans 12:16).

18:13 He who gives an answer before he hears, it is folly and shame to him.

Have you ever heard someone blurt out a wrong or inappropriate answer before hearing the entire question or understanding the entire situation? The results can be amusing.

What is the difference between listening and hearing? Jesus told his disciples that the people's failure to listen was one reason He spoke in parables: "While seeing they do not see, and while hearing they do not hear, nor do they understand" (Matthew 13:13).

Becoming a good listener is very important if we desire to become more like God, for He Himself is always there for us. He listens to us at any time and in all circumstances. (Note: However, there are conditions in which God Himself will not listen. e.g., Job 35:13 and Amos 5:23.) James reminds us to "be quick to hear, [and] slow to speak" (James 1:19).

Listening to God's commands will bring about blessing, while not listening to God's commands will bring a curse (see Deuteronomy 11:26–28).

Elsewhere in scripture, Solomon says a "wise reprover to a listening ear" is like an "earring of gold" (Proverbs 25:12). He also advises us, "Guard your steps as you go to the house of God, and draw near to listen rather than to offer the sacrifice of fools" (Ecclesiastes 5:1).

There is a difference between the physical process of hearing and the internal mental process of listening. Remember Proverbs 18:2, and always be ready to listen rather than reveal only your own thoughts. Focus on the concept, and don't get too hung up on the semantics. The word *hear* can be and often is used to actually mean the same thing as *listen,* e.g., "He who has ears to hear, let him hear."

God will readily listen to us when we seek Him and listen to Him! "[If] My people who are called by My name humble themselves and pray, and seek My face and turn from their wicked ways, then I will hear from heaven, will forgive their sin, and will heal their land" (2 Chronicles 7:14).

18:14 The spirit of a man can endure his sickness, but a broken spirit who can bear?

As Jesus said, "The spirit is willing but the flesh is weak" (Matthew 26:41). This reminds us of a major facet of the human condition, namely, the interrelationship between the spirit and the flesh. The stronger the spirit, the less the flesh can control us, while the weaker the spirit, the greater control the flesh maintains over us.

(Keep in mind that the word *flesh* here deals with physical and moral decisions rather than simply good health.)

Proverbs 15:13 and 17:22 remind us, respectively, "A joyful heart makes a cheerful face, but when the heart is sad, the spirit is broken" and "A joyful heart is good medicine, but a broken spirit dries up the bones."

The New Testament informs us that the spirit brings life while the flesh brings death (see John 6:63 or Romans 8:5–6). Job 34:14–15 sheds some interesting light on our condition as well: "If He should gather to Himself His spirit and His breath, all flesh would perish together, and man would return to dust." See also Colossians 1:17.

The question then arises: How can we build and maintain a healthy spirit and avoid developing a broken spirit? We can walk by the Spirit and develop the fruit of the Spirit (Galatians 5:16, 22–23). We can be baptized with the Holy Spirit (Mark 1:8). We can be filled with the Spirit (Luke 1:5). We can also pray for God's Spirit (Psalm 51:10) and we can allow the Spirit of God to rest on us (Isaiah 11:2).

Proverbs 18:14 has another theological implication. We can view man either as a dichotomy (two parts, i.e., spirit [inner] and flesh [outer]) or as a trichotomy (three parts, i.e., body, soul, and spirit). The contrast of the "spirit of a man" with the physical word "sickness" supports a two-part, or dichotomy, view. However, both views have a great deal of scriptural support. Such theological labels help us to discuss aspects of our nature, but they are also often inadequate, for in whatever way we separate or fragment man to discuss our attributes and nature, we remain a totality that is a whole man. Each of us is simultaneously a sum of our parts.

18:15 The mind of the prudent acquires knowledge, and the ear of the wise seeks knowledge.

How can we acquire knowledge? Simple, just have wise ears and a prudent, discerning mind. Well, maybe that's not so simple.

But at least Solomon also told us where to start: "The fear of the LORD is the beginning of knowledge" (Proverbs 1:7). Where do we find knowledge? Knowledge can be found through nature, the word of God, and in our own hearts via the guidance of the Holy Spirit. Regarding nature, scripture tells us, "The heavens are telling of the glory of God . . . and night to night reveals knowledge" (Psalm 19:1–2). This is sometimes called general revelation. Concerning scripture we read, "All scripture is inspired by God and profitable for teaching, for reproof, for correction, for training in righteousness" (2 Timothy 3:16). This is often referred to as specific revelation. As for the Spirit, "The Helper, the Holy Spirit, whom the Father will send in My name, He will teach you all things" (John 14:26).

Oh, that we would learn more of "the depth of the riches both of the wisdom and knowledge of God" (Romans 11:33)! Keep in mind as you share your knowledge with those around you that "a true knowledge of God's mystery [is] Christ Himself, in whom are hidden all the treasures of wisdom and knowledge" (Colossians 2:2–3).

18:16 A man's gift makes room for him, and brings him before great men.

This verse may have layers of application. Through the use of presents and gifts one can smooth the path before him. In other words, one way to see the king (or to get a politician to listen to you) is to offer him a gift.

There are also examples of other "gifts" that have enabled gifted individuals to be brought before great men. They include Joseph, Daniel, and the apostle Paul. Because of the gifts God had given him, Paul was able to preach the gospel to many "great men," including the high priest Ananias, Felix the governor, the new governor Porcius Festus, King Agrippa, and many others! (See Acts 23–28; 1 Corinthians 12, and Genesis 32:20.)

What are your gifts? Have you examined yourself enough to know what your gifts are?

18:17 The first to plead his case seems just, until another comes and examines him.

Having dealt with true listening, Solomon now turns his instruction to true seeing. Perspective is a fascinating thing. Too often we see things only from one perspective, and often it is a fault-ridden perspective. "When I was a child, I used to speak as a child, think as a child, reason as a child; when I became a man, I did away with childish things. For now we see in a mirror dimly, but then face to face; now I know in part, but then I shall know fully just as I also have been fully known" (1 Corinthians 13:11–12).

We know that two or more people may view the same event in completely different ways. Do not be misled (see Matthew 24:11). Do not see things as a child, except for those things that require faith. We need to attempt to see things from God's perspective. People may blame others and attempt to win you over to their side, but before choosing sides, try to see the whole picture as our omniscient Father does.

18:18 The lot puts an end to contentions, and decides between the mighty.

Solomon offers another solution to some debates, especially if the individuals involved are contentious and hot-tempered. Simply cast lots, because their "every decision is from the LORD" (Proverbs 16:33).

With our western way of thinking, this concept may be difficult to accept. However, focus on the word "contentions." Some issues cannot be resolved by more knowledge and research, which is the typical western solution to resolving a problem. Part of solving a contentious issue rests in both sides wanting a resolution. What does each side value more, peace or the issue at hand? If you can get two sides to agree to accept the outcome of the lots, then they have agreed that peace is more valuable than their personal desire.

> 18:19 A brother offended is harder to be won than a strong city, and contentions are like the bars of a castle.

The deeper one's initial intimacy, friendship, and experiential relationship, the deeper the pain caused by a rift in that relationship.

Consider the example of Cain and Abel. God spoke to Cain, "If you do well, will not your countenance be lifted up?" As it turned out, Cain did not master his sin. Instead he allowed his "contentions" to become a part of his attitude and his actions. When we cease to allow God to define who we are and who we are becoming, then we allow sin to define those things. Cain had to spend the rest of his days being defined by the phrase "I am a murderer."

Scripture contains numerous examples of brothers not getting along, such as Jacob and Esau (Genesis 27:41), Joseph and his brothers (Genesis 37:2, 4, 8), and Jesus' account of the prodigal son and his saturnine older brother (Luke 15:28,29).

The latter part of Proverbs 18:19 also bears a great message for us to muse upon. With our beliefs and attitudes, we create our own prisons "like the bars of a castle." We often insist on this, even while God offers us freedom. What prisons are contained within your own heart and mind?

Consider also how the Christian concept of forgiveness plays into this idea. Without the freedom that comes from forgiveness, you will remain trapped within the "bars of your own castle" of bitterness.

"If you will forgive men for their transgressions, your heavenly Father will also forgive you. But if you do not forgive men . . . ." How do you think this verse ends? Check to see how your ending compares to what Jesus actually said in Matthew 6:14–15.

Paul wrote, "But whom you forgive anything, I forgive also . . . in order that no advantage be taken of us by Satan" (2 Corinthians 2:10–11). See also Ephesians 4:32 and Matthew 18:35.

18:20–21 With the fruit of a man's mouth his stomach will be satisfied; he will be satisfied with the product of his lips. Death and life are in the power of the tongue, and those who love it will eat its fruit.

How powerful are your words? They are more powerful than you imagine. Life and death are often held within the power of one's tongue. In politics, this truth prompted Patrick Henry to proclaim, "Give me liberty or give me death."[14] Thomas Paine (in Common Sense) proved that the pen is mightier than the sword.[15]

Speak from a spirit of love with the goal of fruitful encouragement, and you too will be satisfied with the product of your lips. How joyful would we be if we never had to say again, "Oops, I wish I hadn't said that," or "Sorry, I really didn't mean what I said." Choose your words carefully.

18:22 He who finds a wife finds a good thing, and obtains favor from the LORD.

Genesis records the creation of male and female: "'It is not good for the man to be alone; I will make a helper suitable for him.' . . . For this cause a man shall leave his father and his mother, and shall cleave to his wife; and they shall become one flesh" (Genesis 2:18, 24).

Solomon also points out in Ecclesiastes: "Two are better than one because they have a good return for their labor. For if either of them falls, the one will lift up his companion. But woe to the one who falls when there is not another to lift him up. Furthermore, if two lie down together they keep warm, but how can one be warm alone?" (Ecclesiastes 4:9–11). Enough said, so knock it off with the ball-and-chain bachelor party jokes!

18:23 The poor man utters supplications, but the rich man answers roughly.

The NIV records this verse as "A poor man pleads for mercy, but a rich man answers harshly." We need to keep a proper perspective regarding who we are and what we need. The contrast here between the poor man's attitude and the rich man's attitude is similar to the story Jesus told of the Pharisee and the publican in Luke 18:10–14.

18:24 A man of many friends comes to ruin, but there is a friend who sticks closer than a brother.

Do you have an inner circle of friends you can count on? Extroverts especially may need to heed this advice, as they often make many friends rapidly. As the prodigal son discovered, some friends are only fair-weather friends.

The story of Ittai in 2 Samuel 15:21 is relatively obscure, but it illustrates loyalty and friendship. Ittai said, "Surely wherever my lord the king may be, whether for death or for life, there also your servant will be."

1 Samuel also provides us with a great illustration of friendship in the story of David and Jonathan (see chapters 18–20).

Human friendship is a truly beautiful thing, but friendship with God Almighty fulfills the deepest purpose of our existence. It was for this purpose that God created us. O that our epitaphs would read, "He (or she) was a friend of God!"

Proverbs 19

Proverbs 19:1 Better is a poor man who walks in his integrity than he who is perverse in speech and is a fool.

War on poverty was the watchword of the Johnson administration. This war failed because "we have met the enemy, and he is us." What we need is a war against immorality. Integrity must be our watchword. God is not impressed by human possessions. Rich or poor, God desires our heart. Without integrity, perverse speech will become commonplace along with other foolish behaviors. There are many things worse than being poor.

19:2 Also it is not good for a person to be without knowledge, and he who makes haste with his feet errs.

Do you make a conscious effort to acquire knowledge? Do you value knowledge? Obviously the latter part of this verse is not suggesting that you must stop speedwalking or running for exercise. Rather, it is suggesting that we proceed carefully down the path of life.

This verse is talking about decision-making. Knowledge is crucial to good decision-making. Big decisions should not be made hastily. These are the two elements addressed here. In other words, the two things that can defeat good decision-making are the speed with which we make decisions and the information we possess at the time of the decision. Time is required to process information. But more likely, a hasty decision is an error because we simply didn't value having the information in the first place. This is an error due to laziness. When a person participates in an orienteering race, if he proceeds too rapidly he will err. A mistake in a race is just a mistake in a race, but an error in *life* moves us off our path toward God. Notice again how Proverbs 19:1 reminds us to *walk* in integrity.

> 19:3 The foolishness of man subverts his way, and his heart rages against the LORD.

Immaturity is caused by either a lack of growth or a lack of fundamentals. But foolishness is different. It is the result of a process of rebellious choices. Although the foolish man "subverts his way," he almost always sees his problems as the result of the faults of someone else. He loves to blame others, and no other target is used as often as God Himself.

> 19:4 Wealth adds many friends, but a poor man is separated from his friend.

We are exhorted to be neither tightwads nor overly extravagant. One example of a poor steward who was "separated from his friend" is the story of the prodigal son. When God blesses us, we are to use our blessings to bless others. This is the essence of the Abrahamic covenant. Jesus exhorted the multitudes in this manner: "Let the man who has two tunics share with him who has none; and let him who has food do likewise" (Luke 3:11).

19:5 A false witness will not go unpunished, and he who tells lies will not escape.

In the ninth commandment we are told to not be false witnesses: "You shall not bear false witness against your neighbor" (Exodus 20:16). The purpose of a trial is to get at the truth and ultimately justice. False witnesses destroy the truth and thereby distort justice. The Bible also exhorts us not to gossip, because people who engage in gossip may often be participating in spreading lies. Exodus 23:1 says, "You shall not carry a false rumor; do not join your hand with a wicked man to be a malicious witness."

Proverbs 6:19 lists being a false witness as one of the six things that the Lord hates! In Proverbs 12:17 we read that "he who speaks truth tells what is right, but a false witness, deceit." In addition to this we need to be aware of the contrast between the different types of witnesses: "A faithful witness will not lie, but a false witness speaks lies" (Proverbs 14:5).

These words bear solemn meaning for each of us if we view our very lives as a witness of our faith. I know the true and only living God of Creation. However, if I live my life as though I don't know Him, then I am a false witness.

The penalty for being a false witness is severe. Jesus warned His followers about false witnesses of God in Matthew 24:24: "For false Christs and false prophets will arise and will show great signs and wonders, so as to mislead, if possible, even the elect."

19:6–7 Many will entreat the favor of a generous man, and every man is a friend to him who gives gifts. All the brothers of a poor man hate him; how much more do his friends go far from him! He pursues them with words, but they are gone.

As a wealthy man, Solomon knew a great deal about the psychological relationship between wealth and friendship. Proverbs 18:24 reminds us that "a man of many friends comes to ruin," and from this chapter we have learned that "wealth adds many friends"

(Proverbs 19:4). While a cause-and-effect relationship exists between the two, the effect is not necessarily as desirable as many
people assume. Having given this warning about using wealth to
gain friends for one's own self-esteem, Solomon points out how to
properly utilize this law of relationships. By giving gifts, you can
develop friendships, not to *gain* happiness and joy, but rather to
share your happiness, joy, and peace.

There is another implication contained within these verses involving our work ethic. I take verse 7 to mean that the poor man
spoken of here is hated by his brothers not simply because he is
poor, but because he has created his own poverty. The implication
is that he is lazy and slothful. If the brothers were also as poor as
this man, they would all be in the same boat, so to speak. If the
brothers have worked hard and followed the principles of righteous living, then this verse is easily understood. Having gained
the means to be generous, they are tired of being asked to support
their irresponsible brother's lazy lifestyle.

Scripture teaches that being poor is of no shame at all (Luke
6:20). In fact, Jesus taught that there would always be poor people:
"The poor you have with you always" (Matthew 26:11). But stewardship is a vastly different thing. How do you see the difference
between being a poor person and being a poor steward?

> 19:8 He who gets wisdom loves his own soul; he who keeps
> understanding will find good.

What Hebrew word is used here for the term "wisdom"? It is
the word *leb,* which is a form of *lebab. Lebab* may refer to the most
interior organs, such as the heart or liver. The word *lebab* can also
refer to abstracts like courage and understanding. *Leb* is often used
figuratively in reference to feelings, the will, and even the intellect.
It can be used to refer to the center of anything. "Wisdom" is also a
possible translation, as the NASB team has chosen. However, you can
see that this initial phrase could be translated, "He who gets to the
center of things loves his own soul."

The Bible teaches that all men love themselves—e.g., "No one ever hated his own flesh" (Ephesians 5:29). But in our society we see a dichotomy between those who love their bodies and those who love their souls. Ask yourself what you feed more, your body or your soul.

The latter phrase of this verse implies that understanding may be lost. In other words, if we are exhorted to *keep* understanding, then logically it must be something that we can *lose*. Ask God to safeguard the wisdom He has imparted to you even as you ask for more wisdom and understanding. This also declares again the cause-and-effect relationship between wisdom and good. Solomon himself is the ultimate example. When we allow evil to abound (as Solomon did with his wives' idols), then wisdom is diminished.

19:9 A false witness will not go unpunished, and he who tells lies will perish.

Repetition is important in the learning process; that is why Solomon repeats key concepts so frequently. In case you have forgotten, don't break the ninth commandment, and review Proverbs 19:5 again.

19:10 Luxury is not fitting for a fool; much less for a slave to rule over princes.

Compare this verse to Proverbs 17:7: "Excellent speech is not fitting for a fool; much less are lying lips to a prince." These verses could imply to some that people are not created equal. The biblical perspective is that inasmuch as we are all created in the image of God (see Genesis 1:26–27), people are equal in value and in spiritual needs. However, in gifts and abilities, people are in fact *not* equal (see 1 Corinthians 12:4–11). The contrast here between a slave and a prince, and with luxury and a fool, has to do with ability rather than innate value.

Solomon's main point, however, has little to do with equality. It has more to do with logic and reality. The illustration of a slave ruling over princes is given to aid our understanding of the first line. Why shouldn't a fool have luxury? It's ridiculous, because a fool, as Solomon has defined it, will squander his wealth. He'll be lazy and simply not maintain things properly.

> 19:11 A man's discretion makes him slow to anger, and it is his glory to overlook a transgression.

The ability to forgive, to be merciful, to be slow to anger—these things are all qualities of our heavenly Father. "Then God said, 'Let us make man in our own image . . . ' and God created man in His own image" (Genesis 1:26–27). When we operate according to His image, it is to our glory.

Alexander Pope showed he understood this concept when he penned his famous line, "To err is human, to forgive, divine."[16] Above all else, the message of Christianity is a message of forgiveness.

> 19:12 The king's wrath is like the roaring of a lion, but his favor is like dew on the grass.

Wrath and mercy are both attributes possessed by our heavenly Father. We need to be cognizant of both attributes, else our theology can become easily warped by an overemphasis on only one aspect of God's nature.

> 19:13 A foolish son is destruction to his father, and the contentions of a wife are a constant dripping.

Two things can beat us down faster than almost anything else: a foolish child and a contentious spouse. Family is unquantifiably important. Prioritize your family life. Nothing is more devastating than foolish and contentious family members, for they cause the family to disintegrate from the inside out. Self-check time: Are you a "constant drip" to your spouse?

> 19:14 House and wealth are an inheritance from fathers, but a prudent wife is from the LORD.

Verse 13 pointed out some of the negatives of family living. This verse points out some of the wonderful aspects of family life. Which is of more value—a house, great wealth, or a prudent spouse? Always prioritize the latter! The first two items may be given to you by your earthly father, or perhaps you may earn them (with the Lord's help)—but a prudent spouse cannot be given to you by any human. It is another one of God's wonderful gifts. Like salvation, internal peace, joy, and all the other gifts of God, cherish this gift as well.

If you are not married but plan on marrying at some point in the future, then pray for this future spouse. My wife and I are already praying for the future spouses of our three daughters. We want God's best for each of them.

> 19:15–16 Laziness casts into deep sleep, and an idle man will suffer hunger. He who keeps the commandment keeps his soul, but he who is careless of his ways will die.

Remember the curse of Genesis 3? The curse is real, and if you ignore it, as an idle and lazy man does, you will suffer hunger. This involves a tangible and physical result. Verse 16 goes even deeper. If we do not keep the commands of God, then our very souls become vulnerable! Spiritual laziness brings deadly results. Obedience is a key ingredient in our walk with God. The opposite of obedience is rebellion, which is more commonly called sin. The wages of sin is death.

> 19:17 He who is gracious to a poor man lends to the LORD, and He will repay him for his good deed.

We often speak of giving our tithes and offerings unto the Lord. The commands to tithe in Deuteronomy 14 were given so that "you may learn to fear the LORD your God always" (Deuteronomy 14:23). This is the primary purpose of giving to the Lord. But there is a secondary reason to give to the Lord, namely, to lay up our treasures in heaven. A portion of the tithe (one-third) was to be donated to help feed "the Levite . . . and the alien, the orphan, and the widow" (Deuteronomy 14:28–29). "Whoever in the name of a disciple gives to one of these little ones even a cup of cold water to drink, truly I say to you he shall not lose his reward" (Matthew 10:42). We look forward to our reward. "In My Father's house are many dwelling places . . . I go to prepare a place for you" (John 14:2–3).

It is interesting to note the usage of the word *lend*. In the context of lending to the Lord, you cannot outgive God. Rest assured, you will be repaid!

> 19:18 Discipline your son while there is hope, and do not desire his death.

Solomon suggests there is a window of opportunity regarding the discipline of our children. Perhaps Solomon was thinking of his brother Absalom when he penned this verse. Absalom had his brother Amnon killed near Baal-hazor (2 Samuel 13) in his determination to usurp the throne. So strong was his power that David had to flee Jerusalem. Absalom's own vanity (his long hair) brought about his demise, and he died! Scripture does not tell us all the details, but we may surmise that while David might never have given up hope for Absalom, others near the throne, such as Joab, could see the writing on the wall. Without a recommitment to the Lord, Absalom had reached a point beyond hope. We do not know, but it is possible, that David did not discipline Absalom properly as a child.

Keep this story in mind. Discipline is a painful process for both parents and child. But the alternative is far more painful, often resulting in death! Without discipline we allow our children to practice foolish behaviors until they become habitual.

The general principle is that there is a window of opportunity for parental discipline to be most effective. If we squander that opportunity, it will be difficult to redeem. However, we should always remember the possibility of a spiritual homecoming for any prodigal.

19:19 A man of great anger shall bear the penalty, for if you rescue him, you will only have to do it again.

Anger is often more destructive to its owner than it is to the one toward whom the anger is directed. A fool either does not acknowledge a need to change, or else he chooses not to change. Fools repeat their folly (see Proverbs 26:11).

19:20 Listen to counsel and accept discipline, that you may be wise the rest of your days.

There are people we should listen to, and other people we should not listen to. Some of the people we should *not* listen to are

1. The wicked. "Blessed is the man who does not walk in the counsel of the wicked" (Psalm 1:1).
2. Those who are "wise" in the ways of the world. "Where is the wise man? Where is the scribe? Where is the debater of this age? Has not God made foolish the wisdom of the world?" (1 Corinthians 1:20).

Those whom we should listen to include

1. God Himself:

    I will instruct you and teach you in the way which you should go; I will counsel you with my eye upon you. Do not be as the horse or as the mule which have no understanding. (Psalm 32:8–9)

With Thy counsel Thou wilt guide me, and afterward receive me to glory. (Psalm 73:24)

2. The word of God:

Blessed is the man . . . [whose] delight is in the law of the LORD. (Psalm 1:2)

This is my comfort in my affliction, that Thy word has revived me. (Psalm 119:50)

3. Those who are truly wise:

What king, when he sets out to meet another king in battle, will not first sit down and take counsel whether he is strong enough with ten thousand to encounter the one coming against him with twenty thousand? (Luke 14:31)

Through presumption comes nothing but strife, but with those who receive counsel is wisdom. (Proverbs 13:10)

The simple rule of thumb is to listen to counsel that is eternal in essence. "Forever, O LORD, Thy word is settled in heaven" (Psalm 119:89).

Do you accept discipline? How do you respond to criticism? Do you blame others? Do you look for excuses for your behavior? Or do you say, "Thank you for caring enough to point out this shortcoming"?

Faithful are the wounds of a friend. (Proverbs 27:6)

Do not reject the discipline of the LORD, or loathe His reproof. (Proverbs 3:11)

Know in your heart that the LORD your God was disciplining you just as a man disciplines his son. (Deuteronomy 8:5)

Behold, how happy is the man whom God reproves, so do not despise the discipline of the Almighty. For He inflicts pain and gives relief; He wounds, and His hands also heal. (Job 5:17–18)

While we are on the subject of accepting discipline, don't neglect to accept your own discipline! Acquiring self-discipline is a very valuable aspect of our Christian walk. Paul instructed Timothy to "have nothing to do with worldly fables fit only for old women. On the other hand discipline yourself for the purpose of godliness" (1 Timothy 4:7).

Knowledge is brought about through discipline. Compare Proverbs 19:27.

19:21 Many are the plans in a man's heart, but the counsel of the LORD, it will stand.

Clearly, our primary task is to humbly look for and acknowledge God's counsel and purpose in our lives. This is easier said than done! Compare Proverbs 16:1–3. Listen to the Lord, confess your sins, maintain pure motives, and commit your works to the Lord. As your personal plans develop through this process, they are very likely to be plans that "will stand."

19:22 What is desirable in a man is his kindness, and it is better to be a poor man than a liar.

The prophet Micah wrote about kindness as a spiritual requirement: "He has told you, O man, what is good; and what does the LORD require of you but to do justice, to love kindness, and to walk humbly with your God?" (Micah 6:8). Kindness is a fruit of the Holy Spirit. What does Proverbs 3:3 say about kindness and truth?

Do you value wealth above kindness? Is it worth lying to achieve wealth? Not according to scripture. Honesty, integrity, and kindness are more valuable than wealth.

> 19:23 The fear of the LORD leads to life, so that one may sleep satisfied, untouched by evil.

Here is another astounding truth of kingdom principles. How can fear lead to total and complete peace? Nonbelievers cannot understand a principle that appears to be so ironic. Nothing is more important than our relationship with the Almighty Creator and God of the universe. Because of our relationship we rest in Him and can sleep in peace. David wrote a very similar passage in Psalm 4:4–8: "Tremble, and do not sin; Meditate in your heart upon your bed, and be still . . . . In peace I will both lie down and sleep, for Thou alone, O LORD, dost make me to dwell in safety."

> 19:24 The sluggard buries his hand in the dish, and will not even bring it back to his mouth.

Solomon paints a picture of a ridiculous situation here to make a point: We are often tempted to do less than our best—that is, to be lazy. God provides for our needs, he offers us gifts, and our hand is "in the dish." But so often we refuse to accept His gifts! Why does this phenomenon occur so frequently? Simply take what is in your hand and lift it to your mouth! Take God's promises, mix them with your faith, and rest in Him.

> 19:25 Strike a scoffer and the naive may become shrewd, but reprove one who has understanding and he will gain knowledge.

This verse shows a contrast between two different types of people and two different methods of instructive discipline. Solomon contrasts a scoffer and a person of understanding.

Hundreds of years after Solomon penned these words, the Greek civilization developed a formalized school of thought which taught that self-control was the only means of achieving virtue (the only "good"). However, they believed that all people are motivated by selfishness. They were called the Cynics. From this group we derive our words *cynicism* and *cynical*. Like most philosophies, this one is founded on a great deal of truth, but it suffers from two basic assumptions that are flawed.

First it assumes that God, the Creator of the universe, is *not* the greatest thing. In a rather idolatrous manner, it assumes that the *virtue* is the greatest desirable thing to possess. (Note how this compares with Eastern mysticism's Taoism and the Nirvana of Buddhism.) Secondly, it assumes an oversimplification of the human condition—namely, that all people are alike in all ways. The Bible clearly points out that people are alike in their need for God, in their intrinsic value, and in their original purpose for existence. However, they are clearly different in their relationship with God, in their gifts and abilities, and in their individual functions. Thus the Cynical idea that all men are motivated by selfishness must be altered biblically to state that most men are motivated by selfishness while some men are motivated by love and a desire to please God. Some men have been changed from the inside out! Of course, a Cynic would find such an idea "cynical"!

The "scoffer" is like a cynic. He does not believe that God can change others so he does not believe that God can change him. Because of this attitude, discipline does not cause him to learn, it only causes him to become more sneaky. In Lawrence Kohlberg's[17] classification of moral development, he is at stage 1. His motivation is not to do things because they are morally right, but to avoid punishment.

In addition to this, Solomon contrasts the two styles of learning. No matter what you do to the scoffer, he will not become wise.

But a person of understanding takes even a light rebuke to heart and discerns what he needs to learn.

19:26 He who assaults his father and drives his mother away is a shameful and disgraceful son.

This verse reiterates the theme of honoring your father and mother. Note how this verse is connected conceptually to the next verse.

19:27 Cease listening, my son, to discipline, and you will stray from the words of knowledge.

Discipline and knowledge are symbiotic; each affects the other in a positive way. Great discipline leads to greater knowledge, and great knowledge assists one in the pursuit of any discipline or learning by providing additional areas of connection.

In this verse, the warning is given to prevent us from choosing a poor path. Things such as assaulting one's father (as in verse 26) and not listening to discipline lead to the path of shame and disgrace.

19:28 A rascally witness makes a mockery of justice, and the mouth of the wicked spreads iniquity.

The tongue is small but mighty. With the tongue you can mock justice and spread iniquity. Nothing new here, but still, frequent reminders help us to realize how important justice is.

19:29 Judgments are prepared for scoffers, and blows for the back of fools.

Punishment is the natural consequence for fools and scoffers. However, they will probably not learn from these consequences. As we have seen before, fools and scoffers will more often blame others and place themselves in the role of victim rather than attempt to learn from their errors.

Proverbs 20

20:1 Wine is a mocker, strong drink a brawler, and whoever is intoxicated by it is not wise.

*N*owhere in scripture is drinking condemned as a sin, but this verse points out that being intoxicated is foolish. The avoidance of the fruit of the vine is sometimes seen as a spiritual behavior, as in the Nazirite vow (Numbers 6:4). Solomon wrote, "I explored with my mind how to stimulate my body with wine while my mind was guiding me wisely . . . and behold all was vanity and striving after the wind" (Ecclesiastes 2:3, 11).

At the end of the last supper, Jesus told his disciples, "Truly I say to you, I shall never again drink of the fruit of the vine until that day when I drink it new in the kingdom of God" (Mark 14:25).

In Leviticus the priests were directed to not drink wine or strong drink when they entered the "tent of meeting" upon penalty of death, "so as to make a distinction between the holy and the profane" (Leviticus 10:9–10). Paul wrote that spiritual leaders should not be addicted to wine and that all believers should not be drunk, but filled with the Spirit (see Ephesians 5:18 and 1 Timothy 3:3).

The principle behind the issue of whether or not Christians should drink is illustrated in 1 Corinthians 8. In this chapter, Paul addresses a contemporary issue for that era, namely, whether or not Christians should eat meat offered to idols. Paul expresses two key thoughts to the church at Corinth:

1. "Knowledge makes arrogant, but love edifies" (1 Corinthians 8:1).
2. "Take care lest this liberty of yours somehow become a stumbling block to the weak" (1 Corinthians 8:9).

You may drink. However, many Christians choose not to drink to ensure that they avoid becoming a stumbling block to others.

> 20:2–3 The terror of a king is like the growling of a lion; he who provokes him to anger forfeits his own life. Keeping away from strife is an honor for a man, but any fool will quarrel.

When someone with authority gets riled up, watch out! (Proverbs 19:12 has a similar theme.) How do you relate to authority? Do you resent authority, or are you appreciative of what those in authority do for you and your family?

Scripture exhorts us to strive with the devil (see Ephesians 6), but regarding authority, "keeping away from strife is an honor." There are many types of authority, including God, parents, the church, government, school (for students), or a boss (for those who work). These numerous types of authority add to the complexity of this issue. Whom do we obey when differing authorities conflict? A boss may ask us to do something immoral. A school may teach a false concept and demand that we accept it. A government may be inherently evil and under the dominion of the devil. A parent may be corrupt. But God will never be evil, and He is our highest authority.

When dealing with authority that is corrupt, our first action ought to be prayer. Oftentimes God uses an authority that is externally evil to change an internal evil. (See the book of Judges.) God may use a secular authority for His own end, as He can and often does bring good out of evil.

Our second action should be to attempt to bring about change within the structure of authority. Esther and Daniel are examples of this.

Obey the authority whenever possible, as long as you are not sinning or behaving with injustice or corruption. If the authority asks you to do something that is sinful, unjust, or corrupt, then you must refuse in the name of your higher authority.

Here's an important question to consider: do you seek quarrels and strife, or do you seek unity and truth? See also Romans 13:1–3.

20:4 The sluggard does not plow after the autumn, so he begs during the harvest and has nothing.

Laziness is linked with natural consequences (compare Proverbs 19:23). Our work ethic is connected to our spiritual walk as well. What connection do you think exists between your work ethic and your spiritual walk?

20:5 A plan in the heart of a man is like deep water, but a man of understanding draws it out.

The implication of this verse is that the foolish man vacillates, wanders, and meanders, and that his plans are without direction. The metaphor addresses the utility principle of wisdom. This principle is the idea that knowledge is simply information unless it is actually used for something. When it is used, then knowledge is transformed into wisdom. In the image depicted by this verse, we just look at deep water, but we can use the water only if we are able to draw it out, the way a man draws out water from a well.

The man of understanding has the ability to see a deeper purpose for his life, so that he can look inside of himself and pull a plan out of his heart. This is also a test, a means by which you may know if you are a person of understanding. Do you know your purpose? Are you able to draw forth a plan from your own heart? Compare Proverbs 16:1–3.

> 20:6 Many a man proclaims his own loyalty, but who can find a trustworthy man?

Talk is cheap. Many may proclaim their loyalty, but how do you find people you can really trust? Look first for righteous individuals (see verse 7). Why is this so? A man who proclaims his loyalty and allegiance to God shows you where he stands. Also, work at being the trustworthy person others are looking for. Who can say how God will use you if others see you as trustworthy? The examples of Joseph and Daniel illustrate how God uses such men.

> 20:7 A righteous man who walks in his integrity—how blessed are his sons after him.

Righteous men walk in integrity. You can trust people of integrity. How wonderful it is to see that righteousness and integrity come with a blessing! Righteousness and integrity have another reward: righteous parents have the opportunity to see their children emulate their walk with God. Righteousness is the cornerstone of our relationship with God, and there is another tremendous side benefit of righteousness. Righteousness allows us to bring blessings to others, especially to those whom we love.

> 20:8 A king who sits on the throne of justice disperses all evil with his eyes.

When this was written (circa 900–1000 B.C.), a king functioned more as a magistrate or judge and less as a legislator, compared to a modern politician. There was little need to change or create new laws, because God's law was the law of the land. As an example, one of Solomon's duties was to discern (i.e., "judge") which woman was the rightful mother of an infant (1 Kings 3:16–28). I don't think any modern politician would ever handle such a situation.

The principle of this verse to keep in mind is that when true justice reigns, those who contemplate evil are afraid of being caught and punished. This is why their evil is dispersed.

20:9 Who can say, "I have cleansed my heart, I am pure from my sin"?

No one can cleanse his own heart or purify his sins through his own power. Only the Lord can do these things. Solomon is recommending an attitude of openness to the Lord. David asked the Lord, "Wash me thoroughly from my iniquity, and cleanse me from my sin . . . create in me a clean heart, O God" (Psalm 51:2, 10).

Solomon is directing us to acquire several keys to godly leadership. We are to draw forth a plan from our heart (v. 5), locate loyal and trustworthy companions (v. 6), maintain righteousness and integrity (v. 7), disperse evil (v. 8), and ask the Lord to cleanse and purify us (v. 9).

20:10 Differing weights and differing measures, both of them are abominable to the LORD.

This theme is echoed throughout Proverbs:

Ill-gotten gains do not profit. (Proverbs 10:2)

A false balance is an abomination to the LORD, but a just weight is His delight. (Proverbs 11:1)

It is better to be a poor man than a liar. (Proverbs 19:22)

Despite the clarity of this verse, we often need to be reminded of our need to remain honest. Do not dishonestly seek the wealth of this world. It is fleeting and vain. Seek rather the glory that the Lord Himself wishes to bestow upon you by proclaiming, "Well! bondman good and faithful . . . . Enter into the joy of thy lord" (Matthew 25:21 *The Englishman's Greek New Testament* Thomas Newberry Grand rapids, Michigan: Zondervan Publishing House 1970).

20:11 It is by his deeds that a lad distinguishes himself if his conduct is pure and right.

How is self-esteem developed? Jesus was not bothered when immature people of His generation called Him a gluttonous man and a drunkard, or a friend of tax-gatherers and sinners. He pointed out that "wisdom is vindicated by her deeds" (Matthew 11:19).

Solomon qualifies his statement by saying, "If his conduct is pure and right." We judge others by their deeds. The New Testament commonly uses the figure of speech "fruits" for this. The inverse is also true, for it is by his deeds that a lad dishonors himself as well.

20:12 The hearing ear and the seeing eye, the LORD has made both of them.

God has created us with the means and ability to know Him! Paul wrote in Romans 1:19–20, "That which is known about God is evident within them . . . . For since the creation of the world His invisible attributes, His eternal power and divine nature, have been clearly seen." See also Matthew 13:10–17.

This is also a reference to how wonderfully we are created. Both the ear and the eye are incredibly complex. In fact, they have irreducible complexity[18], which is a great argument to use with your friends who believe in evolution.

20:13 Do not love sleep, lest you become poor; open your eyes, and you will be satisfied with food.

Sleep is not our purpose. God has created us for fellowship and for work (see also Proverbs 20:4). So why did God create us with a need for sleep? Without this need, man might find it too easy to forget God. Sleep imposes a schedule on us, and a schedule allows us to more readily worship God on a daily basis. It reveals our humanity to us on a daily basis and allows us to understand better the concept of resting in God. On the other hand, the point is not to overly indulge in it.

20:14 "Bad, bad," says a buyer; but when he goes his way, then he boasts.

"Little white lies are OK." Thus saith the world. Any lie, any falsehood, is a false balance. A lie is saying something but thinking something else. Do not lie just to get a better deal. Any lie is an abomination to God and serves only to damage our witness and credibility to unsaved people. It also hurts our parenting (our kids are watching!). Some people view such lies as funny, but how can our marriages be helped by such a habit? We hurt our relationships with God and our spouse—and any other significant relationship. Trust is a communication bridge that takes a very long time to build. Always value the truth.

20:15 There is gold, and an abundance of jewels; but the lips of knowledge are a more precious thing.

What do you value? So many people seem satisfied with the knowledge they currently possess. But how many are satisfied with the wealth they possess? Ask yourself, do you crave more spiritual knowledge? "Lay up for yourself treasures in heaven . . . no one can serve two masters" (Matthew 6).

20:16 Take his garment when he becomes surety for a stranger; and for foreigners, hold him in pledge.

This verse at first reading appears to be an incredible juxtaposition. When wealth becomes our goal, debt is often not far behind!

The dilemma is that we naturally want to be "nice" to people, but this verse suggests that we limit our financial obligations, especially to strangers and foreigners. In other words, don't finance people you don't know well.

Good stewardship demands that we balance our heart's desire to give with our head's ability to make rational decisions. God blesses us so that we can bless others. However, if we are foolish and lose our shirts, then we also lose the ability to continually help others. This verse does not mean to avoid helping others, it means we should help others wisely. It may also mean that if the lender is giving to the stranger, and he is borrowing part of the gift or investment from you, then you better take his shirt now as part of the collateral, so that you get at least something out of the transaction.

Often, helping others wisely involves giving counsel and knowledge more than money. Those we help often do not like this, but if they accept it, they will later appreciate it. Note: Those who do *not* accept it are also the people who don't actually appreciate the gift of your money either. They expect it, but they don't appreciate it. In this state of mind, they are likely to learn little anyway, so your help would have been squandered. Understanding this can help you feel less guilty. Helping others is not the same as enabling poor stewardship.

> 20:17 Bread obtained by falsehood is sweet to a man, but afterward his mouth will be filled with gravel.

Can you think of a time when this verse was a reality for you? At times, sin is sweet in a man's mouth. But its wages are bitter (cf. 2 Samuel 13:11–12, 14–15).

> 20:18 Prepare plans by consultation, and make war by wise guidance.

Presumption brings strife, but counsel brings wisdom (Proverbs 13:10). Listen to counsel because it often leads us to develop greater self-discipline and accountability than we might otherwise possess (Proverbs 19:20). We often need many counselors (Proverbs 15:22), and advisors can help us "count the cost" (Luke 14:31).

20:19 He who goes about as a slanderer reveals secrets, therefore do not associate with a gossip.

Not only are we directed by scripture to avoid gossip ourselves (e.g., 2 Corinthians 12:20), but also we are to squelch gossip actively by refusing to hear it. Gossip is no fun to possess unless one can share it with others. By refusing to participate as a listener, we may help someone who has a problem with gossip extinguish that behavior. If nothing else, we demonstrate to the gossiper that we will personally not tolerate it. This verse also points out that a slanderer reveals secrets. What secrets should we pursue? David recorded that "the secret of the LORD is for those who fear Him" (Psalm 25:14). Let us seek the secrets of the Lord rather than the secrets of the world.

20:20 He who curses his father or his mother, his lamp will go out in time of darkness.

To honor our father and mother is a command associated with a blessing of long life. The inverse is just as true, as this verse points out. If you curse and dishonor your parents, you may expect your own lamp of life to be snuffed out when your life is at its darkest moment. The latter metaphor contained within this verse, of the lamp going out in a time of darkness, is a picture of biblical consequential judgment. The Bible is full of many passages that contrast light with darkness. In Matthew 25 He gave a parable of ten virgins preparing for a wedding reception. The five foolish ones had their lamps go out when they needed them (Matthew 25:1–13). Jesus also spoke often of judgment. In John 3:18–

21 Jesus explains how serious consequential justice can be. It is often a matter of life and death!

> 20:21 An inheritance gained hurriedly at the beginning, will not be blessed in the end.

Do not seek the quick fix or the premature inheritance. Seek rather an eternal inheritance. This verse indirectly addresses the issue of maturity. An inheritance can be used for many good uses, but an immature individual is likely to just squander the inheritance.

> 20:22 Do not say, "I will repay evil"; wait for the LORD, and He will save you.

Bitterness will destroy its owner. You begin by "owning" it, but in the end it will own you. This verse also reveals a practical application regarding faith and salvation. When we utter the words, "I will repay," we remove God from the picture. God is our salvation; we must place our trust in Him.

> 20:23 Differing weights are an abomination to the LORD, and a false scale is not good.

True godliness requires true honesty. The illustration of the scale gives rise to two pertinent questions: 1) do you weigh things honestly? and 2) is your own life in balance?

Much of Proverbs deals with the concept of balance. We need to find balance in health issues, in the way we parent (between permissiveness and authoritarianism), in money issues (between risk and safety), and in our spiritual lives (between loving God and loving others). Other areas of spiritual balance include the following: fear God, yet rest in Him; seek truth, balanced with grace; value justice and compassion. This list is unfinished. Can you think of other areas that also require balance?

20:24 Man's steps are ordained by the LORD, how then can man understand his way?

If your way is God's way, you can rest in His promises, but you will not necessarily perceive all of the blessings, trials, tasks, and changes that will be a part of your earthly life. "Oh, the depth of the riches both of the wisdom and knowledge of God! How unsearchable are His judgments and unfathomable His ways!" (Romans 11:33).

God revealed through the prophet Isaiah: "'My thoughts are not your thoughts, neither are your ways My ways,' declares the LORD. 'For as the heavens are higher than the earth, so are my ways higher than your ways'" (Isaiah 55:8–9).

So numerous are the examples of this concept in scripture that we shall mention only three men: David, Moses, and Amos. All were sheepherders at some time during their lives, and all three could not see all that God held in store for them.

How does this verse apply to the concept of knowing and doing the will of God? Read the following verses and see if they in any way alter or bolster your current view of what it means to do the will of God: Proverbs 1:15; 3:6; 5:21; 8:22; 9:6; 14:12.

20:25 It is a snare for a man to say rashly, "It is holy!" and after the vows to make inquiry.

Vow cautiously. Pledge sincerely. Do not take holiness tritely! Note Solomon's words from the book of Ecclesiastes: "Guard your steps as you go to the house of God, and draw near to listen rather than to offer the sacrifice of fools; for they do not know they are doing evil. Do not be hasty in word or impulsive in thought to bring up a matter in the presence of God. For God is in heaven and you are on the earth; therefore let your words be few" (Ecclesiastes 5:1–2).

Remember that when Moses asked God to reveal to him all of His glory, God showed him only a portion—because if He revealed

all of His face, it would have killed Moses right then. We worship
an awesome God!

> 20:26 A wise king winnows the wicked, and drives the thresh-
> ing wheel over them.

Sanctification means to "set apart." Winnowing is done to separate the wheat from the chaff. In the future, the righteous and the
wicked will be separated completely through the vehicles of judgment and resurrection. Scripture reveals that "an hour is coming,
in which all who are in the tombs shall hear His voice, and shall
come forth; those who did the good deeds, to a resurrection of life,
those who committed the evil deeds to a resurrection of judgment"
(John 5:28–29).

Our post-resurrection existence will be one of complete sanctification. But until then we live in a world where righteous men
coexist with evil men. In this context we seek to live a sanctified
life that is set apart from the world and set apart for God. But
Solomon's point here is that a person in governmental authority,
i.e., a king, can do something tangible to benefit the quality of life.
He can seek to separate those who are evil through civil justice.
Perhaps this verse is where we get the phrase "the wheels of justice." Compare Proverbs 20:8.

> 20:27 The spirit of man is the lamp of the LORD, searching all
> the innermost parts of his being.

This is a fascinating observation on which to meditate. Our own
spirit reveals God to us. Thus the more aware and in touch we are
with our own spirit, the more able we are to perceive the spirit of
God because we were created in the image of God.

The Hellenistic goal, "Know thyself," is a worthy task. But apart
from God it is impossible to fully know yourself, because without
God you are missing the key component of your very existence.
The self-knowledge that the ancient Greek philosophers were able

to achieve was always incomplete because of their false polytheistic beliefs.

It is my personal belief that the enchanting and mysterious draw of most false religions is based on the fact that we were created in the image of God. Through meditation on this "image of God," the humanist, Hindu, Taoist, Buddhist, and others do indeed perceive aspects of truth. But they incorrectly assume that these perceptions are of the ultimate reality rather than an image of that ultimate reality. Paul wrote in 1 Corinthians 13:12, "Now we see in a mirror dimly."

Therefore the precepts of such religions may be true. They preach such things as the golden rule, valuing humility, and loving others. These precepts are true. But what they lack is relationship with God; therefore they offer no true salvation for bringing about an internal transformation through a crucified self (Romans 6) and a transformed mind (Romans 12).

Without a relationship with the one true God Almighty (which is the purpose for which we were created), any assessment of the nature of man is foggy and incomplete becuase it is based only on partial truth. Those who address the nature of man without God in the picture are like the people in Plato's cave,[19] they perceive only shadows of the truth (see also Hebrews 8:4–5).

20:28 Loyalty and truth preserve the king, and he upholds his throne by righteousness.

As a leader, you should seek to surround yourself with people of integrity who are loyal and truthful, and you must demand no less of yourself. Today in American politics the question of one's integrity versus one's goals is still, thankfully, an issue. Even Confucius understood in his ancient day and culture that good leaders were more important than good laws.[20]

However, there are many pragmatists who believe that personal integrity should not be an issue. Realistic pragmatism, on one hand, and idealism, on the other, are extremes that should be held in balance. The former asks the question, "OK, what will really work?" The latter asks the question, "What should we be striving for?" This verse suggests that what will really work is loyalty and truth, and what we should be striving toward is righteousness.

> 20:29 The glory of young men is their strength, and the honor of old men is their gray hair.

We all possess something of value. Jesus pointed out to his disciples that they could learn from children regarding their humility (Matthew 18:3–5). In whatever stage of life we find ourselves, we should realize that we have something of value to offer to others. Likewise, we can learn from others in all stages of life. Do not despise others because of their age.

> 20:30 Stripes that wound scour away evil, and strokes reach the innermost parts.

This is another gem, an absolute jewel demonstrating how God has woven His gospel message throughout all of scripture. As a parent I understand this encouragement to discipline my children that they may learn to depart from evil. As a leader in social situations, I see the practicality of this verse in the enforcement of rules and laws. But as a Christian, I see in this verse the stripes of my Savior who suffered and died to "scour away evil" so that I might live.

Proverbs 21

21:1 The king's heart is like channels of water in the hand of the LORD;
He turns it wherever He wishes.

God is in control. The following passage illustrates the hand of God at work with a king's heart: "The LORD had caused them to rejoice, and had turned the heart of the king of Assyria toward them to encourage them in the work of the house of God, the God of Israel" (Ezra 6:22). Paul instructs us to be in "subjection to the governing authorities" (see Romans 13:1–3), not because governments are perfect, but because of the sovereignty of God.

It is interesting to ponder the fact that a king penned these words found here in Proverbs. Solomon observed the work of the hand of God in the heart of his father and in his own heart.

Christians frequently bemoan the state of their imperfect governments. We should promote the biblical concepts of freedom, fairness, truth, and justice in whatever society we find ourselves. However, we should never underestimate God or lose hope. Do what you can to improve things socially and politically, but always realize, God *is* in control.

21:2 Every man's way is right in his own eyes, but the LORD weighs the heart.

Do you examine yourself daily? Do you spend a portion of each day in communion with God? Solomon reminds us to examine ourselves. I believe we should do this daily and spend a portion of each day in communion with God. This is the purpose for which we were created.

As a believer, do not take the statement, "The LORD weighs the heart" as a negative. For those who expect judgment, it definitely is a negative, but for those of us who love the Lord, His weighing of our hearts should be seen as the caring action of our loving Father. Why not actively invite the Lord to weigh your heart, as David did? He wrote, "I have trusted in the LORD without wavering. Examine me, O LORD, and try me; test my mind and my heart" (Psalm 26:1–2). Perhaps we are often too timid in our approach to developing a deeper relationship with God.

For further application, read 2 Timothy 4:2–4 and see if you can discern how Paul's advice to Timothy relates to Proverbs 21:2. A fresh look at Proverbs 16:1–3 may provide additional insights.

Besides these areas of practical application, this verse provides insight into an area of the nature of God. What is important to Him is your heart and your motives.

21:3 To do righteousness and justice is desired by the LORD rather than sacrifice.

This is a profound concept! What does God desire of you? And for what purpose were you created? If you believe your purpose is to have an abiding relationship with your Creator, to lead others into a similar relationship, and to bring glory to God, then you have answered the second question. But the first question gets at the issue of *how* we may live out and accomplish this purpose. How attuned are you to the desires of God?

The prophet Micah wrote, "With what shall I come to the LORD and bow myself before the God on high? Shall I come to Him with burnt offerings, with yearling calves? Does the LORD take delight in thousands of rams, in ten thousand rivers of oil? . . . He has told you, O man, what is good; and what does the LORD require of you but to do justice, to love kindness, and to walk humbly with your God?" (Micah 6:6–8).

Jesus reiterated these ideas when He said to the Pharisees, "It is not those who are healthy who need a physician, but those who are ill. But go and learn what this means, 'I desire compassion and not sacrifice,' for I did not come to the righteous, but sinners" (Matthew 9:12–13). Jesus liked this quote from Hosea (6:6), and He used it again in Matthew 12:7.

This is a key concept in understanding God's grace and in developing our character. Our faith is active when we seek righteousness and justice in the world around us. If we live under a purely sacrificial system, our faith is reactive rather than proactive. James championed proactive faith when he wrote, "Show me your faith without the works, and I will show you my faith by my works" (James 2:18).

21:4 Haughty eyes and a proud heart, the lamp of the wicked, is sin.

The English word *lamp* is translated from the Hebrew word *niyr* (neer), which can be translated as either "plowing" or "lamp." How can this verb and this seemingly unrelated noun have anything in common? According to *The Complete Word Study Old Testament*[21], *niyr* can figuratively have the idea of the gleam of a fresh furrow on newly plowed land.

If we take it the way the NIV and the NASB translation teams have ("the lamp of the wicked is sin"), then this verse suggests that the wicked follow the path (light) of sin. If we take it the way it was translated in the King James Version ("The plowing of the wicked is sin"), then the verse suggests that we can look behind the wicked and see the trail (furrow) of sin they leave. In either case, the wicked can be identified by the trail of sin they either follow or leave behind. In a practical sense, the verse simply means that we can discern who sinful people are by sensing their pride and haughtiness.

21:5 The plans of the diligent lead surely to advantage, but everyone who is hasty comes surely to poverty.

To avoid poverty, there are three needed elements: planning, diligence, and patience. These three elements are the foundation of what is commonly referred to as "good stewardship." Many disadvantages can be overcome by careful planning and hard work. In the parable of the talents and the faithful servant (Matthew 25:14–30), Jesus reveals the idea that good stewardship requires a balance of active planning, diligence, and risk-taking. The overly cautious servant actually took the greatest risk. He unknowingly risked the disfavor of his master.

"He who hesitates is lost" is a nonscriptural proverb that my father was fond of quoting. There is a time to act decisively, but knowing the proper timing requires insight and planning. The fool acts hastily, not because he makes a quick decision, but because he makes a quick decision without forethought, planning, and all the necessary information.

Are you still a little unsure of how to apply this verse? Think of the concept of readiness. A person who is ready has already planned and prepared. When an opportunity arises, he may act quickly. There is a huge difference between acting hastily and acting swiftly because you are ready.

21:6 The getting of treasures by a lying tongue is a fleeting vapor, the pursuit of death.

Are you actively pursuing death? Many people are, although they seldom realize it. Notice that this particular verse does not strictly condemn the acquisition of treasures alone, but only the gaining of treasures through falseness, lies, or deceit. One of the ironies of life is that "he who loves money will not be satisfied with money" (Ecclesiastes 5:10).

21:7 The violence of the wicked will drag them away, because they refuse to act with justice.

Here we see another case of "what goes around" coming around again. The Scriptural principle is that those who refuse to act with justice will actually receive justice! Those of us who have experienced grace know that we have been spared from true justice.

At times, from a temporal perspective, life may appear to be unfair. But from an eternal perspective, we know that God will ultimately act with total and complete justice (except to those who have received His grace). Theologically, we all deserve death. The only exceptions are made to those who have received His redemptive, merciful gift of salvation. A similar idea is seen in Proverbs 11:5–6: "The wicked fall by their own wickedness" and "the treacherous will be caught by their own greed."

21:8 The way of a guilty man is crooked, but as for the pure, his conduct is upright.

The former part of this verse uses the label "a guilty man." This title presupposes former sins and transgressions of which the man is guilty.

The contrast here is between "the way" or conduct of people. How do we know if a person is upright or guilty? This verse implies that the evidence is easy to discern if we simply look at their path through life and their conduct.

21:9 It is better to live in a corner of a roof, than in a house shared with a contentious woman.

The word *contentious* here describes someone unpleasant to live with. Contentious people always seem to look for a fight. They love to debate or dispute any point, but not for the purpose of uncovering greater knowledge or insight. Their purpose seems to revolve more around power and control issues instead of personal growth.

Unity is the key not only to our marriages but even to our own personal happiness. Unity with God and with others is the source of our deepest joy. Such unity is the foundation of our greatest internal peace.

The Gospel of John is full of references to peace and unity. Chapters 14–18 contain numerous references to Jesus' relationship to the Father and to us. John also includes what our relationships to Him and to each other ought to be. Jesus describes for us how the internal development of our hope, faith, and love lead us into "abiding with [Him]" (see John 15).

How then are you to apply this verse? First, do not be a contentious person yourself. A contentious person may believe that his or her contentiousness will achieve something positive, but this is an illusion. It simply drives others away. Many contentious individuals attempt to use the label of "honesty" to excuse their crass behavior. But so-called "honesty" that attempts to put others down is not interested in the truth. It is actually only selfishly interested in gossip.

Sometimes we do need to confront someone. The biblical method is always rooted in love (see Galatians 6:1). The difference between confronting and contending lies within your motivation. It is the internal motive that reveals the heart.

Secondly, this verse can be taken as a warning for those who are yet seeking a mate. Use your discernment wisely.

> 21:10 The soul of the wicked desires evil; his neighbor finds no favor in his eyes.

The latter part of this verse speaks to the fact that those who are wicked look for what is bad and evil in others. This is the bully who complains of others being mean, and the gossiper who complains that others are calling him names and starting rumors about him. This is the critic who complains that he doesn't like so-and-so because that person is always negative and complaining. In essence, this is the man who looks at the speck in his brother's eye but does not notice the log in his own eye (Matthew 7:3–4).

Let us now examine the former portion of this verse: "The soul of the wicked desires evil." What we desire greatly shapes who we are and who we will become. The inverse is also true. Who we are shapes our desires. What is it that you desire?

The reader may find it interesting to note that the Septuagint version renders a slightly different idea here, stating, "The soul of the ungodly shall not be pitied by any man."

> 21:11 When the scoffer is punished, the naive becomes wise; but when the wise is instructed, he receives knowledge.

A scoffer or mocker does not learn from his own punishment, but others can learn vicariously. While the scoffer is trying to figure out how to avoid getting caught the next time (see Proverbs 19:25), those who are simple and naive are developing a healthy fear. "Fear of the LORD is the beginning of wisdom" (Proverbs 9:10).

21:12 The righteous one considers the house of the wicked, turning the wicked to ruin.

This verse can be seen in several different ways. The critical phrase is "righteous one." How shall we interpret this phrase?

Solomon is directing much of his proverbial writing to leaders (or future leaders). If we understand "righteous one" to mean a righteous individual, then we can take this verse to mean, "If you are a righteous leader, then squelch evil wherever you can." However, if we understand the phrase "righteous one" to be a title for God Himself (as the NIV editors do), then we see this verse more as an observation that enables us to rest in the assurance that our righteous Creator is a just God. He will ultimately bring judgment to the wicked. Other scriptures support both ideas, so either interpretation seems possible.

21:13 He who shuts his ear to the cry of the poor will also cry himself and not be answered.

This verse offers a clear illustration of the golden rule: "Whatever you want others to do for you, do so for them" (Matthew 7:12). As Jesus instructed us, "Love your neighbor as yourself" (Matthew 19:19).

As you practice your faith, be compassionate. The parable in Matthew 18:21–35 about the unmerciful slave directs us to remember how great a compassion our Lord has bestowed upon us. We are to emulate His patience and His compassion.

21:14 A gift in secret subdues anger, and a bribe in the bosom, strong wrath.

Given the parallel structure of this verse, it appears that the word *bribe* in this context may be a synonym for the word *gift*. In other contexts, the word *bribe* implies corruption. What do you think are the distinguishing differences between a true gift and a true bribe? Surely at some level, motivation (as in most areas of our spiritual walk) is the critical litmus test.

The Bible condemns bribery (Exodus 23:8) when it is given to obstruct justice (e.g., bribing false witnesses). However, it is often appropriate to give gifts to quell anger.

The offering of a gift is an act of sacrifice, and it demonstrates that you honor the person to whom you are offering the gift. Remember, "A man's gift makes room for him, and brings him before great men" (Proverbs 18:16).

21:15 The execution of justice is joy for the righteous, but is terror to the workers of iniquity.

Because we are created in the image of God (Genesis 1:27), a sense of justice is a part of our innate nature (see also Romans 13:30). Since it is a natural part of us, it brings us joy when we see it.

Revenge is how the natural man copes with feelings of injustice. The problem with revenge is that it is a nonspiritual solution to a spiritual problem. A man with revenge on his mind usually suffers from a one-sided earthly perspective. This inadequate perspective is then coupled with the emotion of impatience, resulting in poor decisions that may ultimately hurt additional innocent people. Such decisions run the risk of creating further injustices.

The main focus of this verse is that we should never be in a position where we ourselves are terrorized by justice. If we live righteously, in relationship with God, we will have inner peace. However, those who practice iniquity will not have peace.

An additional irony to ponder is that we may either be men who fear God (of our own free will), or we will eventually become men who are terrorized by the judgment of God.

21:16 A man who wanders from the way of understanding will rest in the assembly of the dead.

Regardless of your position on "eternal security," the warning here is easily understood. Find the "way of understanding"—and stay on it! The following verses reveal additional insights into the "way": Proverbs 2:11–13; 3:5–6; 4:11–14, 18–19; 10:17; 14:12, 14; 15:9.

For Solomon, the "way" is a symbolic metaphor implying the concept of salvation. Jesus said, "I am the way, and the truth, and the life; no one comes to the Father, but through Me" (John 14:6). Anyone who ignores His advice will also "rest in the assembly of the dead."

21:17 He who loves pleasure will become a poor man; he who loves wine and oil will not become rich.

Here Solomon is pointing out a generalization framed as a warning. If you desire financial security, do not love pleasure or wine. The biblical principle is "Seek first His kingdom . . . and all these things shall be added to you" (Matthew 6:33). Solomon's own personal experience regarding his acquisition of wisdom involved this principle (1 Kings 3:3–14).

If you seek pleasure and things such as wine as your primary pursuit in life, you should realize that even if you were not made "poor" by your own standard, it is still a futile pursuit (see Ecclesiastes 2:1–3). Only what is done for God will last.

21:18 The wicked is a ransom for the righteous, and the treacherous is in the place of the upright.

Theologically, this is a very difficult verse to understand. Clearly it is better to be righteous than to be wicked, for God's sense of justice must be met. But usually scripture illustrates the opposite idea, like the sacrifice of a pure, blameless lamb for one's sins—or as in the case of Messiah, the atoning sacrifice of the Righteous One for the sins of all mankind.

However, we can see that in a sacrificial system the "wicked is a ransom for the righteous." When Jesus bore our sins on the cross, without committing the actual acts of sin, He in essence became the most wicked, sinful man ever (see also Isaiah 53:9–10; 2 Corinthians 5:21; Romans 8:3; Galatians 3:13; and 1 John 2:2). This is what it means for Him to bear our sins, and this is why the Father momentarily had to forsake Him. Through death *all* the sins He bore were paid for. This is the gospel. However, it seems doubtful that this particular verse is actually dealing with theology of this sort.

Perhaps a more likely way to view this verse is to think of Biblical stories such as those of Mordecai[22], Daniel[23], and Shadrach, Meshach, and Abed-nego[24]. In each of these stories God turned something evil into something good. Often, in addition, the instigators of the evil (such as Haman) were themselves punished. In this way, the wicked ransom the righteous.

> 21:19 It is better to live in a desert land, than with a contentious and vexing woman.

Do you know someone who is at a point in life at which he or she is looking for a mate? Perhaps you could suggest the following ideas and supporting passages to that person. It is good to find a suitable mate (Genesis 2:18 and Proverbs 18:22). Understand the value of unity (Ecclesiastes 4:9–12). Study the story of Isaac and Rebekah, because it is both beautiful and didactic (Genesis 24). Seek a "prudent" mate who is "from the LORD" (Proverbs 19:14). Discover the truth that the relationship between a man and a woman should be "too wonderful" for them to completely understand. There should be "zing" or "electricity" in the relationship (Proverbs 30:18–19 and Proverbs 5:18–20). Look for lasting qualities. Understand that "charm is deceitful and beauty is vain, but a woman who fears the LORD, she shall be praised." Physical aspects are fleeting, above all seek a mate who "fears the LORD" (Proverbs 31:10–31, esp. verse 30).

If we encourage young people to pursue such relationships, there will be fewer people living in a "desert land"!

> 21:20 There is precious treasure and oil in the dwelling of the wise, but a foolish man swallows it up.

The wise man accumulates wealth not by methods of greed, but by good stewardship. This is why treasures exist in his dwelling. The foolish man consumes all he acquires.

> 21:21 He who pursues righteousness and loyalty finds life, righteousness and honor.

Think back over the last seven days. What have you pursued this last week? Righteousness and loyalty do not just happen arbitrarily; they must be actively pursued.

The pursuit of righteousness may be seen as a vertical focus on the things of God. The pursuit of loyalty may be seen as a horizontal focus on the things of others. If we are both righteous and loyal, we shall please both God and men as we fulfill the two great commandments.

21:22 A wise man scales the city of the mighty, and brings down the stronghold in which they trust.

Here Solomon uses a wartime illustration to demonstrate the superiority of wisdom over physical strength. See also Ecclesiastes 9:16–18 and 10:10.

Joab accomplished this for David (2 Samuel 5:6–8 and 1 Chronicles 11:4–7), as they were able to sneak in through the water system to conquer Jerusalem.

21:23 He who guards his mouth and his tongue, guards his soul from troubles.

Often we view ourselves in a fragmentary manner. Sometimes we study ourselves in classifications such as body, soul, and spirit. At other times we use concepts like physical, emotional, psychological, social, and spiritual. These are useful terms, but we should never forget our wholeness and the genuine interconnectedness of our entire being.

The point of this verse is that external activities bear internal results. If you read the third chapter of James you will realize two things: 1) the power and danger of the tongue; and 2) how internal things (such as wisdom) influence our outward actions, e.g., good behavior (James 3:13).

It is difficult to "guard" our souls, for such an ethereal idea is very nebulous. How are we to go about accomplishing such a task? Solomon answers this in a practical way. To guard our souls, we need to guard our tongues. This is something we can do, and we can even see the tangible results of our efforts. Are you tempted to gossip? Do you have a critical attitude? Do you struggle with occasional foul language? Why not plan something you can do this week that could be deemed a form of guarding your tongue?

> 21:24 "Proud," "Haughty," "Scoffer," are his names, who acts with insolent pride.

These three titles demonstrate three different things we look at from one egocentric perspective. "Proud" denotes how we view ourselves. "Haughty" denotes how we view others. "Scoffer" denotes how we view God. Pride is a great deceiver, and it is at the root of all three forms of insolence.

> 21:25–26 The desire of the sluggard puts him to death, for his hands refuse to work; all day long he is craving, while the righteous gives and does not hold back.

Solomon continually demonstrates how free will operates. We make choices when we follow our desires. Those choices have natural and spiritual consequences. "His hands refuse to work" because his mind tells his hands what to do.

Look at Matthew 6:19–34 and reread Proverbs 19:21–24. Plan, listen to the counsel of the Lord, have faith when times are tough, be satisfied with what God has given you, and work hard. Do this and you will be able to give and not hold back.

> 21:27 The sacrifice of the wicked is an abomination, how much more when he brings it with evil intent!

This is a sobering verse. While actions speak louder than words to us, motives speak louder than actions to God. He looks at the heart. Isaiah 66:2–4 tells us plainly what the Lord is looking for.

> 21:28 A false witness will perish, but the man who listens to the truth will speak forever.

The first part of this verse is clear in all the translations. A false witness will perish. But the latter part of the verse has some ambiguity. The NASB reads, "But the man who listens *to the truth* will speak forever." The NIV says, "And whoever listens to him will be destroyed forever," while the KJV renders it: "but the man that heareth speaketh constantly." The NASB and KJV are quite similar, but the NIV has a completely different meaning. So which translation is correct? Or are they all good possible renditions.

There are four Hebrew words in the phrase and they can be transliterated as *'ish shama davar netsach. 'Ish* means man. *Netsach* refers to a goal, such as splendor or glory, when it is used as a noun. But when used as an adverb, it means always, forever, until eternity, unceasing, or constantly. So far, nothing too tricky translationally, except all three translations used an adverb while *The Complete Word Study Old Testament*[25] gives *netsach* as a noun (attached with an article and preposition). But, nevertheless, the first word is "man" and the last word is "forever" or a future goal. But *davar* is another matter. *Davar* is one of the most general words in the entire Old Testament. It is one of the basic words for "say" and "speak." About thirty different English words are used to translate it. The main idea is mental or oral communication.

This leaves us with the word *shama*, which basically means "to hear." Its main idea is perceiving a message or sensing a sound.

So pick your translation. While the NASB as usual has attempted the most literal translation, we still run into the problem of connecting that latter part of the verse to the former part. The KJV and NASB teams chose to see them as *contrasts* while the NIV team chose to see the two parts as *parallels*.

21:29 A wicked man shows a bold face, but as for the upright, he makes his way sure.

The contrast here is between style and substance. One man is all show; he represents style. The other is prudent, stable, and mature; he represents substance. Our beliefs, our desires, our attitude toward self and others— these are the things that mold us and make us people of style or substance.

21:30 There is no wisdom and no understanding and no counsel against the LORD.

This is a beautiful statement of theology. All truth is God's truth. There are pseudo-truths and half-truths that are the illegitimate creation of man or the devil. But all true wisdom and understanding and counsel is from the Lord.

21:31 The horse is prepared for the day of battle, but victory belongs to the LORD.

The cliché "God helps those who help themselves" is a useful idea. It shows that there are two parties involved in life's affairs. The danger of the cliché is that it can be seen as an understatement of God's role and an overstatement of man's role.

God is in control, and He will help us as we commit our ways to Him and seek His will. As the latter part of the verse implies, be sure to give honor and glory to God for all of "your" victories.

Proverbs 22

22:1 A good name is to be more desired than great riches, favor is better than silver and gold.

How do others see you? How important is your reputation? How will you be remembered? What would you like as an epitaph on your life? Guard your good name, for once it is tarnished, no amount of cleanser can clean it up entirely in the eyes of most men.

22:2 The rich and the poor have a common bond, the LORD is the maker of them all.

In what ways are people the same and in what ways are we different from one another? In analyzing differences we consider overt things such as gifts, abilities, interests, and physical characteristics. Differences are thus easily observed. However, when we consider universal qualities whereby we may claim to be the same, it is interesting to note that it is difficult to find any major quality of "sameness" that is not directly related to God Himself! Here are some examples. We all possess life and value. We are all sinners. Jesus died for all of us. We are all created in the image of God. We have common bonds in all areas of eternal significance, for the Lord is our maker.

> 22:3 The prudent sees the evil and hides himself, but the naive go on, and are punished for it.

The prudent and the naive (or "simple" in the KJV and NIV) are contrasted here in two ways: First, the prudent man sees, meaning he is discerning and aware. This is an important distinction. In Matthew 23:13ff. the "blind Pharisees" do not see, and this has terrible consequences ("How shall you escape the sentence of hell?").

A second point is that the prudent man's natural consequences differ from the naive man's. Natural consequences are often brought about by spiritual blindness. The next time someone calls you a "prude," tell him, "Thank you for the compliment."

> 22:4 The reward of humility and the fear of the LORD are riches, honor, and life.

This verse demonstrates clearly how the principles of the kingdom of God work. One begins to truly fear God, not because of an expectation of reward, but through a heightened perception of God Himself. This is the beginning of wisdom, and it is also the beginning of humility.

Humility is not namby-pamby groveling, it is the antecedent attitude of a *useful* servant. The greater one's fear of the Lord, the greater will be one's perception of his own value to the Creator! A truly "good and faithful" servant recognizes with joy the gifts and strengths he has received from the Lord. Humility is an attitude of joyful thanksgiving for what God has created one as. It is manifested in a utilitarian fashion under the purpose of bringing glory to God. The prayer of such a man or woman is "Cleanse me, fill me, teach me, use me!" The rewards are there, as they are listed in this verse, but the focus of an individual of humility who fears the Lord is not on the rewards, but on the actual relationship with God.

22:5–6 Thorns and snares are in the way of the perverse; he who guards himself will be far from them. Train up a child in the way he should go, even when he is old he will not depart from it.

Have you ever heard any of the following clichés?

"Boys will be boys."

"Everybody does it."

"It's just teenage rebellion, you can't do anything about it."

These outlooks have a unifying thread. They are all fatalistic statements. God's word is replete with examples of what we can do about it! It is your choice whether or not to accept God's gift of salvation. It is your choice to put on the full armor of God or not. True, the Fall brought many thorns, and Satan certainly has set many snares, but you may choose to expose yourself openly or to guard yourself from these thorns and snares. This is also the point of much of our child-rearing.

The word "perverse" in the NASB is rendered "froward" in the King James and "wicked" in the NIV. It is our desire to avoid the "thorns and snares" for ourselves, and as parents we hope for our children to avoid these things as well. Therefore, we must train our children in a morality that seeks to avoid perversity, frowardness, and wickedness. Webster[26] defines *perverse* as "deviating from what is considered right or good," or "obstinately disobedient." To be *froward* is to be "not easily controlled; willful; contrary." To be *wicked* is simply to be "morally bad."

Verse 6 brings up one further point for rumination. How are we to view good Christian parents whose kids have gone astray? Actually, the Bible has quite a few examples of this. The verse is not stating a promise but rather a general principle. Each child maintains his own free will and sin nature.

Most children raised in good Christian homes will remain faithful throughout their lives. Some will stray, as did the prodigal, and return after a few years. A few will never truly accept or will reject outright the teachings of the Bible. I view this as a result not of poor parenting, but rather of the reality of living in a free-will system.

Some scholars and pastors (e.g., Charles Swindoll) believe that Proverbs 22:6 is to be understood by translating the verse as "Train up a child according to *his* way." The idea here is that each of us is unique, each of us has "a way." Parents are to perceive "the way" of their child and teach him accordingly, with his own personal uniqueness in mind.

However, I prefer the more traditional interpretation, as is seen by emphasizing the phrase "the way." With this view, we read it as "Train up a child in *the* way he should go." Although we are free in God, there are *shoulds* and *oughts* taught throughout scripture for our safety, greater joy, the fulfillment of our potential, and the glory of God. Throughout Proverbs Solomon has woven the concept of the "way" by contrasting man's way and God's way. Let us train our children God's way! This, I believe, is the real flow of the verse.

> 22:7 The rich rules over the poor, and the borrower becomes the lender's slave.

If possible, do not borrow. Referring to compound interest, Albert Einstein is quoted as saying, "It is the greatest mathematical discovery of all time. "Albert Einstein is credited with discovering the compound interest "Rule of 72." [27]

Solomon points out that a relational difference exists between the rich and the poor. In Proverbs 22:2 he writes about a point of similarity, for all men are made by God, whether they be rich or poor. Nevertheless, in verse 7 he points out that it is the rich who rule over the poor. Your relationship to God is in no way dependent upon your wealth, but if you choose the oxymoron of becoming a voluntary "slave" to a lender, then you must also accept the natural consequences of this action.

> 22:8 He who sows iniquity will reap vanity, and the rod of his fury will perish.

This verse offers us a poetic rendition of "The wages of sin is death." The progression of self-destruction begins with sin. It then becomes vanity, or pride ("I am more important than others"). This then leads to violence ("Others are not valuable, even their lives"). Violence eventually leads to one's own self-destruction.

22:9 He who is generous will be blessed, for he gives some of his food to the poor.

Why not plan a way in which you can be generous in the near future? You will be blessed! Read this verse a second time and answer this question: Which comes first, the generosity or the blessing? The answer really is quite logical, spiritually speaking, but it's funny how often we think the other way around and ask, "Lord bless me, and then I will become generous."

22:10 Drive out the scoffer, and contention will go out, even strife and dishonor will cease.

Tough love is never easy, but here we see a biblical precedent for it. "Scoffer" (NASB), "mocker" (NIV), and "scorner" (KJV) are terms used throughout the wisdom literature in reference to one who does not honor or believe in God. This person is characterized by constant cynicism. Do you know someone of this ilk? Perhaps it is time to begin disassociating with this person.

22:11 He who loves purity of heart and whose speech is gracious, the king is his friend.

Matthew 20:20–28 reminds us to seek greatness in the kingdom of heaven by having a servant attitude. Do you wish to influence the leaders around you? Solomon gives us two key concepts here to help develop the attitude of a good servant.

The first attribute is rather abstract, as he encourages us to love "purity of heart." Loyalty, righteousness, honor, integrity, peace, and holiness may all be a part of this phrase. If you're looking for a more concrete concept to help you apply the idea of loving purity of heart, then realize that what Solomon probably means is for us to have motives that are guileless. The second attribute is practical. He instructs us to keep our speech gracious. This is something tangible that we may all practice overtly.

A final thought regarding this verse is that we should seek these qualities in our lives because we truly want them and not only because of what they can get us.

22:12 The eyes of the LORD preserve knowledge, but He overthrows the words of the treacherous man.

The metaphor "eyes of the LORD" demonstrates the ubiquitous manner in which the Lord observes what we do and say. We may infer that the word *knowledge* here means truth, because of the contrast between "knowledge" and "the words of a treacherous [unfaithful (NIV)] man."

Observe also that God's role is active rather than passive when it comes to preserving truth and overturning falseness.

22:13 The sluggard says, "There is a lion outside; I shall be slain in the streets!"

Rationalizing, even to the point where we become paralyzed, is epidemic in our society. It is small comfort to see that even three thousand years ago it was also a problem. Human nature is still the same.

Agatha Christie wrote, "Imagination is a great servant but a cruel master."[28] This verse points out that it is only a small step from laziness to phobia. This is a fascinating psychological observation regarding the self-inflicted victimization mindset of many in our society!

22:14 The mouth of an adulterous is a deep pit; he who is cursed of the LORD will fall into it.

Remember the commandment, "You shall not commit adultery" (Exodus 20:14). Such commands enable us to preserve our own lives! Review Proverbs 5:1–6.

This verse reminds us of the power of the mouth. If an adulterer uses flattery, why would you believe it? The answer is simple, you will believe it because you want to believe it.

22:15 Foolishness is bound up in the heart of a child; the rod of discipline will remove it far from him.

We are not born wise. Foolishness is an inherent aspect of our human nature. The humanists claim that children are basically good. I always wonder if they've spent much observation time on a preschool or elementary school playground! When it comes to changing human behavior at a young age, the current methods espoused by such humanists generally involve rationalizing and seeking to understand *why* the child behaved that way, and then considering other, more appropriate choices the child could have made. This approach falsely assumes that children can (or will) be rational, and that they will try to follow the golden rule once they have been educated in this rule.

The way to remove foolishness is to use the rod of discipline. The truth of the matter is that most children are actually quite low on the Kohlberg scale of moral development. Young children live at a concrete operational level (as Piaget[29] demonstrated) and need to experience concrete discipline if they are to both learn and adjust their behavior. God knows this much better than any social scientist will ever know.

Never hurt a child just to be punitive. Always use discipline, which implies learning. In discipline, there is always a lesson. Pain is involved to make the lesson memorable and meaningful.

22:16 He who oppresses the poor to make much for himself or who gives to the rich, will only come to poverty.

In the movie *It's a Wonderful Life*, Lionel Barrymore played a character named Mr. Potter, who seeks to benefit by oppressing the poor in his community. In this story, good (represented by the inimitable Jimmy Stewart as George Bailey) finally overcomes the evil.

The consequence of oppressing the poor is poverty itself. This is another repetition of the theme "What you sow is what you shall reap." Sometimes it seems to not be so, but eventually justice is brought about (see Psalms 73:2–19). Prior to the French Revolution, the aristocracy in France oppressed the poor. Those aristocrats found it unthinkable that the peasants would lead a successful revolt. Yet that is precisely what happened, and those who were rich lost it all.

There is a rather puzzling aspect to this verse, concerning giving to the rich. What is wrong with this? Why does it receive the same condemnation as oppressing the poor? In answering this question, perhaps we should consider motives. Why would one give to the rich? Most likely, one would give to the rich to receive personal favoritism or to gain power in a particular sphere of influence. Or perhaps Solomon is simply revisiting his statement in 22:7 that "the rich rules over the poor, and the borrower becomes the lender's slave."

22:17 Incline your ear and hear the words of the wise, and apply your mind to my knowledge;

Regarding Proverbs 22:17–21, it is interesting to compare these verses with Proverbs 1:1–7. The authorship of this section of Proverbs is in question, according to some scholars. There is a stylistic change if you look at the last part of chapter 22 along with chapter 23 and then compare this to chapters 16, 17, or 18, for instance. Of course Solomon may simply have adjusted his style. The main internal clues we have to the authorship of this passage are the style comparison and the phrase "Hear the words of the wise" here in verse 17.

Other passages in Proverbs refer to "the wise" (such as Proverbs 15:7 and 12) as well, but the debate seems to overlook these verses. Other similarities exist as well between all the chapters we could compare. Thematically they are very similar, and some transitional phrases like "My son" can be found throughout all of Proverbs. My conclusion is that there is not enough evidence to make a valid judgment. Since Proverbs 1:1 is clear, I am not interested in speculating any further without valid data.

Regardless of who wrote this section, it bears the obvious influence of the Holy Spirit. The author has a hungering for the spiritual growth of his readers, just as Solomon demonstrated when he introduced the first section of Proverbs (see 1:1–7). We are urged to get ready to learn by listening and applying our minds.

22:18 For it will be pleasant if you keep them within you, that they may be ready on your lips.

Words of wisdom should be ready upon our lips. This does not automatically happen without effort on our part! In 2 Timothy 2:15, Paul wrote to Timothy advising him to "be diligent to present yourself approved to God as a workman who does not need to be ashamed, handling accurately the word of truth." This is a part of our personal discipleship.

When God directed Moses to impart the *Shema* ("Hear, O Israel! The LORD is our God, the LORD is one!" [Deuteronomy 6:4]) and the greatest commandment ("And you shall love the LORD your God with all your heart and with all your soul and with all your might" [Deuteronomy 6:5]), He did not intend for His people to forget these words quickly, or ever!

In Deuteronomy 6:6–9 we read what God wanted His people to do with His words of wisdom. He wanted them to teach their children, wear the words on their hands and foreheads, and write them outside of their houses. Constant reminders help us to witness and to always be ready.

22:19 So that your trust may be in the LORD, I have taught you today, even you.

In what do you trust? Many people trust in money, or the government, or themselves, or other people. All these will disappoint.

Proverbs 3:5–6 reminds us to "trust in the LORD" and to acknowledge Him "in all your ways." Immerse yourself in the words of God's wisdom and trust in Him.

> 22:20–21 Have I not written to you excellent things of counsels and knowledge, to make you know the certainty of the words of truth that you may correctly answer to him who sent you?

This is a rhetorical question that the author intends for us to answer in the affirmative.

How do you know that what you know is certainly the truth? When it comes to the epistemology of the Bible, Christians have faith, but it is not blind faith. The Bible validates itself through prophecy. (My personal favorite is Psalm 22 compared to the gospel accounts of Jesus' crucifixion.) The faith of other believers throughout history, and their changed lives and their willingness to die, also testify to the validity of the Bible (see Hebrews 11 and Foxe's *Book of Martyrs*[30]). The promises of the Bible, both blessings and curses, can be readily witnessed in our own lives and in the lives of those around us.

In this verse, the author offers one additional method for knowing the truth. The test he mentions is the test of "excellent things." J. B. Phillips wrote a book entitled *Ring of Truth*[31] in which he argued that the Bible, when compared to other works, has the ring of truth about it. The "excellent things" work! They are true, because they are valid.

Before a standardized test is used in the classroom, the test itself is tested for validity and reliability. Validity refers to the question of whether it does what it claims to do. Reliability refers to whether or not someone could take the test numerous times with basically the same results. The advice given here in the book of Proverbs is both valid and reliable.

> 22:22–23 Do not rob the poor because he is poor, or crush the afflicted at the gate; for the LORD will plead their case, and take the life of those who rob them.

These verses remind us that we should not rob the poor because it is unjust. But if our sense of justice has become warped due to greed or a desire for power, then we should know that the Lord Himself will "plead their case." He is the consummate lawyer (for he made the true laws) and He is also the great Judge. If this fear does not deter us, then death will be our ultimate reward.

22:24–25 Do not associate with a man given to anger; or go with a hot-tempered man, lest you learn his ways, and find a snare for yourself.

The nature-or-nurture debate shows up in many settings. When it is applied to this verse, the question arises: Is anger innate or learned? Anger is a universal quality, so we must assume that it is innate. If something is innate, then it must be a result either of being created in "the image of God" or of our fallen state of being! It would appear that the most satisfactory answer is that some forms of anger are innate (due to selfishness) and some forms are learned (due to righteous morality). The Bible identifies two types of anger—righteous anger and harmful anger. Bitterness and an unforgiving attitude may bring about the latter type.

When it comes to habitual anger, it is apparently a learned trait. Even the word *habitual* implies this. Anger in scripture is a fascinating subject. It is not condemned in and of itself. In many parts of the Old Testament we read that God can become angry with either individuals or entire nations. Jesus became angry when His Father's house was run as a robbers' den rather than a house of prayer (Matthew 21:12–13), and Paul wrote, "Be angry, yet do not sin" (Ephesians 4:26).

This verse, however, seems to be talking about habitual anger rather than true righteous anger. Do not associate with people who chronically fly off the handle.

22:26–27 Do not be among those who give pledges, among those who become sureties for debts. If you have nothing with which to pay, why should he take your bed from under you?

241

If you heed this word of advice you should literally sleep better at night! At least you'll have a bed! Note also that dealing with debt is not a modern problem. It has been around for thousands of years.

22:28 Do not move the ancient boundary which your fathers have set.

If we take the verse literally, then the implication is that we should not cheat by moving boundary markers to try to gain more land fraudulently. Proverbs 23:10 is a similar verse lending credence to this literal view.

But there may be a deeper meaning to this verse as well. The word translated "ancient" comes from the Hebrew *'olam,* which may refer to something eternal, perpetual, lasting or everlasting. It may also refer to something concealed, as from a vanishing point, or because it is just "out of mind." We need to follow in the footsteps of our spiritual fathers, such as Abel, Enoch, Noah, Abraham, Moses, and numerous others. The boundaries we should not seek to move are the spiritual and moral boundaries set forth by God, and tried and proven by such great heroes of the faith.

22:29 Do you see a man skilled in his work? He will stand before kings; he will not stand before obscure men.

Compare the notes for Proverbs 18:16: "A man's gift makes room for him, and brings him before great men." One example of this is seen in Genesis 41:46, where we find Joseph standing before Pharaoh because of his skill. Throughout history God has used men such as Nehemiah, Daniel, and Paul to stand before the rulers of their time.

Proverbs 23

23:1–3 When you sit down to dine with a ruler, consider carefully what is before you; and put a knife to your throat, if you are a man of great appetite. Do not desire his delicacies, for it is deceptive food.

How would you define the figure of speech "deceptive food"? The world is full of deceptive food, and not all of it is stuff that we eat. The corrupting influence of excessive desire has been revealed throughout history since the Fall. In one example, Daniel "made up his mind not to defile himself with the king's choice food" (Daniel 1:8).

The main message of this passage deals with the sin of covetousness. The Buddhist solution is to follow the eight-step path until you eventually rid yourself of all desire. As good as this sounds (at least, to Buddhists), it simply does not work. The Christian solution is to replace the desire with a different desire, namely, a desire to please God.

David's prayer in Psalm 141 reveals the heart of a man devoted to God: "Set a guard, O Lord, over my mouth; keep watch over the door of my lips. Do not incline my heart to any evil thing; To practice deeds of wickedness with men who do iniquity; and do not let me eat of their delicacies" (Psalm 141:3–4).

> 23:4–5 Do not weary yourself to gain wealth, cease from your consideration of it. When you set your eyes on it, it is gone. For wealth certainly makes itself wings, like an eagle that flies toward the heavens.

The subtle truth of this passage involves an understanding of the kingdom of God. All wealth truly belongs to the Lord. Yet we are children of the King! We are heirs of the kingdom! Wealth flies upward, not to escape our grasp, but to return to its Master in glory. We *are* wealthy beyond imagination. The Father asks us to "cease striving, and know that I am God" (Psalm 46:10). In this sense, true wealth comes to us as we stay in the presence of the Father, instead of vainly seeking after it here on earth.

As we come to Him, we lay up "treasures in heaven" (Matthew 6:20), and this truth sets us free (John 8:32). If you are "free from the love of money, being content with what you have" (Hebrews 13:5), then you are free to focus on godliness, which Paul reminds Timothy "is a means of great gain" (1 Timothy 6:6).

> 23:6–8 Do not eat the bread of a selfish man, or desire his delicacies; for as he thinks within himself, so he is. He says to you, "Eat and drink!" but his heart is not with you. You will vomit up the morsel you have eaten, and waste your compliments.

What do you think of when you hear the word *bread* in the Bible? I counted 362 references to bread in Strong's Concordance.[32] The Bible uses the term *bread* both literally and figuratively. Bread is necessary to support life, but it is also a part of the Curse! "By the sweat of your face you shall eat bread" (Genesis 3:19).

Bread has been used as a tool by God Himself. Note the following passage: "He humbled you and let you be hungry, and fed you manna which you did not know . . . that He might make you understand that man does not live by bread alone" (Deuteronomy 8:3).

Satan also attempts to use bread as a tool. In the wilderness he tempted Jesus to turn stones into bread (Matthew 4:3), in response to which Jesus quoted the scripture above. The interested reader may look at Appendix C for a deeper look at the biblical concept of bread.

Let us now reconsider Proverbs 23:6–8. The five verses prior to this passage all deal with the idea of covetousness, and so too, is this passage. One of the biggest snares we can fall into is desiring what evil people around us possess. As verse 3 says, it is "deceptive food." Be discerning. There are people who are simply selfish, and it is a waste of time for you to attempt to cultivate a relationship with them because of their extreme selfishness.

23:9 Do not speak in the hearing of a fool, for he will despise the wisdom of your words.

Jesus put it another way: "Do not throw your pearls before swine, lest they trample them under their feet" (Matthew 7:6).

It is not enough for us to *possess* wisdom, we must also *use* wisdom in discerning when we elect to share the wisdom God has given us (or will give us—see James 1:5), as well as with whom we elect to share it. Keep this in mind regarding evangelism. We are stewards not only of our money, but also of our time, our knowledge, and our relationships with God and others.

By heeding this word of caution we can avoid useless strife and wasted energy. By ignoring this advice, we can do more damage than we might at first imagine. By stirring up the despiteful ire of a fool, our well-intentioned words of wisdom can bring about a great deal of destructive activity at the hands of someone influenced by Satan or the philosophies of the world.

Does this verse discount the need for boldness in sharing the gospel? No. But it *does* reveal the need for true discernment. Can you think of a circumstance in your life in which the reality of this verse was manifested?

23:10–12 Do not move the ancient boundary, or go into the fields of the fatherless; for their Redeemer is strong; He will plead their case against you. Apply your heart to discipline, and your ears to words of knowledge.

Don't prey upon the weak. "You shall not afflict any widow or orphan" (Exodus 22:22). James 1:27 points out that *true religion* helps widows and orphans.

What does the author tell us we should do instead of taking from the weak (verse 12)? What do you do with your time and energy?

23:13–14 Do not hold back discipline from the child, although you beat him with the rod, he will not die. You shall beat him with the rod, and deliver his soul from Sheol.

Gary Ezzo, in his video series *Growing Kids God's Way,*[33] talks about "permissive parenting." He points out that one sign of the permissive parent is that the child's happiness and psychological health are elevated above the child's moral and spiritual health.

Discipline is designed for learning rather than just being a punitive action. Proverbs demonstrates how physical action can bring about spiritual gain. Are spiritual growth and maturity the goals of your parenting? Regardless of *how* you discipline your children, always be sure of *why* you discipline. Spiritual gain (i.e., to "deliver his soul from Sheol") is our ultimate goal.

23:15–16 My son, if your heart is wise, my own heart also will be glad; and my inmost being will rejoice, when your lips speak what is right.

As we gain in wisdom, we bless and bring joy to others. Luke wrote that Jesus "kept increasing in wisdom and stature, and in favor with God and men" (Luke 2:52). How can Proverbs 23:9 and these two verses both be true? Of course the answer is that speaking wisdom in the presence of wise individuals brings them great joy, while the same statement may irritate those who are foolish.

23:17 Do not let your heart envy sinners, but live in the fear of the LORD always.

How ridiculously shortsighted it is for us to envy people who do not understand the purpose for their existence and who will die for their actions (Romans 6:23). Yet it is something we are all susceptible to. Even such a great prophet as Jeremiah asked God, "Why has the way of the wicked prospered?" (Jeremiah 12:1). Asaph also struggled mightily with this question (see Psalm 73).

As Christians, we are to live proactively rather than reactively in our walk with the Lord. It is reactive to see someone in possession of something and desire what he possesses. It is proactive to live in the fear of the Lord on a daily basis. The author here uses the word "always" (NASB), which can be translated literally as "all the day." Our awareness of God must be continual and constant.

David wrote, "Who is the man who fears the LORD? He will instruct him in the way he should choose. His soul will abide in prosperity . . . the secret of the LORD is for those who fear Him" (Psalm 25:12–14).

When we covet, our souls wither. When we fear the Lord, our souls prosper.

23:18 Surely there is a future, and your hope will not be cut off.

Hope is focused on the future. A true understanding of the future is essential for any Christian. Understanding that we will be raised and receive a resurrected body gives us a hope more powerful than the world can understand. When hope is applied to the present, it may manifest itself as *faith*. Faith is a deep and abiding internal quality, yet when it is directed outwardly, it grows into *love*.

In John 11:23–26 Jesus used the death of Lazarus to teach an important lesson to Martha:

Jesus said to her, "Your brother shall rise again."

Martha said to Him, "I know that he will rise again in the resurrection on the last day."

Jesus said to her, "I am the resurrection and the life; he who believes in me shall live even if he dies."

But, you may ask, isn't the idea of a resurrection a post-Christ idea? No, it isn't. The ancient believers also believed in a bodily resurrection! Psalms 16:10–11 and 41:9–10 address the concept of the resurrection of the Messiah.

One the greatest testimonies ever recorded is found in Job 19:25–27: "And as for me, I know that my Redeemer lives, and at the last He will take His stand on the earth. Even after my skin is flayed, yet without my flesh I shall see God; Whom I myself shall behold."

Yes, as the author states, "Surely there is a future!"

23:19 Listen, my son, and be wise, and direct your heart in the way.

Step 1 in the pursuit of true wisdom is to "fear the LORD" (Proverbs 9:10). The author points this out in verse 17. Step 2 is to listen. But what are we to listen to? Read Proverbs 8:1, 32–36 to see Solomon's answer to this question.

The phrase "direct your heart" serves as a reminder that you control your heart. It is the seat of your free will. There is not an inkling of fatalism in this phrase.

Consider the phrase "in the way" (cf. Proverbs 1:15, 31; 2:8, 20; 3:6; 4:11–12, 18–19; 6:23). There is *a* way. It is God's way, and it is *the* way in which we should walk.

Are you open to change? "Listen . . . be wise . . . direct your heart." This process is not always easy. There are many possible roadblocks. We may hear but not listen. We may choose to be foolish rather than wise. We may begin to direct our hearts, but our hearts may not want to change! Perhaps my heart enjoys harboring hate, covetousness, lust, greed. etc. This sets up a tremendous internal battle. Paul wrote about this battle in Romans 7: "Wretched man that I am! Who will set me free from the body of this death?"

It is through the grace of our Savior that we gain salvation. It is through His power that we gain the means to truly listen, be wise, and direct our heart in the way! (Note: I believe that every time we read Romans 7, we should read Romans 6 and 8 twice. The emphasis is not on the problem of sin, but on conquering sin through the power of the Spirit and the work of Christ that has already been completed!)

> 23:20–21 Do not be with heavy drinkers of wine, or with gluttonous eaters of meat; for the heavy drinker and the glutton will come to poverty, and drowsiness will clothe a man with rags.

Some may ask, why not associate with drunkards and gluttons? Jesus did this. He associated with Samaritans, tax gatherers, prostitutes, and other known sinners. The man who asks such a question demonstrates a lack of knowledge regarding context. Jesus did not become these things; rather, He ministered to them. There is quite a difference. Even those of His own generation made such accusations: "The Son of Man came eating and drinking, and they say, 'Behold, a gluttonous man and a drunkard, a friend of tax-gatherers and sinners!' *Yet wisdom is vindicated by her deeds*" (Matthew 11:19 [see also Luke 7:34]).

Some may ask an even more basic question: What is wrong with drinking wine and eating in a gluttonous manner? Deuteronomy 21:18–21 paints a picture of a young man who is classified as a "glutton and a drunkard." The primary adjectives describing him are "stubborn" and "rebellious." It is interesting to note that in *all* of these passages both words (drunkard and glutton) always appear together.

The Hebrew word used in both Proverbs 23 and Deuteronomy 21 is the word *zalal*. My Hebrew dictionary[34] defines its figurative usage as "to be loose morally, or worthless, or to be a vile and riotous (eater)." Clearly, as we understand these words, we see that we are not just talking about sipping a few sips of wine or enjoying a good meal. To describe someone as a glutton and heavy drinker implies a lifestyle that is primarily rebellious.

Beyond the spiritual implications of rebellion, Proverbs 23:20–21 gives us a practical reason to avoid this lifestyle choice as well, for otherwise we will be led to poverty.

> 23:22 Listen to your father who begot you, and do not despise your mother when she is old.

How do we honor our fathers and mothers? Listen to them. Honor them in their old age. See Proverbs 23:24–25 for another way to do this. Let them be glad. Look back again at verse 16. As sons or daughters, when we "speak what is right," we will make our parents glad. This is a means of honoring them as well.

> 23:23 Buy truth, and do not sell it, get wisdom and instruction and understanding.

"Buy truth." Jesus spoke about the kingdom of God in a similar manner:

> The kingdom of heaven is like a treasure hidden in the field, which a man found and hid; and from joy over it he goes and sells all that he has, and buys that field.

> Again, the kingdom of heaven is like a merchant seeking fine pearls, and upon finding one pearl of great value, he went and sold all that he had, and bought it. (Matthew 13:44–46)

Do you value truth? Buy it "and do not sell it." Cherish truth and keep it!

"Get wisdom." The acquisition of wisdom is not a one-time thing. It is a process of growth. It is something we must continue to ask for (see James 1). The most foolish thing Solomon did in his life was to quit asking God for more and more wisdom. Do not get it and then cease striving for it.

> 23:24–25 The father of the righteous will greatly rejoice, and he who begets a wise son will be glad in him. Let your father and your mother be glad, and let her rejoice who gave birth to you.

This is one of the most profound yet practical ways in which we can honor our fathers and mothers. Be righteous and become wise, and you will bring rejoicing to your parents.

> 23:26–28 Give me your heart, my son, and let your eyes delight in my ways. For a harlot is a deep pit, and an adulterous woman is a narrow well. Surely she lurks as a robber, and increases the faithless among men.

In the phrase "Give me your heart," who is the "me" of this passage? I believe that it is not the author who penned the words (a literal interpretation) but rather the personification of wisdom (a figurative interpretation). Heed the metaphor. Engaging in illicit sex is like falling into a deep pit or a narrow slippery well. Once you're in, it is very difficult or impossible to climb out. If you fall in, you'll need someone holding a rope for you to get out.

> 23:29–35 Who has woe? Who has sorrow? Who has contentions? Who has complaining? Who has wounds without cause? Who has redness of eyes? Those who linger long over wine, those who go to taste mixed wine. Do not look on the wine when it is red, when it sparkles in the cup, when it goes down smoothly; at the last it bites like a serpent, and stings like a viper. Your eyes will see strange things, and your mind will utter perverse things. And you will be like one who lies down in the middle of the sea, or like one who lies down on the top of a mast. "They struck me, but I did not become ill; they beat me, but I did not know it. When shall I awake? I will seek another drink."

This section points out the folly of lingering over wine. The rhetorical questions bring the issue of free will to bear once again. Verse 35 illustrates the power and distortion of reality brought upon by the abuse of drugs. As stated previously, drinking wine in moderation is not a sin, but great caution must be used, else the liquor itself can become your own master.

Proverbs 24

24:1–2 Do not be envious of evil men, nor desire to be with them; for their minds devise violence, and their lips talk of trouble.

Envy of others is never to be condoned. It can never lead to good. But envy of evildoers? This is craziness! Nonetheless, it is a type of craziness we are all susceptible to. Proverbs 24:1 suggests that we limit our time with them (see also Proverbs 3:31; 23:17; and 24:19 and Psalm 73:3).

Verse 2 gives a rationale to prevent us from desiring to be with evil men. They will devise violence and talk of trouble. Do you know people who always, always, always talk only of troubles? You can live without their additional violence and trouble. Put your time to better use for the kingdom. When your heart and mind are fully focused on God, it is impossible to be envious of others. I challenge you to prove that statement incorrect.

24:3–4 By wisdom a house is built, and by understanding it is established; and by knowledge the rooms are filled with all precious and pleasant riches.

What plans, dreams, and tools are you using to build your house? Make sure you utilize and include wisdom, understanding, and knowledge. Remember also the words of the Psalmist, "Unless the LORD build the house, they labor in vain who build it" (Psalm 127:1).

Solomon also wrote, "Wisdom has built her house . . . whoever is naive, let him turn in here" (Proverbs 9:1, 4). Additionally, Jesus gave a parable that compared the house of a foolish man with the house of a wise man (Matthew 7:24–27). Jesus also pointed out that a "house divided against itself falls" (Luke 11:17).

With all the divorce and marital problems in our society, perhaps right now would be a good time for you to consider the present condition of your own house!

> 24:5–6 A wise man is strong, and a man of knowledge increases power. For by wise guidance you will wage war, and in abundance of counselors there is victory.

Of what benefit is wisdom? Wisdom gives us the strength, power, and ability to wage war and gain victory.

You may then respond by saying, "I'm not at war right now." Consider Ephesians 6:12: "For our struggle is not against flesh and blood, but against the rulers, against the powers, against the world forces of this darkness, against the spiritual forces of wickedness in the heavenly places." Do not attempt to be a spiritual pacifist. Rather, "fight the good fight" (1 Timothy 1:18, 6:12).

True wisdom understands the truth of the phrase "The LORD will fight for you" (Exodus 14:14, Nehemiah 4:20).

The two major parts of our "fight" plan should be to 1) put on the full armor of God; and 2) pray as David did, "Contend, O LORD, with those who contend with me; fight against those who fight against me" (Psalm 35:1).

Can you think of any examples of how the spiritual forces of wickedness are waging war with you right now?

In addition to the above, the phrase "In abundance of counselors there is victory" is also important to consider. How does this phrase tie in with fighting a spiritual fight? What role does Christian fellowship play in helping us to fight the good fight?

24:7 Wisdom is too high for a fool, he does not open his mouth in the gate.

In the writings of the prophet Isaiah we read that God "will deal marvelously with this people . . . and the wisdom of their wise men shall perish" (Isaiah 29:14). The apostle Paul quotes this verse in his letter to the Corinthians before he begins a string of rhetorical questions: "Where is the wise man? Where is the scribe? Where is the debater of this age? Has not God made foolish the wisdom of the world?" (1 Corinthians 1:20). Paul goes on to present an inspired message contrasting worldly philosophies and the power of the gospel.

Are you intimidated by conversations regarding evolution, the existence of God, explaining why you are a Christian, and other topics of debate? If you have the fear of the Lord, then your wisdom already surpasses that of the most intelligent Ph.D. who is an atheist. The weakness of their arguments lies within their basic assumptions.

In Matthew 11, Jesus offered the prayer, "I praise Thee, O Father, Lord of heaven and earth, that Thou didst hide these things from the wise and intelligent and didst reveal them to babes."

Why doesn't the fool open his mouth in the gate? The "gate" is the place of gathering where people discussed religion, current events, and life in general (see Ruth 4:1–12). In this context, a fool has nothing worth saying.

24:8–9 He who plans to do evil, men will call him a schemer. The devising of folly is sin, and the scoffer is an abomination to men.

The English word "plans" here is the Hebrew word *chashab,* which means to fabricate or contrive (usually in a malicious sense). It can also mean to invent, devise, or imagine.

God created us with minds, and with them we can glorify or dishonor God. Your mind craves stimulation. It *will* find something to do. You can (for the most part) control the input. You may stimulate your mind with good things that are "true . . . honorable . . . right . . . pure . . . lovely . . . and of good repute" (see Philippians 4:8). Read Proverbs 16:1–3 again to review how we can avoid planning evil.

Is sin only doing the "don'ts" of God's commandments? According to this verse, it would appear that sin can also be something we create with our own imagination.

24:10 If you are slack in the day of distress, your strength is limited.

What is the point of strength? I mean, what is its value? According to Proverbs 24:5, "A wise man is strong." Acquiring this strength has a purpose, because the days of distress are coming! Trials, temptations, strife, and contentions exist all around us. None of us escape these all the time. The point is, *are you ready?*

If you have planned and prepared for the "day of distress," you should be ready to take decisive action when it comes. But you must be ready. If the day comes and you are "slack," then all your preparation has been for nought.

24:11–12 Deliver those who are being taken away to death, and those who are staggering to slaughter, O hold them back. If you say, "See, we did not know this," does He not consider it who weighs the hearts? And does He not know it who keeps your soul? And will He not render to man according to his work?

There are two types of death to consider as we begin to meditate upon these verses. There is physical death, which is the separation of the body from the spirit. And there is spiritual death, which is the separation of the spirit from God Himself, who is the Supreme Spirit.

Regarding premature physical death (i.e., nonnatural causes), there are voluntary deaths (suicide), involuntary deaths (e.g., murder/ manslaughter) and *subvoluntary* deaths. This last category I have included to discuss deaths related to lifestyle choices, such as substance abuse, daredevil activities, and associations with dangerous people or situations. Death due to natural causes is not listed here because it would not be considered premature.

Regarding involuntary situations, there is little we can do except warn people of impending danger if we perceive it. I believe the author of Proverbs 24:11–12 is aiming his advice here toward peacemaker approaches we can take on behalf of people in suicidal or subvoluntary life-threatening situations.

But there is another aspect to strongly consider in our understanding of these verses. All men who do not have salvation are "staggering to slaughter"! Consider what you can do to "hold them back." When Cain asked God, "Am I my brother's keeper?" (Genesis 4:9), God's implied answer was *Yes you are!* "He who wins souls is wise" (Proverbs 11:30 NIV).

Is apathy acceptable? Is mediocre Christianity acceptable? You know the answer without me stating it. We must rise to a higher standard.

> 24:13–14 My son, eat honey, for it is good, yes, the honey from the comb is sweet to your taste; know that wisdom is thus for your soul; if you find it, then there will be a future, and your hope will not be cut off.

Wisdom is "sweet," and it is good for our souls because it is food for our souls. Compare this verse to Psalm 19:7–10.

Consider the phrase "If you find it." Wisdom must be sought. It is not an automatic gift. To obtain it you must pray for it (James 1), meditate upon God's word, and accept it.

The author points out that "then there will be a future." Wisdom is active rather than passive. It operates in the *now,* enabling us to make choices and decisions here in the present, but it does so with an ever watchful eye on the future and on what is truly important.

> 24:15–16 Do not lie in wait, O wicked man, against the dwelling of the righteous; do not destroy his resting place; for a righteous man falls seven times, and rises again, but the wicked stumble in time of calamity.

Are these verses really addressed to the "wicked man" as they suggest? Actually, the author seems to be using a rhetorical device, and his true audience are those who seek wisdom. These verses emphasize hope by stating the value of righteousness (see also Proverbs 24:1). This verse reminds me of the cliché "You can't keep a good man down."

The righteous man has *hope*. No matter how bad things get, he knows that God will *always* be there for him! His strength is in the Lord. Not so for the evil man; his strength is completely in himself.

Notice that the phrase describing the righteous man includes the idea that he "rises again." Once again we see how the author connects the concept of resurrection to that of righteousness. The evil man has no such hope.

> 24:17–18 Do not rejoice when your enemy falls, and do not let your heart be glad when he stumbles; lest the LORD see it and be displeased, and He turn away His anger from him.

"Love your enemies" is a command we have from our Lord. Remember that justice and mercy are both aspects of God's nature. Compare Proverbs 25:21–22 and Romans 12:17–21. How do these verses apply to the suggestion of Proverbs 24:17 that you should not "rejoice when your enemy falls"?

To follow this advice requires the utmost in humility. However, notice the rationale. If we do not rejoice, then God is more likely to continue His just punishment of our enemy.

How, then, do we love our enemies at the same time we seek for God to continue punishing them—even as we humbly avoid mocking their predicament? Once again we must step back from the present situation and see the greater picture as God Himself may view it. God justly punishes, but He is ready to forgive and demonstrate mercy whenever our enemies repent and lament their sins. The passage from Romans mentioned above urges us to "overcome evil with good." Keep in mind also that these are the times when our enemies may be open to God and the truth. In this, do not imitate Jonah, who became displeased and angry when God relented in His punishment of the Ninevites (Jonah 4:1).

> 24:19–20 Do not fret yourself because of evildoers, or be envious of the wicked; for there will be no future for the evil man; the lamp of the wicked will be put out.

Where should our thoughts be focused if we are not to fret about the evildoers? Let us trust in the Lord. "Rest in the LORD and wait patiently for Him" (Psalm 37:7). Read the prior verses of Psalm 37 (vss. 1–6) for a broader discussion on this theme.

"The lamp of the wicked will be put out" indicates that the judgment of the wicked will be total and complete destruction.

"Behold then the kindness and severity of God; to those who fell, severity, but to you, God's kindness, if you continue in His kindness; otherwise you also will be cut off" (Romans 11:22). Make sure that *you* are walking with the Lord before you worry about whether or not others are walking with Him.

> 24:21–22 My son, fear the LORD and the king; do not associate with those who are given to change; for their calamity will rise suddenly, and who knows the ruin that comes from both of them.

"The LORD and the king" represent the primary sources of authority. We should fear God out of our relationship to Him. We fear (verb) Him, because we see who He truly is. When we possess the fear (noun) of the Lord it is the beginning step of wisdom.

The Bible reminds us to "be subject to rulers, to authorities, to be obedient, to be ready for every good deed" (Titus 3:1).

The advice to avoid the company of people "given to change" suggests a need on our part to carefully observe the habits and patterns of those around us. We should not associate with a man who is a "double-minded man, unstable in all his ways" (James 1:8). If we associate with those prone to calamity, then their woe may overflow and become ours as well.

> 24:23–26 These also are sayings of the wise. To show partiality in judgment is not good. He who says to the wicked, "You are righteous," peoples will curse him, nations will abhor him; but to those who rebuke the wicked will be delight, and a good blessing will come upon them. He kisses the lips who gives a right answer.

What does it mean to show partiality in judgment? Basically, it means to allow yourself to be influenced. We cannot walk rightly with the Lord and still call that which is evil "good" and that which is good "evil."

Christianity is proactive even as it seeks balance. While we are directed to control our mouths in many contexts, the author reminds us that there is also a time to stand up to the wicked, confront them, and even rebuke them.

> 24:27 Prepare your work outside, and make it ready for yourself in the field; afterwards, then, build your house.

Prepare your foundations and your external structures before you begin to build. Have you done this in your Christian walk with the Lord?

This verse is about taking prophylactic actions that are necessary to carry out a plan. Before you build, you must prepare.

24:28–29 Do not be a witness against your neighbor without cause, and do not deceive with your lips. Do not say, "Thus I shall do to him as he has done to me; I will render to the man according to his work."

Regardless of your personal feelings toward someone, you cannot condemn that person or bear false witness against him for something he has not done, no matter how badly you would like to see him get what you feel he deserves. Remember to allow God alone to take vengeance (Hebrews 10:30, see also Proverbs 20:22).

Feelings of revenge are very passionate, but they also represent very strong emotional prisons! This is why forgiveness is such an essential aspect of true Christianity. The power of revenge can set into anyone.

Does this verse mean you should *never* be a witness? No, this is not what it is saying. When is it appropriate to be a witness? When you have truly observed something pertinent to a case. At that time your testimony is essential for truth and justice to be upheld.

24:30–34 I passed by the field of the sluggard, and by the vineyard of the man lacking sense; and behold, it was completely overgrown with thistles, its surface was covered with nettles, and its stone wall was broken down. When I saw, I reflected upon it; I looked, and received instruction. "A little sleep, a little slumber, a little folding of the hands to rest," then your poverty will come as a robber, and your want like an armed man.

What does it take for poverty to set in? In this passage, the sluggard bears two qualities: 1) he is lazy; and 2) he is lacking in sense. For those of us who observe, there are external signs for us to identify the sluggard. The signs are there if we pay attention to them. The examples in verse 31 illustrate long-term neglect. They reflect a lifestyle.

This passage also contains a method of self-education that we should be attuned to. In verse 32 we read, "When I saw, I reflected upon it; I looked, and received instruction." Make observations, and then reflect upon what you have seen. By doing so we may learn vicariously, and thus avoid the mistakes others around us may make.

Proverbs 25

25:1 These also are proverbs of Solomon which the men of Hezekiah, king of Judah, transcribed.

This passage was authored by Solomon, but compiled some 250 years later by the "men of Hezekiah." Hezekiah reigned from 728 to 686 B.C. The biblical information we have concerning Hezekiah can be found in 2 Kings 18–20 and 2 Chronicles 29:2–31:21. Hezekiah "did right in the sight of the LORD . . . he removed the high places and broke down the sacred pillars and cut down the Asherah . . . the LORD was with him, wherever he went he prospered. And he rebelled against the king of Assyria."

Hezekiah was one of Judah's greatest kings, even though Judah was taken into captivity during his reign. He was a great spiritual leader. We do not know for certain who the "men of Hezekiah" were, but they may have included Isaiah and Micah, who were contemporaries of Hezekiah.

The Hebrew word *athek* translated in 25:1 as "transcribed" or "copied" may mean that Hezekiah's men collected, edited, or re-copied these proverbs—perhaps some degree of all three. Scholars have various opinions about it.

Hezekiah ruled 42 years, although the first 13 were as a co-regent. His father, Ahaz, had been pro-Assyrian, but Hezekiah was anti-Assyrian. However, he did not openly rebel as long as Sargon II ruled (722–705). When Sargon's less able son, Sennacherib (705–681), came to the throne, Hezekiah joined an alliance of other kings (apparently with the Egyptians and Philistines) against Assyria. He later averted bloodshed by sending tribute to Sennacherib when he saw that the rebellion would fail.

25:2 It is the glory of God to conceal a matter, but the glory of kings is to search out a matter.

We feel a part of God's glory as we observe the mysteries of nature all around us. God reveals Himself through *specific revelation* via His word and occasionally through dreams and visions. He also reveals Himself through *general revelation,* which includes both the universal morality within human nature (all people possess knowledge of right and wrong) and through the actual existence of nature itself. One example of general revelation is spoken of in Psalm 19: "The heavens are telling of the glory of God . . . there is no speech . . . [where] their voice is not heard."

The point is that without revelation, the mysteries of the kingdom of God remain enigmatic mysteries. But God does not seek to conceal His truths from us, that we might never know them. However, neither does He openly reveal things to everyone. His desire is that we "seek first His kingdom and His righteousness" (Matthew 6:33). He wants us to be a holy people, ever questing after Him. When John the Baptist inquired of Jesus, "Are you the coming one, or shall we look for someone else?" (Matthew 11:3) Jesus did not announce outright, "Yes, it's me, God in the flesh." Instead, He told the messenger, "Go and report to John the things which you hear and see: the blind receive sight and the lame walk."

Another passage that illustrates this is found in Matthew 13: "And the disciples came and said to Him, 'Why do You speak to them in parables?' And He answered and said to them, 'To you it has been granted to know the mysteries of the kingdom of heaven, but to them it has not been granted. For whoever has, to him shall more be given, and he shall have an abundance; but whoever does not have, even what he has shall be taken away from him. Therefore I speak to them in parables; because while seeing they do not see, and while hearing they do not hear, nor do they understand'" (Matthew 13:10–13).

Although the Greeks and Romans popularized the idea of philosopher-kings, I believe the best models are actually found in Hebraic history. David and Solomon both exuded a desire to "search out a matter." Likewise, Hezekiah also fits this mold, for he sought to reestablish God as Judah's first priority.

> 25:3 As the heavens for height and the earth for depth, so the heart of kings is unsearchable.

In the next four verses, we see that kings can be righteous or wicked. They can be ready and willing to bestow honor or to ridicule. We can identify what is in someone's heart after we have observed his or her actions and fruit, but for us this observation is always in past tense. God alone can look into someone's heart in future tense, before any outward deeds are done, and predict what that person will do.

> 25:4–5 Take away the dross from the silver, and there comes out a vessel for the smith; take away the wicked from before the king, and his throne will be established in righteousness.

This is an interesting comparison. The king is compared to silver, which is a precious, yet pliable metal. In this we see the humanity of the king revealed. The king is valuable because of his function. He should be pure and pliable himself, but he is not a deity. He can be influenced.

When we surround ourselves with wicked people, we become influenced by their views and perceptions. Pilate did not listen to his own conscience or his wife because of the shouting of those around him (see Luke 23:20–24). Likewise, Herod the tetrarch was influenced by his dinner guests, and he beheaded John the Baptist even though he didn't really want to (Matthew 14:1–12).

A truly righteous king should remove the wicked from his presence. He should surround himself with righteous advisors and counselors. But what shall we do if the king is *not* righteous? In that case we ought to seek to place righteous people as close to the king (ruler/decision-maker) as possible. When a leader's counselors are righteous, he will tend to make wise decisions if he listens to them. A great example of this can be found in Daniel 6:1–4, 17, 24, 26.

> 25:6–7 Do not claim honor in the presence of the king, and do not stand in the place of great men; for it is better that it be said to you, "Come up here," than that you should be put lower in the presence of the prince, whom your eyes have seen.

One of the condemnations that Jesus proclaimed against the Pharisees of His time was that "they love the place of honor at banquets" (Matthew 23: 6, see also Luke 14:7–11).

Along this line of thought, consider Proverbs 15:33: "The fear of the LORD is the instruction for wisdom, and before honor comes humility."

> 25:8 Do not go out hastily to argue your case, otherwise, what will you do in the end, when your neighbor puts you to shame?

"The beginning of strife is like letting out water, So abandon the quarrel before it breaks out" (Proverbs 17:14). Are you quick to anger? Do you have to get in the last word? Does your arrogance prevent you from abandoning the quarrel? If so, remember that we should be humble rather than arrogant. Scriptural "shoulds and oughts" and "dos and don'ts" are not given to us whimsically. They are given to us that we might have life, and that we might have it more abundantly!

The other lesson here, is don't try to be first when defending yourself. The first person to speak *tells* what happened (often from a biased perspective), often leaving out details and facts. The second person to speak *explains* what happened and provides additional information. Thus, the second person's position is more powerful and convincing. Offering an explanation is more powerful than just relating a story.

> 25:9–10 Argue your case with your neighbor, and do not reveal the secret of another, lest he who hears it reproach you, and the evil report about you not pass away.

How tiresome are the gossiping and backbiting that go on because of injustice, stupidity, and simple revenge. Biblically, we are to keep our matters of personal affronts with other Christians "in house" (cf. Matthew 18:15–17 on church discipline). This means that we are not to complain behind someone else's back. We need to care enough to confront our neighbors (see Proverbs 27:5–6). But if you cannot do it in love, don't do it at all. You will only do more damage to all involved. Another reason for this approach is that it may preserve your own reputation (see Ecclesiastes 7:1). You may well avoid being labeled as a gossiper, a busybody, or even a slanderer.

When you respect your neighbor as he should be respected, you will follow the advice of Solomon (see also Proverbs 11:12–13). It is when you do not respect your neighbor that you "reveal the secret of another."

> 25:11 Like apples of gold in settings of silver is a word spoken in right circumstances.

Would you like to be able to speak with a golden tongue? Here are a few steps to follow toward meeting this goal:

1. Ask God to help you. "Let the words of my mouth and the meditation of my heart be acceptable in Thy sight, O LORD" (Psalm 19:14).

2. Exercise self-control by avoiding evil words. "Keep your tongue from evil, and your lips from speaking deceit" (Psalm 34:13).

3. Speak with a godly purpose in mind (e.g., healing or edification). "There is one who speaks rashly like the thrusts of a sword, but the tongue of the wise brings healing. Truthful lips will be established forever" (Proverbs 12:18–19).

4. Make the most of your opportunities. "A man has joy in an apt answer, and how delightful is a timely word!" (Proverbs 15:23).

5. Seek to edify (build up) others. "Let no unwholesome word proceed from your mouth, but only such a word as is good for edification according to the need of the moment" (Ephesians 4:29).

6. Seek to glorify God. "Whoever speaks, let him speak, as it were, the utterances of God . . . so that in all things God may be glorified" (1 Peter 4:11). Consider your circumstances before you speak, and when it's right, do not hesitate to speak good words.

25:12 Like an earring of gold and an ornament of fine gold is a wise reprover to a listening ear.

Who is a "wise reprover"? The answer is one who reproves out of love. God Himself is our great example, for "whom the LORD loves He reproves" (Proverbs 3:12). Paul instructed Timothy to "reprove . . . with great patience and instruction" (2 Timothy 4:2). Read Matthew 18:15. How valuable it is to have someone who is willing to reprove us. The great test is whether or not we have a "listening ear." If we have pride, we will not. But if we have humility and discernment we will likely heed the reproof. If indeed we do heed the reproof, then we will grow and mature.

25:13 Like the cold of snow in the time of harvest is a faithful messenger to those who send him, for he refreshes the soul of his masters.

Good help is hard to find. If you read the story of Genesis 24, in which Abraham's servant locates a wife for Isaac, you will understand the value of a good messenger. John the Baptist came as a messenger of the Messiah. Indeed, each of us is called to be a messenger of the gospel. The word *angel* in the Bible means "messenger." Have you refreshed the soul of your Master today? What kind of a messenger are you?

> 25:14 Like clouds and wind without rain is a man who boasts of his gifts falsely.

The general meaning of this verse is easy to discern. The weather analogy illustrates how fickle many men are. We need to be promise keepers—people whose word means something. We need to be people who follow through and avoid hypocrisy.

However, the more specific meaning of the phrase rendered in the NASB as "who boasts of his gifts falsely" is subject to interpretation. The translators of the NIV render this phrase "boasts of gifts he does not give." These subtle differences in no way distort the truth. A humble man of God boasts only in the Lord *and* means what he says (see 2 Corinthians 11:30 and 12:9–10).

> 25:15 By forbearance a ruler may be persuaded, and a soft tongue breaks the bone.

There is great power in patience combined with a gentle tongue. What is it you wish to accomplish in the near future? Improved relationships with your spouse, friends, boss, or in-laws? Why not give a gentle tongue coupled with patience a try? Note: A gentle tongue is not the same as a silent tongue!

The Hebrew *'aph* (translated "forbearance" here) suggests to me that passionate patience is the key to persuading. *'Aph* comes from a root word meaning "nostril." In this form it may mean rapid breathing in passion or worthy anger. The word picture implies that by passionate breathing, your intensity and desire is communicated. When a ruler witnesses this intensity, he may be persuaded.

When you pray, are patience and intensity a part of your prayer life? In what ways does Jesus' advice on praying persistently (Luke 11:5–9) relate to this verse? Picture in your mind the passionate prayer of Jesus in Gethsemane.

> 25:16 Have you found honey? Eat only what you need, lest you have it in excess and vomit it.

How important is self-control? List five areas of your life where self-control is vital. Be as specific as you can. Here are a few possibilities to get you started: Marital fidelity, alcoholic consumption, possessions, thoughts, etc.

Don't waste your honey! How do you determine the "balance point" of moderation? The key idea is the word *need*. Eat only what you need. Buy only what you need. Drink only what you need, etc.

> 25:17 Let your foot rarely be in your neighbor's house, lest he become weary of you and hate you.

What results may occur if we do not follow this advice? How is the moderation spoken of here similar to the self-control of verse 16? The principle is to think of others above yourself. Love your neighbor. We should be there in need and be friendly and helpful, but we should not be a suffocating leech.

> 25:18 Like a club and a sword and a sharp arrow is a man who bears false witness against his neighbor.

Compare Proverbs 24:28–29. The Hebrew word used here (in both texts) for "neighbor" is the word *reya*, meaning an associate, brother, companion, friend, husband, lover, or neighbor. An expert in the Mosaic law asked Jesus, "Who is my neighbor?" (Luke 10:29). Jesus answered by relating the story of the good Samaritan. It is interesting that the word used here may mean either "brother" or "neighbor."

> 25:19 Like a bad tooth and an unsteady foot is confidence in a faithless man in time of trouble.

The metaphors of the bad tooth and the unsteady foot are problems that can be continual and chronic, or sudden, acute, and unexpected. Imagine a beautiful meal prepared. You sit down to dine with relish and great anticipation. You take a big bite, and suddenly you are overwhelmed with intense pain. This is what may happen to you if you rely on an unfaithful person. A project involving an unfaithful person may suddenly become a bad and painful experience in your business.

The phrase "in time of trouble" reminds us that when everything is going along fine, faithfulness may not appear to be much of an issue. But when things get rough, it certainly will be! Compare the prodigal's fair-weather friends to the steadfast relationship of Jonathan and David.

The classifying title "a faithless man" requires a mental and moral judgment on our part. We look at a person's past actions, his current statements of morality, and his goals for the future, and we formulate a character judgment. Yes, character does count!

Finally, take a moment for self-analysis. How would your friends, spouse, and God Himself classify you on a Likert scale[35] of faithfulness, from 1 to 5?

> 25:20 Like one who takes off a garment on a cold day, or like vinegar on soda, is he who sings songs to a troubled heart.

Solomon apparently enjoyed a good science experiment as much as anyone. Try this: Put some baking soda in a balloon, pour in some vinegar and quickly pinch the opening closed. The reaction creates a bubbling auditory noise and generates quite a bit of carbon dioxide gas. This reaction is the metaphor Solomon uses.

Romans 12:15 reminds us to "rejoice with those who rejoice, and weep with those who weep." We need to exercise sensitivity to those around us and not be bombastic bubblers when someone is in a state of grief. Paul had a desire to be "all things to all men" (1 Corinthians 9:22) that he might win some to the Lord. How good are you at adjusting your attitude in sensitivity to those around you?

> 25:21–22 If your enemy is hungry, give him food to eat; and if he is thirsty, give him water to drink; for you will heap burning coals on his head, and the LORD will reward you.

How are we to respond to our enemies? According to this, we are to take care of their needs! Paul quotes this passage in Romans 12:20. He then summarizes it: "Do not be overcome by evil, but overcome evil with good."

The verb used for the word "heap" here is the Hebrew word *chathah,* which means "to lay hold of; especially to pick up fire; heap or take away." The translators for the NASB point out that this verb can be literally translated as "snatch." This can, therefore, be understood in two ways. To "heap" burning coals *on* the head of your enemy (as most English translations read) implies that you help prick his conscience with your good deeds. The other way to interpret the word is to emphasize the Hebrew meaning of *chathah* as to snatch or take away fire. This implies that as you aid your enemy, he will see God's love through your actions, and he may then begin to be pulled away (i.e., snatched) from the fire (as of hell).

Your motivation is *not* merely improving your personal relationship with your enemy. If the relationship improves, it is a great bonus. Your motivation should be desiring the relationship of your "enemy" to improve with *God.* This was the great struggle of Jonah. But even if your personal relationship with your enemy deteriorates or improves, your reward is from the Lord for being a faithful ambassador.

How does God treat His enemies? Although ultimate destruction is the result of those who continually deny God's call to salvation, He invites them to accept His gift of grace, and He provides for their basic needs on this planet throughout their lives.

Keep in mind that at one time we were all the enemies of God. "When a man's ways are pleasing to the Lord, he makes even his enemies to be at peace with him" (Proverbs 16:7). Finally, remember Jesus' admonition as He quoted Hosea to the Pharisees: "But go and learn what this means, 'I desire compassion, and not sacrifice,' for I did not come to call the righteous, but sinners" (Matthew 9:13).

25:23 The north wind brings forth rain, and a backbiting tongue, an angry countenance.

This metaphor demonstrates a cause-and-effect relationship. There is a direct correlation between anger and the improper usage of the tongue. "A gentle answer turns away wrath, but a harsh word stirs up anger" (Proverbs 15:1).

25:24 It is better to live in a corner roof than in a house shared with a contentious woman.

When faced with a choice between internal peace and joy, or external perks (with strings attached) and the illusory "happiness" they may bring, opt for peace. Though we may chuckle when we read this verse, its point is clear, easily understandable, and powerful.

25:25 Like cold water to a weary soul, so is good news from a distant land.

When Jacob sent his sons into the land of Egypt to buy food, he was worried about their safety. When he finally learned that Joseph was still alive—indeed, doing very well and being used of God—what joy must have flooded his soul!

The gospel is a joy to our "weary soul[s]." It comes to us from the distant land of God's throne and kingdom. How blessed we are as we hunger and thirst after His righteousness!

25:26 Like a trampled spring and a polluted well is a righteous man who gives way before the wicked.

Jesus said, "If any man is thirsty, let him come to Me and drink. He who believes in me, as the scripture said, 'From his innermost being shall flow rivers of living water'" (John 7:38–39). We who have partaken of the living water of life must beware of spiritual pollution! What a travesty we make of God's gift if we allow ourselves to become polluted. As Revelation 2:18–28 reveals, "Blessed is he who overcomes."

Do not confuse the ideas of tolerance and mercy. They are completely different. God is merciful and full of grace, but He is *not* "tolerant." Make it your request that God strengthen you and make you to be a sweet, flowing stream of living water, overflowing with the water of life, who is our Savior, the Lord Jesus Christ! We must be compassionate, loving, and merciful. But we must be unwavering in regard to the truth.

25:27 It is not good to eat much honey, nor is it glory to search out one's own glory.

Compare this verse to Proverbs 25:16. Putting forth your own glory may seem to be sweet, but in the end you will only be stuck up! Pride is a deadly disease that destroys from within.

25:28 Like a city that is broken into and without walls is a man who has no control over his spirit.

Do you control your spirit (see also Proverbs 16:32), or do circumstances? Can you list several consequences that may befall someone who does not control his own spirit?

How can we control our spirits? Scripture suggests that we may begin this process by doing things that draw us closer to God. We should read the word of God. We should confess our sins and ask God to help us. As Paul wrote in Philippians 4:8, we should let our minds dwell on things that are true, honorable, right, pure, and lovely.

Proverbs 26

26:1 Like snow in summer and like rain in harvest, so honor is not fitting for a fool.

*I*t is interesting to compare this verse to a similar proverb, "Like the cold of snow in the time of harvest is a faithful messenger to those who send him" (Proverbs 25:13). The imagery is similar, but the point of similarity within the metaphor is completely different. 25:13 refers to a situation you wish would occur, while 26:1 refers to an absurd and potentially harmful situation. Harvest rain is unwelcome. It may damage crops or at the very least prevent a proper harvest from occurring.

Our society often honors fools. For example, we exalt celebrities and seek out their views regarding politics, religion, and life in general—even though they may be "fools" in regard to their relationship with God. We're tempted to think that wisdom automatically accompanies fame. In my experience, this is seldom the case. Beware of phrases such as "Well, they must be doin' something right!" Learn to define success as God defines it!

26:2 Like a sparrow in its flitting, like a swallow in its flying, so a curse without cause does not alight.

Are there different types of curses? In what ways does a curse with a cause differ from a curse without a cause? Is it ever appropriate for a Christian to curse something? Let's take a moment to explore these seldom-addressed issues.

There are different types of curses. God cursed the serpent and Adam and Eve (Genesis 3:14–19). In some ways, a curse can be a benefit (not to the one cursed, but to others). In God's covenant with Abraham He stated, "I will bless those who bless you, and the one who curses you I will curse" (Genesis 12:3). In God's eyes, people may bring a curse upon themselves. In 1 Samuel 3:13 we read that Eli's sons "brought a curse on themselves."

Some curses are definitely out of bounds. Even though his story may have been written before the Torah, Job was probably familiar with the concept of Exodus 22:28: "You shall not curse God."

Curses can also be used to prove a point. For example, Jesus cursed a fig tree because it was barren of fruit (Matthew 21:19). In this case, Jesus taught His disciples a lesson about faith and prayer (see also Matthew 21:20–22). Whenever God curses, there is always a cause.

In rare instances it may be appropriate for a Christian to issue a curse. As one example, Paul wrote, "If any man preaches to you a gospel contrary to that which we have preached to you, let him be accursed [Greek *anathema*]" (Galatians 1:9).

Cursing is a form of judgment, and should be applied only in areas of special circumstances (such as the above example about the Gospel and truth). Paul instructed us to "bless those who persecute you; bless and curse not" (Romans 12:14).

This brief study of curses would not be complete if we left out an amazing aspect of the gospel. In Galatians 3:13 we read a remarkable statement: "Christ redeemed us from the curse of the Law, *having become a curse for us*—for it is written, 'Cursed is every one who hangs on a tree.'" Praise God for His unsearchable blessings as you meditate upon this fascinating concept.

26:3 A whip is for the horse, a bridle for the donkey, and a rod for the back of fools.

The whip, the bridle, and the rod are all tools for guidance, direction, and proper "goading," not simply punishment for its own sake. Take care that you do not need to have such a tool applied to your own foolishness! Compare Psalm 32:8–10.

> 26:4–5 Do not answer a fool according to his folly, lest you also be like him. Answer a fool as his folly deserves, lest he be wise in his own eyes.

Your responsibility is not to make fools feel good about themselves. Use caution when dealing with foolish people. Measure your words carefully, lest you become a fool yourself. But do speak forth. Verse 5 tells us to answer the fool as his folly deserves. This does not mean you have to enter into a huge debate about anything and everything. Let the second part of the verse guide the motivation of your answers: "Lest he be wise in his own eyes." Your goal in such a setting is to simply try to get him to see the truth of Proverbs 26:12: "Do you see a man wise in his own eyes? There is more hope for a fool than for him." Point out his presuppositions, his irrationalities, and the places where his logic breaks down. I can assure you that no modern man who is not a Christian can live with the logical conclusions of his own convictions. The Bible presents truth and the only realities. For more on this point, read Francis Schaeffer's *The God Who Is There*.[36]

> 26:6 He cuts off his own feet, and drinks violence who sends a message by the hand of a fool.

Many romantic comedies have been based on this simple truth. A forlorn and desperate lover sends a message to the recipient of his unreturned affection via the hand of a friend or servant. But somehow, along the way, the message gets bungled. Shakespeare's *Two Gentlemen of Verona*, Rossini's *The Barber of Seville*, and Mozart's *The Marriage of Figaro* all have similar themes of poor or mishandled communication. How important is communication to you? The point of Proverbs 26:6 is that you should not use a fool to deliver your messages.

26:7 Like the legs which hang down from the lame, so is a proverb in the mouth of fools.

This interesting metaphor illustrates a critical difference between wisdom and knowledge (as the word *knowledge* is commonly used). It is one thing to possess knowledge; it is quite another to be able to use that knowledge in a beneficial way.

If your legs cannot be used, they have no utilitarian value. In this way a proverb has no utilitarian value to the fool. He may be able to quote the proverb, but he does not integrate its truth into his life. This is a type of hypocrisy that makes far too many people *lame* in areas of spiritual consequence.

26:8 Like one who binds a stone in a sling, so is he who gives honor to a fool.

A sling only works when the stone flies free upon release of the strap! The stone must be unfettered so it can hit the target. The point of this illustration is that honor is utterly useless for a fool because it is meaningless. It is a shame to give honor to a fool.

When a master performs on an instrument (such as a violin), we do not honor the instrument itself. We may appreciate the instrument, but we do not honor it. We applaud for the musician. When we apply this to our spiritual lives, we see that all honor and glory belong to our Master—God Himself! We are only His instruments, and we allow Him to perform through us. Honor is real; however, it also has intangible qualities. If we attempt to "bind" it to ourselves, as if it were something tangible, it merely stagnates. In this way honor is like the stone in a sling. We must set it free and allow it to go to its intended target, which is God. Anything less is the act of a fool.

26:9 Like a thorn which falls into the hand of a drunkard, so is a proverb in the mouth of fools.

My dad used to say, "A little knowledge is a dangerous thing." Put a thorn in the hand of a drunkard and he will most likely injure himself. However, he could inadvertently stick someone else with it as well! Watch out whenever fools proclaim themselves to be wise. See also verse 7 and Romans 1:21–22, 25.

26:10 Like an archer who wounds everyone, so is he who hires a fool or who hires those who pass by.

Fools are very destructive, and if you hire one, you may actually be enabling his destructiveness. If you want to help someone who actually is a fool, don't give him a critical job. What else might you do in order to help such a person out?

Do not be "an archer who wounds everyone." There are times when you must weigh the value of a single individual over the opinion of the majority. If it is biblically and morally right, you must obey God rather than men. However, very often we are faced with the inverse dilemma. We must consider the needs of the many over the foolishness of one. One common example of this is a classroom at school. Can you think of other situations where the needs of the many outweigh the needs of a fool?

26:11 Like a dog that returns to its vomit is a fool who repeats his folly.

Do you learn from your mistakes? Fools do not learn. They repeat their mistakes time and time again. This is a major part of the label "fool." We all make mistakes, but fools repeat them. Then they usually blame others, circumstances, fate, or God.

26:12 Do you see a man wise in his own eyes? There is more hope for a fool than for him.

Solomon has been pointing out the shortcomings of fools. There is a type of fool who laughingly acknowledges that he is indeed a fool. There is another type of fool who takes himself and his opinions very seriously. In fact, he believes that actually he is quite wise! This fool is the greatest fool of all. His destructive ability is also greater. The foolishness of Darwin has done more damage to humanity than many other fools whose influence was restricted to a smaller domain.

> 26:13 The sluggard says, "There is a lion in the road! A lion is in the square!"

A lazy man will invent any excuse to avoid work. Do you invent excuses to cover up your bad habits?

> 26:14 As the door turns on its hinges, so does the sluggard on his bed.

The sluggard is a practiced procrastinator. He sleeps when he should be working. But if you attempt to wake him up, be prepared to listen to plenty of moans and groans, just like a door with poor hinges.

> 26:15 The sluggard buries his hand in the dish; he is weary of bringing it to his mouth again.

Of the various types of fools, the sluggard is not the most dangerous, but he is certainly the most disgusting. The sluggard is so lazy he doesn't even want to feed himself.

One application: Reading the Bible is our spiritual food. Ask yourself if you ever become weary of feeding yourself. The Christian life requires self-discipline for maturity to develop. Be wary of becoming a spiritual sluggard.

> 26:16 The sluggard is wiser in his own eyes than seven men who can give a discreet answer.

The sluggard is not open to any advice from others, no matter what their credentials may be. Observe the following possible thoughts of a sluggard: "Why should I follow this man's advice? I didn't even ask him for his opinion. I hate when people stick their noses into my affairs. I know my situation best. I don't need any help. The reason my marriage stinks is because my wife is an idiot [blaming and name-calling]. Why should I attend counseling for *her* problems? The counselor won't tell me anything I don't already know" [rationalizing].

Sound like anyone *you* know?

26:17 Like one who takes a dog by the ears is he who passes by and meddles with strife not belonging to him.

In certain contexts, you should learn to mind your own business. If you do not, you may become a meddler, or a gossip, or a busybody. On the other hand, you should always be ready to help others and not be apathetic. Read Deuteronomy 22:1–4. Wisdom is required to discern which situations would be meddling and which situations will be neglectful.

Let's look a bit closer at the metaphor. If you grab a dog by the ears in the hope of subduing it, boy, do you have a big surprise coming! In all likelihood, the dog will turn on you and bite you! Often when you attempt to pacify a heated situation, one or both of the parties involved will actually turn on you. This is why policemen hate getting in the middle of domestic violence cases. How can you tell whether you are acting as a "good Samaritan" or as a meddler? The answer, as we have often discussed, is to check your motivation.

26:18–19 Like a madman who throws firebrands, arrows and death, so is the man who deceives his neighbor, and says, "Was I not joking?"

People who use the phrase "I was just joking" like to think this magic phrase will cover a multitude of sins. It doesn't. Read 1 Pe-

281

ter 4:8 to discover the only thing that does cover a multitude of sins.

Having a sense of humor is fine, but it should always maintain the spirit of the golden rule. If it does this, then people will be laughing together rather at an individual.

> 26:20–21 For lack of wood the fire goes out, and where there is no whisperer, contention quiets down. Like charcoal to hot embers and wood to fire, so is a contentious man to kindle strife.

Firefighters know there are three main ways to extinguish an inferno: remove the oxygen, cool the fire, (e.g., with water), or remove the fuel. In many situations, the easiest way is to just remove the fuel.

Do you want a contentious situation to become less heated? Remove the contentious man. If this is not possible, get ready to watch the water boil! Remember how powerful the tongue is!

> 26:22 The words of a whisperer are like dainty morsels, and they go down into the innermost parts of the body.

Gossip hurts many people, but it doesn't hurt only "other" people. It does not impact only those the gossip is about. Actually it injures those who take part in the act of gossiping as well, for the "whispering" corrupts them internally. The process actually changes them from the inside out. They become increasingly judgmental, prejudicial, and insensitive.

> 26:23 Like an earthen vessel overlaid with silver dross are burning lips and a wicked heart.

The dictionary[37] defines *dross* as scum on molten metal, refuse, or rubbish. Lips that say evil things are bad, like the dross of the silver, but they hide something even more base, like a wicked heart.

The NIV renders this phrase as "a coating of glaze." From this interpretation, we arrive at the idea that external appearances may look good, but they may be deceiving. Don't be deceived by a glossy exterior hiding a morally bankrupt interior.

26:24–26 He who hates disguises it with his lips, but he lays up deceit in his heart. When he speaks graciously, do not believe him, for there are seven abominations in his heart. Though his hatred covers itself with guile, his wickedness will be revealed before the assembly.

"*Et tu, Brute?*" Beware of backstabbers. To understand the phrase "seven abominations" more clearly, you may wish to reread Proverbs 6:16–19.

These verses clarify further the idea of verse 23 (Look at the inside of people more than the outside). Ultimately, the deceitful man's wickedness will be exposed. The story of Esther reveals this principle in great detail.

26:27 He who digs a pit will fall into it, and he who rolls a stone, it will come back on him.

A man of violence will fall by violence. A man of deceit will himself be trapped by deceit. Trust in the Lord. "'Vengeance is mine, I will repay,' thus says the Lord" (Romans 12:19).

26:28 A lying tongue hates those it crushes, and a flattering mouth works ruin.

Beware of those who flatter you if they have reason to gain by your favor. A lying tongue can be used to "crush" people.

Proverbs 27

27:1 Do not boast about tomorrow, for you do not know what a day may bring forth.

The future is in God's hands. We can plan, set goals, be disciplined, work hard, and seize opportunities when they come our way, but the success of our plans and actions is in God's hands. God warned His people in Deuteronomy 8:7–14 about taking credit for His blessings by interpreting them as their own success. What is the danger of boasting about tomorrow?

James' answer to this question (James 4:13–17) is that such statements are based on incomplete knowledge, for we "do not know what . . . life will be like tomorrow." This is the same conclusion Solomon had.

27:2 Let another praise you, and not your own mouth; a stranger, and not your own lips.

We live in a "now"—and "me"—oriented culture (actually, all cultures are), and it comes with a trap. If we focus on the "now" because of some feelings of angst or anxiety, it becomes easy to find our self-esteem in the now also. This may result in a desire for us to receive praise *now*. If it does not come in a "natural" and immediate manner, we may then be tempted to *manufacture* our own praise. All this may occur because of our focus on ourselves and the elusive *now* experience. When we focus instead on God and the future hope He offers, we tend to be more content with our current station, and we long for the words of praise, "Well done, good and faithful servant" (Matthew 25:21 NIV).

> 27:3 A stone is heavy and the sand weighty, but the provocation of a fool is heavier than both of them.

The actions and words of a fool can wear you out and drain your energy. Being around a fool is a burden—in fact, it's a drag!

> 27:4 Wrath is fierce and anger is a flood, but who can stand before jealousy?

This interesting verse contrasts three negatives. Usually we think of how much damage can be done by anger and rage. These emotions are often clearly manifested overtly. However, jealousy is presented as being worse than both of these. Jealousy may be more covertly hidden than anger and rage; however, its damage may be more deadly and permanent. Indeed, jealousy itself is often the motivator of much hate and rage!

A classic example of this is the story of Othello and Desdemona from Shakespeare's *Othello*. Because of Iago's deceit (compare Proverbs 26:24–26), Othello begins to believe that Desdemona, his wife, has been unfaithful to him with Cassio. In a jealous rage Othello suffocates Desdemona. However, upon learning of Iago's deception and Desdemona's faithfulness, Othello says these words just before plunging a knife into his own heart:

> When you shall these unlucky deeds relate, speak me as I am . . .
> Of one that lov'd not wisely, but too well;

Of one not easily jealous, but, being wrought,
Perplex'd in the extreme; of one whose hand . . .
threw a pearl away.[38]

It is almost as if Shakespeare wrote *Othello* to illustrate the truth of Proverbs 26 and 27.

As a point of interest, let us also glance at Exodus 20:5: "I the LORD thy God am a jealous God." The Hebrew word used here is *qanna*. This word can be used in a positive or a negative manner. Used positively, it means to be zealous. Used negatively, it means to be envious. In Proverbs 27:4, the word translated by the NASB as "jealous" is the Hebrew *qinah*. While this can also mean zeal, it appears to have envy as its primary meaning in this context.

Jealousy is a deeply motivating emotion. It combines fear (i.e., the fear of losing something) with lust, possessiveness, and a self-centered perspective. These ingredients combine to form a powerful mental drug that temporarily stupefies normal reasoning ability. The resulting rationalizations transform the jealous individual's perspective so that he views a loved one as an object rather than as a person.

27:5–6 Better is open rebuke than love that is concealed. Faithful are the wounds of a friend, but deceitful are the kisses of an enemy.

The NIV renders this as "Better is open rebuke than hidden love." What is "hidden love"? When someone says, "I love you, but I just have trouble showing it," perhaps he doesn't love as much as he thinks! Look at 1 Corinthians 13:4–8 to see how true love is defined. How does the word *motive* tie into the outward actions of this type of love?

When we take verses 5 and 6 together, we see that the author is contrasting two distinct types of love. One is conventional, concerned with proper etiquette and being tactful. Occasionally it may even be deceitful. The other is unconventional, perhaps even radical. It is honest, motivated by what is best for the other person, and faithful to the end.

Wounds from a friend may be painful (as all wounds are), but they do heal. They are made from pure motives. Ultimately, true friends have your best interests at heart. They can be trusted.

Compare Proverbs 26:24–26 again in reference to the kisses of an enemy. Perhaps the most famous kiss in all of history was the kiss of Judas as he betrayed Jesus. It is interesting to note that David foretold this event in verse 9 of his messianic Psalm 41: "Even my close friend, in whom I trusted, who ate my bread, has lifted up his heel against me." Also worth cross-referencing is Proverbs 28:23.

27:7 A sated man loathes honey, but to a famished man any bitter thing is sweet.

Hunger is a fascinating phenomenon. Jesus said that we ought to hunger and thirst after righteousness.[39] Hunger affects our perspectives. If we are hungry, we are more likely to be seeking nourishment. If we are hungry, we are more likely to receive what is offered. We are also more likely to enjoy it. Pray that God will make you hungry for Him and His righteousness.

27:8 Like a bird that wanders from her nest, so is a man who wanders from his home.

When a female bird has laid her eggs, what is our expectation for her behavior? She should care for her eggs and her young after the eggs have hatched. She should not be wandering off. (Note: Looking quickly for food and then returning to feed her chicks is not considered "wandering.") Should we expect less of a man? A man who neglects his family is displaying less wisdom than a birdbrain!

In a culture where lyrics such as Lynyrd Skynyrd's "I'm a free bird" and The Allman Brothers' "Lord, I was born a ramblin' man" exult independence and lack of responsibility, we must stand upon the word of God. By the way, no one is actually "born" a ramblin' man.

> 27:9 Oil and perfume make the heart glad, so a man's counsel
> is sweet to his friend.

Good counsel is like a sweet fragrance. You can make another person's heart glad! What an opportunity we have to help others while bringing joy to the heart of someone else. Do you take advantage of your opportunities to bring greater beauty to those around you?

As a side note, consider 2 Corinthians 2:15–16, in which Paul tells us we are to be "a fragrance of Christ to God." John reminds us that the prayers of the saints are like incense to God (Revelation 8:4). I'm sure He delights to smell their fragrance!

> 27:10 Do not forsake your own friend or your father's friend,
> and do not go to your brother's house in the day of calamity.

Be loyal and trustworthy, but do not expect your family to solve all of your problems. In the story of the good Samaritan, the priest and Levite were "brothers" to the injured man, but the Samaritan was a true neighbor. There is a value to proximity, but closeness is not defined only in terms of distance, but also of the heart as well.

To me, this verse seems to say that I should always be ready to help others, but I should rarely seek the help of others. Another way of saying this is that it is better to be the helper than the helpee. Don't be afraid to ask for help when you need it. But don't be characterized as always being needy.

> 27:11 Be wise, my son, and make my heart glad, that I may
> reply to him who reproaches me.

Wisdom is a means of great gain. One of the greatest benefits is the joy it brings to others, both directly and indirectly.

Picture if you will, two men sitting together, chewing the fat. The conversation gets around to the son of one of the two men. Joe points out that Bob's son Tom won't amount to much. However, Bob would just love to be able to brag to Joe about Tom. In our Christian walk, Satan plays the role of Joe—accusing us before the Father.

Our Father would love to be able to turn to Satan and say, "Have you considered My servant Job, or Bill, or Beth, or Laura, or Tom, or Amy, or . . . ?"

> 27:12 A prudent man sees evil and hides himself, the naive proceed and pay the penalty.

This is a major difference between a fool and a prudent man. Being alert, observing signs, looking before leaping, being aware of potential danger and planning accordingly, these are qualities of a prudent man.

American culture suggests that prudence is of little value. In our culture, being a bold risk-taker is seen as a key ingredient of success. But half-truths are often the most dangerous. There is some truth to the motto of "Take a risk or stagnate." Frozen inactivity will not lead to success, but any message can be distorted until it is out of balance.

Our first tendency to interpret the phrase "and hides himself" may be to see this as a passive behavior. However, it is actually a very proactive response to danger. It is not cowardly to take precautions when you see impending evil. To stand before the fury of a hurricane is not macho, it is ludicrous and naive.

> 27:13 Take his garment when he becomes surety for a stranger; and for an adulterous woman hold him in pledge.

Read this verse with verse 12 in mind. There are two common ways for a naive man to get into trouble: debt and adultery. A prudent man hides himself from these areas.

27:14 He who blesses his friend with a loud voice early in the morning, it will be reckoned a curse to him.

Keep your behavior in context. This is not advice to be hypocritical, it is merely an area of wisdom to understand the "whens" of life. There is a time to be silent, and a time to speak (Ecclesiastes 3:7). Reread Proverbs 27:14. Do you think the emphasis is on the blessing or on the loud voice?

The timing, tone, and volume of your voice can influence how your message is received. Proper timing considers the other person's feelings and thoughts. Keep in mind two basic rules of communication: 1) consider your audience; and 2) be aware of how your audience reads between the lines based on your inflections, tone, and volume.

Think once again of love as it is defined in 1 Corinthians 13. Love takes others' situations into consideration. Remember what 1 Corinthians 13:1 says about clanging cymbals.

27:15–16 A constant dripping on a day of steady rain and a contentious woman are alike; he who would restrain her restrains the wind, and grasps oil with his right hand.

These two verses represent observations, the application of which is left to our own minds and present situations. Ask yourself: Am I characterized by contentiousness? In choosing a mate or business partner for myself, have I considered whether the person I have in mind is highly critical of others, but unable to receive criticism in return? Are my children getting involved with friends who are constantly sarcastic? If this is the case, these verses supply a warning.

The author points out the futility of trying to change such a person. It is like restraining the wind. Have you ever continued in a relationship (before commitment) expecting to change something about the person you were interested in? It *is* possible for people who love deeply to change themselves to please their partners, but this change is almost always wrought through their own free will. You may change yourself because of your love for me, but seldom is it me who changes you.

27:17 Iron sharpens iron, so one man sharpens another.

This verse is one of my personal favorites. In the past I have used it as a motto for sports teams that I have coached. Hebrews 10:24 reminds us to "consider how to stimulate one another to love and good deeds, not forsaking our own assembling together." I believe that certain aspects of growth and maturity cannot occur in a vacuum. The stimulation of others is vital! Reread Proverbs 27:5–6. These verses show a practical application for verse 17. David wrote, "Let the righteous smite me in kindness and reprove me; it is like oil upon my head; do not let my head refuse it" (Psalm 141:5).

27:18 He who tends the fig tree will eat its fruit; and he who cares for his master will be honored.

This verse illustrates the fairness principle of work: those who sow and toil should reap the benefits of their labor. Relationships also are a part of this formula. They can and should be cultivated. Much of our labor should be directed toward developing relationships.

Those who do not understand will point fingers (mockery) and use terms of derision (name-calling) to try to prevent a peer from getting an edge over them with the authority figure in nearly any scenario. Ignore it and remember this verse. This is especially important when we apply this to caring for our Lord and Master, Almighty God. Remember the stories of Daniel and Joseph!

Don't do something just because it makes you feel comfortable; do it because it is the right thing to do.

27:19 As in water face reflects face, so the heart of man reflects man.

Is a reflection the "real" you? No, but it helps you to understand the real you! To see the real you, you need only to gaze upon your own heart. "The heart of man reflects man." God looks at the heart (1 Samuel 16:7; 1 Chronicles 28:9; Psalm 44:20–21).

How do we see the hearts of others? Matthew 6:21 says that where your treasure is, there is your heart also.

How important is the heart? "With the heart man believes resulting in righteousness" (Romans 10:10). You can deceive your own heart (James 1:26) because now we "see dimly" (1 Corinthians 13:12). We are commanded, "Love the Lord your God with all your heart and with all your soul and with all your might" (Deuteronomy 6:5).

27:20 Sheol and Abaddon are never satisfied, nor are the eyes of man ever satisfied.

Few men are ever completely satisfied. The interesting aspect of this metaphor is that the eyes of want are compared to death. Paul wrote that he had learned how to be "content in whatever circumstances" he found himself in, and that he could "do all things through Christ" (see Philippians 4:11–13). Rate yourself on a Likert scale of 1–10 regarding how satisfied you are. Is it possible to have a hungry heart and yet have eyes that are satisfied?

For more on Sheol and Abaddon, see the notes on Proverbs 15:11 and Appendix B.

27:21 The crucible is for silver and the furnace for gold, and a man is tested by the praise accorded him.

A crucible is a heat-resistant container for melting ores and metals. Metaphorically, it can also refer to a severe trial.

The phrase "A man is tested by praise" is a very fascinating expression. Do we praise a man because he has weathered a test, or is the praise itself the test? How does praise test a man?

Once again we see how external behavior can reveal the heart. The manner in which a humble man handles praise is completely different from how a proud man handles it.

27:22 Though you pound a fool in a mortar with a pestle along with crushed grain, yet his folly will not depart from him.

There is a type of foolishness that can never be transformed by human external means. Without the intervention of God Himself, fools will not be rehabilitated. Our penal system demonstrates that this is true. Perhaps this is why capital punishment was mandated so frequently in the Mosaic law. Our humanistic system, based on a belief in the ultimate goodness of man, attempts to change people from the outside. Issues of the heart can be changed only in the heart.

27:23–27 Know well the condition of your flocks, and pay attention to your herds; for riches are not forever, nor does a crown endure to all generations. When the grass disappears, the new growth is seen, and the herbs of the mountains are gathered in, the lambs will be for your clothing, and the goats will bring the price of a field, and there will be goats' milk enough for your food, for the food of your household, and sustenance for your maidens.

A good steward pays careful attention to his means of livelihood (v. 23). This verse also has applications for parents, teachers, and leaders in any situation, be it war, business, or politics. Be attuned to the pulse of those under and around you. Also be aware that money, fame, and glory are fleeting commodities (v. 24). Verse 25 provides an interesting picture of the cycle of harvest. When death occurs, new growth soon appears, and harvest follows soon after. How often this pattern is echoed in our spiritual lives! The harvest of hay is also a part of caring for your flocks. This prudence will be repaid to you in the form of clothing, land, and food (vss. 26–27).

Proverbs 28

28:1 The wicked flee when no one is pursuing, but the righteous are bold as a lion.

*W*ickedness brings with it a mixture of guilt and fear. False illusions come easily to a wicked man. This illustrates the difference between a wicked man and an evil man. The wicked man (like Shakespeare's Macbeth) possesses a conscience that he must wrestle with. His sense of right and wrong has not yet been totally corrupted. This is not true of the evil man, as we shall see when we get to verse 5.

"The righteous are bold" because righteousness is the result of faith (Genesis 15:6), and faith allows us to see God Himself, to rest in Him, and to trust His promises. This comfort of ultimate peace brings great confidence. Faith thus renews and begets further faith. However, pride leads to fear, for one can lose status, position, power, money, and even family.

28:2 By the transgression of a land many are its princes, but by a man of understanding and knowledge, so it endures.

The NIV gives this translation: "When a country is rebellious, it has many rulers." There is a relationship between a country's general state of morality and the morality of its leaders. Throughout history it has been demonstrated that good leaders are more important than good laws. This verse implies that a fragmentation of the land occurs when there are many leaders ("princes"). A unified nation is always stronger than a divided one. Transgressions divide a nation by weakening it through a loss of morality, which in turn leads to a wide variety of factions and further weakening by numerous leaders with differing agendas.

> 28:3 A poor man who oppresses the lowly is like a driving rain which leaves no food.

Jesus illustrated this clearly in His parable about forgiveness in Matthew 18:23–35. Whether you are poor or rich, don't oppress others. Solomon's observation is that when poor people oppress other poor people, they strip them the way a severe rain might strip crops from a field.

> 28:4 Those who forsake the law praise the wicked, but those who keep the law strive with them.

Have you analyzed your sense of justice lately? Those who esteem the wicked diminish the law. This too is seen easily in our current justice system and even in our politics.

Wickedness loves company. Those who forsake the law desire the company of others who also forsake the law. Rare is the man who enjoys committing wickedness alone and in isolation—there is no enjoyment in it. The opposite may be true of an evil man, who actually may very much enjoy doing the evil alone. See the comments for Proverbs 28:5.

> 28:5 Evil men do not understand justice, but those who seek the LORD understand all things.

The path of wickedness leads to evil deeds. Eventually the wicked man (partially corrupt) may evolve into an evil man (fully corrupt). The evil man no longer needs temptation or the goading of others to commit sin. His entire way of viewing people, life, and God has been transformed so that he simply cannot understand justice. Because he is now *completely* self-centered, justice is beyond his comprehension. To this man's thinking, if God *is*, He is unfair, because the idea of anything superior is unfair. In Kohlberg's definition of stages of moral development, he has evolved backward to level I, stage 1 (preconventional, heteronomous morality). According to Kohlberg, someone on this stage doesn't consider the interests of others or recognize that they differ from his own. This is someone who doesn't relate two points of view. His actions are considered physically rather than in terms of the psychological interests of others. He sees his own perspective as being authoritarian, and does not recognize any outward person or institution as being an authority.[40]

Fortunately a contrast does exist, and there are those who seek Yahweh.

> 28:6 Better is the poor who walks in his integrity, than he who is crooked though he be rich.

How much value do you place on your integrity? Poverty and riches have this in common: they are both fleeting. Integrity is of lasting value. Never choose riches over integrity. God is not looking for men and women who love money more than Him. To be spiritually impoverished in favor of temporal wealth is to be a prince of fools.

> 28:7 He who keeps the law is a discerning son, but he who is a companion of gluttons humiliates his father.

We choose our companions, but how do we discern whether their companionship will be healthy or detrimental to us? The law is our tutor. It does not make us perfect, but it does teach us and offer a guide to us. John Donne wrote:

No man is an island, entire of itself;
Every man is a piece of the continent.[41]

Donne meant that we influence and affect others. This influence is especially evident with our own family members. Our choices and decisions influence them to a very great degree, as they influence us in turn.

The author contrasts two types of behavior and two types of father/son relationships. One is honorable; the other is dishonorable. The choice is ours.

28:8 He who increases his wealth by interest and usury, gathers it for him who is gracious to the poor.

In regard to money, the cliché "You can't take it with you" is quite true. What we have accomplished for God's kingdom, and what we allow Him to mold us into, are all we will take with us. Through His law of reciprocity we learn that if we will not help those around us in need, God will eventually find a way to transfer the wealth to someone who will help them. Be gracious to the poor, for God loves all men. God is at work, and He is sovereign. Other scriptures that bear reference to this concept include Exodus 22:25, Leviticus 25:35–37, and Deuteronomy 23:19–20.

28:9 He who turns away his ear from listening to the law, even his prayer is an abomination.

Although God desires a personal relationship with each of us, prayer alone is not the panacea that will bring this relationship about. The act of praying can be false or genuine. It can also be one-way or two-way communication. When it is one way, we tell God what we want, but we do not listen to what He wants. Our prayers should be influenced deeply by our time in the word *and* the genuine application of the Law into our lives. We would do well to heed Jesus' advice regarding prayer in the Sermon on the Mount in Matthew 6:5–7.

> 28:10 He who leads the upright astray in an evil way will himself fall into his own pit, but the blameless will inherit good.

Doom is imminent for false prophets and false teachers. But in the meantime, believers also need to beware, "for false Christs and false prophets will arise and will show great signs and wonders, so as to mislead, if possible, even the elect" (Matthew 24:24). Ezekiel 13:1–10 offers more insight into this theme. Ezekiel points out that there are those who follow "their own spirit" and who prophesy even though they really have "seen nothing." These are the types of prophets who say "'Peace!' when there is no peace."

> 28:11 The rich man is wise in his own eyes, but the poor who has understanding sees through him.

Hard work is a part of biblical ethics, but self-sufficiency (e.g., via hard work) is actually a Christian oxymoron. We exist because of, through, and for God Almighty. In Deuteronomy 8:1–16 God warned the nation of Israel about being wise in their own eyes. When the rich man thinks that his wealth is of his own doing rather than the result of God's blessing, he is setting himself up for a reality check from the Lord.

Being poor does not mean you automatically have discernment, but according to this verse, if you possess discernment and happen to be poor, you will sense the truth regarding others. Proverbs often points out that wealth can be acquired and the loss of wealth prevented through the use of wisdom, but that is an entirely different theme. The main point of this verse is that true wisdom does not depend on the possession of wealth and that rich people may also be fools.

28:12 When the righteous triumph, there is great glory, but when the wicked rise, men hide themselves.

We should never give up on the political process, no matter how many wicked men rise to power. The truth of this verse was seen clearly in the early 1940s, when members of the French Resistance hid from the German invaders. When the Germans conquered, they hid. But when the Allies arrived, there was great glory.

28:13 He who conceals his transgressions will not prosper, but he who confesses and forsakes them will find compassion.

Forgiveness is a crucial aspect of Christianity. The primary precursor of forgiveness is remorse and asking for forgiveness. When one conceals his transgressions, it is clear that shame or self-preservation (or both) are the most likely motivators of these actions. To confess is morally painful, but it has long-term benefits. Notice also that confession alone is not prescribed here, but rather confession coupled with forsaking one's transgressions. Anything less is only pseudo-confession. As Jesus told the woman caught in adultery, "Go, and sin no more" (John 8:11).

28:14 How blessed is the man who fears always, but he who hardens his heart will fall into calamity.

Blessing or trouble—the choice is ours, based on our personal relationships with God. If we fear God, acknowledge His greatness, and seek to please Him by following His precepts, we will be blessed. But if we harden our hearts and live for our own selfish motivations, we shall reap trouble.

28:15 Like a roaring lion and a rushing bear is a wicked ruler over a poor people.

When Solomon was a boy, perhaps David shared stories with him about his own boyhood memories. David had experiences with rushing bears and roaring lions that served to develop his faith in God. This faith carried itself into the realm of war and politics. David had no desire to be a despot. He knew how destructive they could be, but he also knew that they could be defeated.

28:16 A leader who is a great oppressor lacks understanding, but he who hates unjust gain will prolong his days.

What type of leader are you? Are you a servant-style leader or an oppressor? By looking at the contrasts, we may observe from this verse that the motivation for an oppressive leader is "unjust gain." We can identify those who would make good leaders by analyzing their sense of justice and what motivates them. Oppressive leaders accomplish what they want through fear. The gain they seek is for themselves and their own glory. Servant leaders accomplish what they want by meeting the needs of those under them—thus providing internal motivation. The gain such leaders seek is centered on others, and their desire is simply that the glory goes to God.

28:17 A man who is laden with the guilt of human blood will be a fugitive until death; let no one support him.

Today in our society, murderers have "support" from various sources. Many interpret the life of the murderer from the fatalistic perspective of victimhood. This is an attempt to shift the blame for the murderer's actions from the free will of the individual to a variety of possibilities. The clear indictment here is "Let no one support him."

28:18 He who walks blamelessly will be delivered, but he who is crooked will fall all at once.

Will you fall all at once (i.e., suddenly), or will you be delivered? The answer depends not on guesswork, but on how you choose to walk.

28:19 He who tills his land will have plenty of food, but he who follows empty pursuits will have poverty in plenty.

A fascinating connection exists between free will and the sovereignty of God. Our choices yield a pattern of consequences, but they *are* choices. Hard work is extolled and empty pursuits condemned here. Why? Because God *is* in control. His laws apply whether a man is aware of them or not. Thus, the idea that a man makes his own fate is partially correct. Yet it is incorrect to view this statement as a true humanist would, for ultimately it is not the man who is in control, but rather God Himself and His laws.

28:20 A faithful man will abound with blessings, but he who makes haste to be rich will not go unpunished.

This verse presents another precept in biblical conduct that may seem odd according to worldly standards. Do I wish to be rich? This is *not* the question I should ask myself when I desire to follow the guidelines espoused in scripture. Rather I should ask, "Do I wish to be blessed?" Instead of focusing on wealth, I should focus on being faithful. It is less a matter of what I *do,* and more of what I am *becoming.*

Of course, there is a relationship between doing and becoming that James points out in his epistle. What I do affects what I am becoming, and what I am becoming affects what I do, but the point of consideration is my motive. Remember also that the Abrahamic covenant contains two parts. God wants to bless us that we may bless others. Examine your motives this week in regard to "haste[ning] to become rich."

28:21 To show partiality is not good, because for a piece of bread a man will transgress.

The word *partiality* refers to treating some people differently than others, usually with a motive involving personal gain. It is not good to be inconsistent, wishy-washy, wavering, partial, and relativistic in our morality. If we are, then we will develop a morally lost society that will rationalize all of its poor decisions. Even in the small things, like a piece of bread, our motives need to be pure and our thinking clear. In verse 20 above we learned to analyze our motives. Now let us also analyze our rationalizations!

> 28:22 A man with an evil eye hastens after wealth, and does not know that want will come upon him.

What does an evil eye focus on? Often the answer is wealth. But man's purpose is not to find wealth. When you think you've found it, you will still not be content, because God has created you in His own image, and a part of that image is a need for communion with Him. Apart from that relationship, an internal vacuum exists that denies complete satisfaction (small wonder the Rolling Stones can't find any). What Proverbs 28:22 also teaches is that a man with an "evil eye" who "hastens after wealth" will come to want. O, the irony of life without God—when what one seeks most of all does not satisfy and in the end will be lost!

The Hebrew word for "eye" here is *ayin*, which may refer to either a literal or figurative eye. It may also refer to one's countenance or "look."

A Brief Look at the Biblical Usage of "Evil Eye"

In Genesis 16:4, Sarai was despised in the sight of Hagar. Judges 21:25 records that "everyone did what was right in his own eyes." When Queen Vashti refused to come before King Ahasuerus "to display her beauty" (Esther 1:10–17), Memucan's advice to Ahasuerus was to quell all forms of women's liberation as quickly as possible—"for the queen's conduct will become known to all the women, causing them to look with contempt on their husbands."

In Job 16:9 we read, "My adversary glares [literally, 'sharpens his eyes'] at me." Solomon noted in Proverbs 16:2, "All the ways of a man are clean in his own sight" and in Proverbs 27:20, "The eyes of man are never satisfied."

Peter wrote about people "having eyes full of adultery, and that never cease from sin" (2 Peter 2:14).

Another warning found in Proverbs is "Do not eat the bread of a selfish [literally, 'evil eye'] man" (Proverbs 23:6). Though not stated explicitly here in verse 22, I think we may infer that we should also avoid those with the evil eye as much as possible, for two reasons: so that their goals do not become our own, and also so that their impending calamity does not encompass us as well.

> 28:23 He who rebukes a man will afterward find more favor than he who flatters with the tongue.

Don't be afraid to rebuke someone whom you love. But a word of caution: make sure you do it in love. See also Proverbs 27:5–6, 17.

> 28:24 He who robs his father or his mother, and says, "It is not a transgression," is the companion of a man who destroys.

There are people who live their whole lives in denial through hyperbole and rationalization. They overstate their accomplishments. They dismiss their weaknesses. They are the people who call evil good. But we can never dismiss the Ten Commandments. We are to honor our father and mother. Solomon also wrote, "Fools mock at sin, but among the upright there is good will" (Proverbs 14:9).

How did Jesus handle this attitude? Read Matthew 15:2–9. Clearly this matter of honoring demonstrates the nearness or distance of our heart to God.

> 28:25 An arrogant man stirs up strife, but he who trusts in the LORD will prosper.

Arrogance leads to strife. Compare this verse with 28:20. Note, the verse does *not* read, "He who trusts in himself." The humanist manifesto of our society declares, "You must believe in yourself. Trust in your own heart. You can do it! Have confidence!" All this sounds great until we come to the Bible and realize our trust must be in God alone.

28:26 He who trusts in his own heart is a fool, but he who walks wisely will be delivered.

Notice how wisdom is displayed. It is not a quality of intellectual capacity or of mystical "Zen" views of the universe. Wisdom is displayed by *walking*, a simple everyday task and a means of mobilization. As you get to know God, you realize you *can* trust in His heart, and you align yourself to walk in His paths. "The fool has said in his heart, 'There is no God (Psalm 14:1).'" A. W. Tozer wrote in his classic *The Knowledge of the Holy*: "Unbelief is actually perverted faith, for it puts its trust not in the living God but in dying men."[42]

28:27 He who gives to the poor will never want, but he who shuts his eyes will have many curses.

Passivity is a choice. But more than a choice, it is also an action. Jesus' parable of the good Samaritan illustrates the act of shutting one's eyes. If you want to see God, keep your eyes open, even to the needs of those around you!

28:28 When the wicked rise, men hide themselves; but when they perish, the righteous increase.

A survey of world history records that a remnant always exists of those faithful to God. During times of oppression they sometimes become less visible, but they are still there. Usually difficult times serve to strengthen the faithful. Sometimes oppression serves to drive people back to God. Sometimes oppressions create a *diaspora* or "scattering" of the people of God. Oftentimes in history, such a diaspora has served to spread the gospel to the far reaches of our planet.

Proverbs 29

29:1 A man who hardens his neck after much reproof will suddenly be broken beyond remedy.

A reed bends in the wind, yet it survives great winds—while a tree that is unbending may snap completely. Are you flexible? In the context of this verse, flexibility refers to the ability to grow and change "after much reproof." None of us is perfect; therefore we all need reproof from time to time. The point of this verse is, how will you handle such reproof? Will you accept it as David accepted Nathan's reproof, or will you need to be broken like Pharaoh[43]?

29:2 When the righteous increase, the people rejoice, but when a wicked man rules, people groan.

All people benefit when righteous people increase. Righteous people bring greater justice, peace, and safety. All people suffer when unrighteous, wicked people are in control (compare Proverbs 28:28). Under wicked leadership, bribery, immorality, corruption, and unfair practices of all sorts will abound.

29:3 A man who loves wisdom makes his father glad, but he who keeps company with harlots wastes his wealth.

One of the greatest ways you can honor your father and mother is to live a righteous life that makes them proud and glad.

The phrase "wastes his wealth" may imply more than just the simple loss of money paid to a prostitute. Throughout the book of Proverbs, advice about maintaining a strong work ethic, managing your money, and avoiding unnecessary financial losses has been tied to the concepts of prudence and wisdom. Here the sin of keeping "company with harlots" is contrasted with the act of loving wisdom. While Proverbs points out that wisdom is better than riches, it also reveals that God desires to bless His obedient stewards. The harlot-visitor has forfeited more than just a bit of money. He has become spiritually bankrupt, forfeiting future blessings and wealth.

29:4 The king gives stability to the land by justice, but a man who takes bribes overthrows it.

The standard of justice acceptable in any society is a reflection of its basic morality. Bribery destroys a nation from the inside out. Any nation characterized by the common practice of bribery will always be unstable and full of injustice. Bribery dilutes morality because standards, trust, and loyalty are eliminated while behavior is controlled not by a system of belief but only by the highest bidder.

29:5 A man who flatters his neighbor is spreading a net for his steps.

This verse is a warning: Do not listen to flattery. Flattery may be defined as the self-centered praise of another person for the purpose of achieving one's own ends. There are two types of flattery. Destructive-greedy flattery attempts to get something from the impending fall of the recipient of the flattery. The idea is that the misinformation given will eventually result in destruction of the recipient, and then the flatterer will gain something. A second type, pseudo-flattery, is less destructive. It is insincere, but it hopes to get something directly from the recipient. The main difference between flattery and true praise is that the latter seeks to gain nothing.

29:6 By transgression an evil man is ensnared, but the righteous sings and rejoices.

People are trapped by their own sins. The beauty of this verse is the clear contrast between a righteous man and an evil man. One will become miserable and the other will be joyful.

29:7 The righteous is concerned for the rights of the poor, the wicked does not understand such concern.

Clearly, as Christians, we need to be concerned for the needs of others. We find joy in several aspects of our Christian walk, such as being in the presence of the Lord, fellowshipping with other believers, and seeing others we love (such as our children) grow into a meaningful relationship with God.

But another simple way to find joy is to reach out and help others in need (compare Proverbs 31:8–9 and Psalm 41:1). Have you evaluated the level of your own compassion recently? If you find yourself feeling a bit depressed for any reason, try helping someone else out! (Note: the inverse is *not* true—being concerned for the poor does not automatically make one "righteous," as many liberals and "works"-oriented people like to think. See Matthew 26:8–11.)

29:8 Scorners set a city aflame, but wise men turn away anger.

Men have the capacity to be destroyers or builders. You can tear down or edify, and you can criticize or encourage. Notice the phrase "Wise men turn away anger." How can you and I learn to turn away anger? Here are three ideas: 1) understand the problem and identify solutions (Genesis 13:8–9); 2) walk in integrity (Proverbs 19:1); and 3) speak gently and compassionately, so as to make knowledge acceptable (Proverbs 15:1–2, 18). But please note this word of warning: you will not always be successful in turning away anger, no matter how wise you become (see Proverbs 29:9). Remember that Jesus was wise, but many were angry with Him!

> 29:9 When a wise man has a controversy with a foolish man, the foolish man either rages or laughs, and there is no rest.

Fools react predictably, either by getting mad or by laughing off a reproof. Part of the *modus operandi* of a fool is to refuse to change or to accept blame. The reason "there is no rest" is that a fool will laugh, rant, blame, or rave, but he will not solve a problem. Therefore the problem will continue and actually get worse.

> 29:10 Men of bloodshed hate the blameless, but the upright are concerned for his life.

This verse reminds us that evil men hate righteous and blameless men. Let us explore *why* this occurs.

Why did Cain murder Abel? His complaint should have been with God, for it was God, not Abel, who rejected his offering. Abel did nothing to Cain. He simply brought an offering to God to show that He loved God and wanted to honor Him as God.

Clearly, from this example we learn that a righteous man does *not* need to do anything directly offensive to an evil man to incur his hatred, because darkness abhors light. Telling the truth can also get you on an evil man's blacklist. In 1 Kings 22:8 we read, "And the king of Israel said to Jehoshaphat, 'There is yet one man by whom we may inquire of the Lord, but I hate him, because he does not prophesy good concerning me, but evil.'" See also 2 Chronicles 18:7.

There are those who hate, but pretend to love (Psalm 81:15). Of this type of man, we must discern who their master is. Jesus stated, "You cannot serve two masters" (Matthew 6:24). Jesus also warned His disciples, "You will be hated by all on account of My name" (Matthew 10:22). However, He gave us a motivating reason to endure with these words: "But it is the one who has endured to the end who will be saved" (Matthew 10:22, Mark 13:13). In His Sermon on the Mount Jesus gave us the words, "Blessed are you when men hate you . . . for the sake of the Son of Man" (Luke 6:22). In the famous passage from John 3 Jesus said, "For everyone who does evil hates the light, and does not come to the light lest his deeds be exposed" (v. 20).

John had more to say about this idea, as we can read in 1 John 2:9; 3:13–16; and 4:19–21. How would you summarize John's position on hating the blameless? For additional insight, compare Luke 21:17; John 15:18; and Titus 3:3.

29:11 A fool always loses his temper, but a wise man holds it back.

Many modern psychologists tell you to "get your anger out." The implication is that anger itself is an entity, and that as you release your angst you are freeing yourself of something, not unlike a physical virus or disease that must be expelled. It is true that anger should be dealt with, but it should be dealt with spiritually as well as physically. Dealing with anger on a spiritual level *always* means implementing some aspect of forgiveness and justice. Grace relates to forgiveness and truth relates to justice. This is in part what John meant when he proclaimed, "And we beheld His glory . . . full of *grace* and *truth*" (John 1:14). To treat anger only physically and verbally is to treat only its symptoms and not its roots. Anger is an issue of the heart. May God grant us His infinite grace and His eternal truth, and may we see His glory as John did!

29:12 If a ruler pays attention to falsehood, all his ministers become wicked.

This verse is a warning: Don't pay attention to lies and falsehoods. If you do, those around you will become increasingly wicked. Ethical behavior on your part will tend to inspire ethical behavior from peers and underlings (even if they do not completely buy into your standards of morality). However, if you are gullible and readily believe lies, this can become like a feeding frenzy for individuals who lie because it's fun to watch you "freak out," or because they are lazy or vindictive (see Proverbs 29:5).

> 29:13 The poor man and the oppressor have this in common: the LORD gives light to the eyes of both.

This verse demonstrates two important aspects of Christianity. The first point is this: While we are all different and unique (e.g., rich or poor, oppressive or thoughtful), in the larger picture we are all the same. We are all created in the image of God. We all need salvation because of our sins. We all use the light of the sun.

The second point is this: We were all created to *see* the *light!* Physically, light is essential to life. The light of the sun provides energy and food through photosynthesis. Light is the result of a Creator.

Spiritually, light has even more meaning to Christians. Light is a symbol of seeing and of revelation, and it is the means of revealing sin and evil.

Following our own resurrection, we shall see as John did: "There shall no longer be any night; and they shall not have need of the light of a lamp nor the light of the sun, because the Lord God shall illumine them" (Revelation 22:5). In Genesis 1 we read that after God created light (with only the power of His voice!), He "saw that the light was good . . . and God separated the light from the darkness." This is why the Psalmist can declare with conviction, "The LORD is my light and my salvation; whom shall I fear?" (Psalm 27:1).

Solomon wrote one of his most poetic passages about light: "But the path of the righteous is like the light of dawn, that shines brighter and brighter until the full day" (Proverbs 4:18). Following are a few other passages from scripture with some interesting comments about light: Micah 7:7–10; Matthew 5:14–16; John 8:12; and Ephesians 5:8–9.

29:14 If a king judges the poor with truth, his throne will be established forever.

If you are in a position of authority and leadership, then be fair. Don't show partiality to the rich or famous. King George III of England, the French aristocracy, and the Russian czars all learned this lesson the hard way. We should always judge with truth; judging with anything else mocks justice.

29:15 The rod and reproof give wisdom, but a child who gets his own way brings shame to his mother.

Don't be fooled by pop-psychology tips on parenting. The beginning of wisdom is the fear of the Lord. Begin by instilling this into your kids. Secondly, instill into them a healthy respect for you as their parent. The commandment to "honor your father and mother" should be taken seriously by all Christians.

Man is born with a great deal of freedom (witness the fall of Adam). But this freedom must be counterbalanced with responsibility. Freedom is self-oriented while responsibility is other-oriented. Wisdom often comes from boundaries.

What kind of wisdom can a simple rod yield? Here are three pearls of wisdom a rod may announce to someone:

1. You are not alone on this planet (egocentrism is a pseudo-reality).
2. My parents mean what they say (fear becomes trust).
3. If others can inflict pain on me, then perhaps I have the ability to inflict pain on others (therefore I should be more sensitive).

Some readers may be interested in a brief word study of the term *rod*. The following is provided for their enrichment. There are at least six aspects of the *rod* in the Bible. It can be used for punishment or "crushing" (Psalm 2:9; Proverbs 26:3; Isaiah 10:5; Jeremiah 51:20; Ezekiel 20:37), measurement (Ezekiel 40:5), ruling over (Revelation 19:15), protection (Psalm 23:4), a sign (Moses' rod in Exodus 4:2 et al., Numbers 17:8; Hebrews 9:4), or as a tool of discipline or learning (2 Samuel 7:14–16).

Other proverbs that use this word include Proverbs 10:13; 13:24; 14:3[44]; 22:8, 15; 23:13–14; and 26:3.

> 29:16 When the wicked increase, transgression increases; but the righteous will see their fall.

Rather than contrast the wicked directly with the righteous, the author points out the cause-and-effect "big picture." Evil will not increase merely of itself. Evil will increase only because evil, wicked *people* increase. The contrast, however, focuses on hope. Even when we see the rise of the wicked, we are promised that we will also witness their judgment and fall.

> 29:17 Correct your son, and he will give you comfort; he will also delight your soul.

Tough love has its rewards. It is good to note that the verb used here is *correct* rather than *punish*. The latter has many misconceptions attached to it. In scripture, whenever punishment is connected to children and parenting, the idea is always to discipline, correct, and impart wisdom and learning.

The verse closes with a wonderful promise to diligent parents who will experience delight.

> 29:18 Where there is no vision, the people are unrestrained, but happy is he who keeps the law.

The Hebrew *chazown* means a revelation or vision. It comes from the verb *chazah,* which means to perceive mentally, to contemplate (with pleasure), or to behold.

But the Hebrew verb *para* is much more surprising. The King James renders it "perish" while the NASB and the NIV use "unrestrained" and "restraint," respectively. The word *para* means to loosen, to expose, or dismiss. When used figuratively, it may mean to strip naked, to perish, or to uncover. When used of hair, *para* has the sense of cutting. According to *The Complete Word Study Old Testament,* "In Proverbs, the sense is to let something slip through the fingers by ignoring an opportunity. It probably means undisciplined in Proverbs 29:18."[45]

What is the application of this verse? The answer lies in answering this question: How important is *hope*? According to the Bible, hope is a fundamental aspect of faith (see Hebrews 11:1). Proverbs 29:18 points out the importance of future-oriented thinking in the setting of today's goals. Hope allows us to see the big picture, even in the midst of circumstances that demand our immediate attention to the details of life. People of hope are people of vision. We obey the law because we love God, and we see the benefits and also the ramifications of not keeping the law.

29:19 A slave will not be instructed by words alone; for though he understands, there will be no response.

Here the author observes that most people need external motivation. When you make an imperative statement but do not see a change in people's behavior, you might be tempted to give them the humanistic benefit of the doubt: "Oh, they probably just didn't hear me. Or maybe they heard me but just didn't understand what I meant." More likely, they just didn't want to do it!

People are by nature self-willed and fond of freedom. If a slave does not act, he may be a slave in name, but in this act of refusal he is free. For a fascinating look at slavery and what it means to be truly free, read Paul's epistle to Philemon.

29:20 Do you see a man who is hasty in his words? There is more hope for a fool than for him.

In attempting to solve problems, we often jump to conclusions and react to situations. This is common in our society, which values action and decisiveness. Biblically, however, we should live proactively rather than reactively. Basically, the hastily speaking man *is* a fool. Remember both the power and danger of the tongue (see James 3:3–10)!

29:21 He who pampers his slave from childhood, will in the end find him to be a son.

Because of ambiguities in the Hebrew text, this verse has several differing interpretations in English Bibles. Every language has words with multiple meanings, and this is exacerbated in languages with fewer words. Ancient Hebrew had only about 6,000 words. By contrast, modern American English has about 50,000 words, while the Queen's English has over 100,000 words! Whatever the reason, this verse seems to have been a problem for the translators.

The NASB has "He who pampers his slave from childhood will in the end find him to be a son." The NIV has "If a man pampers his servant from youth, he will bring grief in the end." The KJV renders it, "He that delicately bringeth up his servant from a child shall have him become his son at the length." Clearly the NIV is at odds with both the KJV and the NASB. The word translated "son" is the Hebrew *manown*, which means continuator or heir. It is not the "normal" word (*ben*) for son. Perhaps the NIV translators based their interpretation on the Septuagint version (a Greek translation of the Hebrew circa 250 B.C.), which reads, "He that lives wantonly from a child, shall be a servant, and in the end shall grieve over himself."

Blood is not always the tightest bond. I believe the KJV and NASB interpretations make the most sense, as we can see examples of adoption and people putting faithful servants in their wills.

29:22 An angry man stirs up strife, and a hot-tempered man abounds in transgression.

Imagine, if you will, a glass of crystal-clear water with a few insoluble sand particles thrown into it. After some time, gravity will pull the sediment down to the bottom of the glass. The clear water will remain at the top until someone comes along to stir it up! We who have been cleansed by the blood of the Lamb are like this glass of pure water. An angry man comes along and tries to stir up trouble. An angry man *looks* for problems! This directly influences the lives of those around him. Furthermore, the latter part of this verse points out that a hot-tempered person will be more likely to sin. This fresh sin is likely to create more problems, and the cycle of blame goes on.

29:23 A man's pride will bring him low, but a humble spirit will obtain honor.

The biblical consequences of pride and humility are clear throughout all of scripture (compare 1 Peter 5:5–6; Proverbs 8:13; and 16:18).

29:24 He who is a partner with a thief hates his own life; he hears the oath but tells nothing.

With whom do you associate? There are dangers connected to your associations if your associate is involved in sin. This danger is especially perilous when this associate is a partner! First, you will be susceptible to mimicking his behavior. Secondly, even if you don't become corrupted, the eventual consequences of his transgressions will be more likely to fall upon you as well.

"He hears the oath but tells nothing." The King James Version gives, "He heareth cursing, and betrayeth it not." This implies a loyalty to evil, but we are called to live by a higher standard.

29:25 The fear of man brings a snare, but he who trusts in the LORD will be exalted.

Whom do you fear? What are the consequences of fearing man? Biblically, the concepts of fear and trust are connected much more closely than the world generally defines them. If you fear God, you learn to trust Him. Jesus told His disciples, "My friends, do not be afraid of those who kill the body, and after that have no more that they can do. But I warn you whom to fear: fear the One who after He has killed has authority to cast into hell" (Luke 12:4–5). This verse also reveals the cause-and-effect relationship brought about by misplaced fear versus that of trust in the Lord.

29:26 Many seek the ruler's favor, but justice for man comes from the LORD.

Seek ye not the favor of men.
Desire not accolades again and again.
Esteem peace and love over lascivious fun.
Look unto God for your justice to come.
Take your Bible down off of the shelf,
Compare Matthew twenty-three two through twelve.

29:27 An unjust man is abominable to the righteous, and he who is upright in the way is abominable to the wicked.

This verse demonstrates the age-old scenario of good versus evil. Darkness hates light. Light hates darkness. Wickedness despises justice and justice despises wickedness.

What does the word "abominable" mean? The Hebrew word is *toebah* (pronounced: tow-ay-baw): it is used regarding something disgusting. The English word means unequivocally detestable or loathsome.

Proverbs 30

We now move into the sixth and final section of the book of Proverbs. This section brings a change in authorship and has three parts: 1) Agur, chapter 30; 2) Lemuel, 31:1–9; and 3) an alphabetical poem (stylistically similar to Psalm 119) on the virtuous woman.

> 30:1–4 The words of Agur the son of Jakeh, the oracle. The man declares to Ithiel, to Ithiel and Ucal: Surely I am more stupid than any man, and I do not have the understanding of a man. Neither have I learned wisdom, nor do I have the knowledge of the Holy One. Who has ascended into heaven and descended? Who has gathered the wind in His fists? Who has wrapped the waters in His garment? Who has established all the ends of the earth? What is His name or His son's name? Surely you know!

We do not know much about Agur or the other three men mentioned here. However, Agur appears to be overly modest. He claims to possess little wisdom, but his fascinating questions demonstrate a great deal of wisdom. Let's consider his five questions.

"Who has ascended . . . and descended?" The most logical answer to this question is God Himself. Heaven, by definition, is God's domain. The latter part of the verse suggests that this One who dwells in heaven will descend to the earth. This is very messianic language. Agur's next few questions continue the messianic theme. "Who has gathered the wind in His fists?" Who except God alone could do this? As we continue to read Agur's questions we echo the same reply, "God alone can do this."

Finally, we get to Agur's last question. What is God's name? The fascinating thing about this verse is that Agur also asks, "What is his son's name?" The ancient authors of the Old Testament knew that Messiah would be the Son of God (see also Psalm 2:7, 12).

Agur's technique here in Proverbs 30:1–4 bears a similarity to the way Jesus used parables. For those who have ears to hear, it creates a desire to look for the deeper meaning. In using a riddle-like format, he doesn't just tell you what to believe, he allows you to reach an insight as you discover the meaning of the words for yourself.

> 30:5–6 Every word of God is tested; He is a shield to those who take refuge in Him. Do not add to His words lest He reprove you, and you be proved a liar.

Compare Revelation 22:18 and Deuteronomy 4:2. That which is real is often hidden by what we perceive, because what we perceive is often real only in our minds. But the truth of God is real whether we perceive it or not. This is why we must always test our beliefs and theology against the word of God.

> 30:7–9 Two things I asked of Thee, do not refuse me before I die: keep deception and lies far from me, give me neither poverty nor riches; feed me with the food that is my portion, lest I be full and deny thee and say, "Who is the LORD?" Or lest I be in want and steal and profane the name of my God.

This is Agur's prayer for truth and balance in life's necessities. "Keep deception and lies far from me." Have you made this your own prayer? It is at moments when we least expect it that weakness and lack of discernment attack us. Aaron (Exodus 32) and King Saul (1 Samuel 28:5–7) are examples of how easy it is to be deceived when we are not fully in the presence of God.

Next let us look more closely at the phrase "Neither poverty nor riches." I find this to be a fascinating prayer! How does Agur's prayer here compare to Jesus' instructions to pray, "Give us this day our daily bread" (Matthew 6:11)? What reason does Agur give for God not to grant him riches? What reason does he offer for God *not* to give him poverty? Agur's wisdom demonstrated in this prayer has many implications for us regarding our own prayers, lifestyle, and goals.

> 30:10 Do not slander a slave to his master, lest he curse you and you be found guilty.

Slander may backfire! Morality should prevent us from doing it in the first place, but if this is not a strong enough motivation, then let fear stop us. Before we put someone down we should consider this warning and the possible consequences. Griping is rampant in our society. It almost seems as if some have raised complaining to an art form! Christians should never be characterized by this trait.

In the phrase "Lest he curse you," to whom does the pronoun *he* refer—the master or the servant? A look at the original language does not help, nor does the context. But regardless of who is doing the cursing, the cause-and-effect consequence is clear. We should heed the warnings of scripture and carefully watch our tongues.

> 30:11–14 There is a kind of man who curses his father, and does not bless his mother. There is a kind who is pure in his own eyes, yet is not washed from his filthiness. There is a kind—oh, how lofty are his eyes! And his eyelids are raised in arrogance. There is a kind of man whose teeth are like swords, and his jaw teeth like knives, to devour the afflicted from the earth, and the needy from among men.

Here Agur talks about different kinds of people. What I think he is really doing is describing a negative progression similar to the one Paul described in Romans 1:21–31. The man who does not honor his father and mother focuses on himself rather than others. With this perspective, he sees all that he does as "pure," regardless of how it may hurt others. This results in arrogance, with a feeling of superiority toward others. Others are then seen as objects that are a step or two below him. Finally he becomes a man of violence, because it is easy to rationalize the pain and abuse inflicted upon inferior objects.

Other scriptures to compare with these verses include the following: for v. 11, see Proverbs 20:20; for v. 12, see Luke 18:9–14; for v. 13, see Proverbs 16:18; and for v. 14, see Psalm 57:4.

We can observe another type of progression here in these verses, from the concrete to what is more abstract, figurative, and imaginative. This may be, to a degree, reflective of the mental state of a man as he progresses from being just sinful to becoming wicked and finally to becoming absolutely evil.

We now arrive at several riddles written by Agur. What place do riddles have in wisdom literature? Stories and parables such as those told by Nathan and Jesus are not dissimilar to riddles. Solomon's introduction to the book of Proverbs mentions riddles: "A wise man will hear and increase in learning, and a man of understanding will acquire wise counsel, to understand a proverb and a figure, the words of the wise and their riddles" (Proverbs. 1:5–6).

In the book of Judges we read about a very famous riddle given by Samson: "Out of the eater came something to eat, and out of the strong came something sweet" (Judges 14:12–19 [compare Ezekiel 17:2]). Riddles are valuable because they stimulate thinking.

30:15–17 The leech has two daughters, "Give," "Give." There are three things that will not be satisfied, four that will not say, "Enough": Sheol, and the barren womb, earth that is never satisfied with water, and fire that never says, "Enough." The eye that mocks a father, and scorns a mother, the ravens of the valley will pick it out, and the young eagles will eat it.

Agur begins this section with a humorous anecdote in verse 15. The leech has two daughters. One is named Give. The other one is also named Give. There is also a numerical device employed here to show emphasis. A singular leech has two daughters. They are followed by three unsatisfied things, which in turn are followed by four things that will not say "enough." Poetically he is showing a pyramid structure of how want expands.

Agur's illustrations are from nature, but they are intended to teach us something about the dangers of human desire and selfishness. Verse 17 contains a "judgment day" type of warning and echoes the theme of honoring one's father and mother, just as verses 11–14 do. What should we learn from this passage? Don't be a leech!

> 30:18–19 There are three things which are too wonderful for me, four which I do not understand: the way of an eagle in the sky, the way of a serpent on a rock, the way of a ship in the middle of the sea, and the way of a man with a maid.

I call this Agur's second riddle. His wonderment here deals with the concept of unity. The examples he gives show the blending of things in the universe. There is an innate beauty contained in things that demonstrate a natural flow of unity.

> 30:20 This is the way of an adulterous woman: she eats and wipes her mouth, and says, "I have done no wrong."

This verse juxtaposes clearly the ugliness of adultery to the beauty of marital unity. The adulterous woman's response to her actions shows that she is not only callous, but also self-deceived. She destroys a marriage even while she declares that it is OK and that she has "done no wrong." Clearly, her sense of right and wrong has become warped.

> 30:21–23 Under three things the earth quakes, and under four, it cannot bear up: under a slave when he becomes king, and a fool when he is satisfied with food, under an unloved woman

when she gets a husband, and a maidservant when she supplants her mistress.

In verses 18–19 Agur illustrates what is natural, right, proper, and normal, if you will. The opposite of this is shown in verses 21–23. Here Agur describes abnormal and unusual events. These events are accompanied with a warning. If they occur—watch out!

> 30:24–28 Four things are small on the earth, but they are exceedingly wise: the ants are not a strong folk, but they prepare their food in the summer; the badgers are not mighty folk, yet they make their houses in the rocks; the locusts have no king, yet all of them go out in ranks; the lizard you may grasp with the hands, yet it is in kings' palaces.

Agur's fourth riddle deals with the theme of "small yet wise." The wisdom he discusses here includes saving up food (i.e., planning for future tough times), building a house that is safe and solid, having friends, and being with people of like mind and purpose.

Remember, as Christians we do not save for the future out of fear, for we know God will supply our needs. We save so that we may bless others and thus bring glory to God. Saving for the hard times is simply good stewardship (compare Genesis 41). It is a part of being wise.

Regarding the badger's house in the rocks in verse 26, consider what Isaiah wrote: "He who walks righteously . . . will dwell on the heights; His refuge will be the impregnable rock; His bread will be given him; His water will be sure. Your eyes will see the king in His beauty; they will behold a far-distant land" (Isaiah 33:15–17).

As Christians, we also live in "the Rock"—Jesus Christ. Make your home completely in Him, and not in the world!

(Here is a fascinating study of Messianic references to Jesus as "the Rock." I encourage any interested reader to spend the time going through them to see more clearly this aspect of the Messiah. Deuteronomy 8:15; 32:1–6, 15, 18; 1 Samuel 2:2; 2 Samuel 23:3; Psalm 27:5; 61:2; 62:2; 71:3; 78:16, 35; 89:26; 92:15; 95:1; 118:22;

Isaiah 8:13–15; 28:16; 30:29; 33:16; 44:8; 51:1; Habakkuk 1:12. See also Matthew 21:42; John 1:5, 10; Romans 9:33; and 1 Peter 2:6–8.)

Agur may not have been thinking of the Messiah when he wrote about the badgers in the rock, but the principle of building on a solid foundation is demonstrated throughout scripture. The wise man builds his house upon the rock.

The metaphor of the locusts in verse 27 reminds me that we do not need an earthly king to do the work of God, for He alone is our true King. Jesus said that the fields are white for the harvest. Could not the world be turned upside down if we all went out in ranks as the locusts?

Verse 28 illustrates humility. No matter how rich and powerful an earthly king becomes, he can never totally escape nature.

> 30:29–31 There are three things which are stately in their march, even four which are stately when they walk: the lion which is mighty among the beasts and does not retreat before any. The strutting cock, the male goat also, and a king when his army is with him.

This represents Agur's fifth riddle, a riddle about pride juxtaposed in contrast to the previous riddle about living life normally, wisely, and in humility.

> 30:32–33 If you have been foolish in exalting yourself or if you have plotted evil, put your hand on your mouth. For the churning of milk produces butter; so the churning of anger produces strife.

This represents the moral of the story. The riddles are given not just for fun, but so that we may examine ourselves. Riddles 1, 3, and 5 are negatives. Riddles 2 and 4 are positives. As we read through the riddles, we should ask questions. Am I like the leech, or like the eagle in the sky? Am I like the ants, or like the strutting cock?

Agur ends his section with yet another interesting lesson from nature by comparing the churning of milk to the churning of anger. Are you in the habit of creating strife, or do you prevent it and reduce it? Our actions always have a byproduct. What is the product of your actions?

Proverbs 31

31:1 The words of King Lemuel, the oracle which his mother taught him.

*R*egarding the name "Lemuel," *The Complete Word Study Old Testament* points out that this word means, literally, "from or belonging to God."[46] Some scholars believe that "King Lemuel" may be a pseudonym for Solomon. Regardless of who the author is, he praises his mother for teaching him about the attributes needed for living a godly life and for leadership. The virtuous qualities written about in this chapter seem to have been modeled for him by his mother. Modeling is always one of the most powerful methods of teaching.

31:2 What, O my son? And what, O son of my womb? And what, O son of my vows?

As a mother, she identifies her relationship to her son. First, she identifies him as "my son." This is a simple familial relationship. Secondly, she uses the term "son of my womb." This addresses the physical and emotional connection that she feels for him. Thirdly, she calls him the "son of my vows." This testament bears witness to her spiritual and psychological interconnectedness and her deep commitment to him. The overriding tone of verse 2 demonstrates a sense of pathos through the deep love of a mother for her son. There is a sense of poetry and passion in this address.

> 31:3 Do not give your strength to women, or your ways to that which destroys kings.

If Solomon is the author of this passage, this note of warning from his mother is one of the greatest ironies in recorded history. Bathsheba was intensely aware of how close her relationship with David had come to completely destroying David, if not for the grace of God. Solomon himself did not heed this advice. His affection for women was his main downfall.

This verse is a warning to all rulers. Many leaders allow their power to have a corrupting influence on themselves. God has called us to a higher standard.

> 31:4–9 It is not for kings, O Lemuel, it is not for kings to drink wine, or for rulers to desire strong drink, lest they drink and forget what is decreed, and pervert the rights of all the afflicted. Give strong drink to him who is perishing, and wine to him whose life is bitter. Let him drink and forget his poverty, and remember his trouble no more. Open your mouth for the dumb, for the rights of all the unfortunate. Open your mouth, judge righteously, and defend the rights of the afflicted and needy.

The biblical ideal of a ruler is that he be a servant. His role is not to be tyrannical. Only as a servant does a ruler demonstrate true nobility as he strives for the rights of the oppressed (v. 5). Strong drink will only serve to impair a ruler's ability to do this. Verses 6 and 7 are not suggesting that drinking can solve the problems of someone in misery. They serve first of all as a contrast to a ruler. Secondly, verses 6–9 here show that our role is to comfort, encourage, and advocate for those who are less fortunate. Jesus gave us the illustration of the good Samaritan (Luke 10:30–37) to show us how to comfort others. The third point I would like to make here is that if you understand the rest of the book of Proverbs and you trust in the Lord, then you should never be in such total despair that you need to drink your problems away—even if others around you may demonstrate this type of need.

The final section of Proverbs, 31:10–31, is an alphabetical acrostic poem in the original Hebrew. Each of the twenty-two letters in the Hebrew alphabet is used in sequence to begin the first word of each verse (see also Psalm 119). This great passage extolling the worth of an excellent woman who fears the Lord is perhaps the most famous passage in the entire book of Proverbs.

> 31:10 An excellent wife, who can find? For her worth is far above jewels.

When you are considering finding a mate, set your standards high. An excellent spouse should be considered far more valuable than money. An excellent marriage begins with an excellent spouse. What qualities make up an excellent mate? If you are currently looking for a mate, what exactly should you be looking for? Verses 11–29 seek to answer this, so keep reading!

> 31:11 The heart of her husband trusts in her, and he will have no lack of gain.

Fidelity and trust are at the heart of a great marriage. Trust is earned over time. It comes by seeing someone's actions, understanding her deepest beliefs, and by realizing the purity of her motives. When you completely trust your spouse, it brings a freedom to your own actions that allows you to attain your own greatest potential.

> 31:12 She does him good and not evil all the days of her life.

Each of us has the ability to bring good to those whom we love. But we also have the ability to bring hurt, pain, sorrow, and harm to them.

Marriage is forever ("all the days of her life") for the virtuous woman. Her commitment is both pure and complete.

31:13–15 She looks for wool and flax, and works with her hands in delight. She is like merchant ships; she brings her food from afar. She rises also while it is still night, and gives food to her household, and portions to her maidens.

The virtuous woman works hard. She takes care of the needs of her family and those around her.

31:16 She considers a field and buys it; from her earnings she plants a vineyard.

She is bold yet wise in her investments. She makes money and reinvests it rather than just spending it all. She doesn't buy a large item on impulse. Before she buys the field, she considers it. She plans. In the example given, when she purchased the field, she already had an idea of what she would do with it. She would make it into a vineyard. She follows through with her plans.

31:17 She girds herself with strength, and makes her arms strong.

Having first provided for the needs of her family, she now looks after her own needs (not the other way around). She keeps herself in good health. The verse uses the euphemism "She girds herself with strength" to describe how she builds herself up physically. Whether this refers to exercise, good nutrition practices, or simply maintaining a good mental attitude, we cannot be sure. But as far as personal application of this verse goes, I feel confident that we should do what we can to make ourselves feel good. When we feel good, we tend to have a better attitude about things in general.

31:18 She senses that her gain is good; her lamp does not go out at night.

To have a sense that you have been truly blessed by God is one of the great gifts of peace that God can bestow on us. The latter part of this verse reminds me of the parable of the ten virgins told by Jesus in Matthew 25:1–13. She is a prudent woman, prepared for the entire night.

31:19 She stretches out her hands to the distaff, and her hands grasp the spindle.

What is a distaff? It is a staff that holds on its cleft end the unspun flax, wool, or tow from which thread is drawn in spinning by hand. See also 31:13. She is industrious.

31:20 She extends her hand to the poor; and she stretches out her hands to the needy.

She is generous. She cares first for her husband (v. 11), second for her family (v. 15), third for herself (v. 17), and then also for the poor and needy. Proverbs 22:9 reminds us that generosity will be rewarded with blessing. On a literary note, there may be a strong connection metaphorically with both verse 19 and 20. She "stretches" out her hand in both verses. In verse 19, she stretches out her hand to work, which enables her to stretch out her hand in verse 20 to help others. There is a very poetic feel within these two verses. Consider how you can "stretch out" and improve the world around you.

31:21–22 She is not afraid of the snow for her household, for all her household are clothed with scarlet. She makes coverings for herself; her clothing is fine linen and purple.

Snow is a cyclical event. In those portions of the world where it occurs, it usually occurs annually. This means that it can be anticipated, and hence it can be prepared for. Yet I would dare say that every year in this country the snow comes and many people aren't ready for it. They didn't get the heaters fixed in their cars or buy new tires or chains—or maybe their children outgrew their winter coats and they didn't purchase new ones, etc. The virtuous woman is not among this group of people. Being prepared enables one to have less fear. In fact, we should fear nothing except God Himself. The five foolish virgins were afraid that the bridegroom would come before they could get more oil (see the note for verse 18). What are some of the "snow" events in your life? Are you prepared for them?

> 31:23 Her husband is known in the gates, when he sits among the elders of the land.

A mutual love and respect exists between this virtuous woman and her husband. This respect is shared by others in the community. This is yet another blessing to her.

Another thought to consider here is that she has helped him to become the man he is. We can imagine that her encouragement and prompting have enabled him to become a leader within the community.

> 31:24 She makes linen garments and sells them, and supplies belts to the tradesmen.

Once she and her household's clothing needs are met, she continues to be productive so that she may sell her products at a profit.

31:25–28 This next passage consists of four couplets of comparison praises for the virtuous woman. Altogether she is praised for eight different things.

> 31:25 Strength and dignity are her clothing, and she smiles at the future.

King Lemuel takes the discussion about clothing from the practical realm into the metaphorical. Not only does she create clothing, but she is also clothed in the fine qualities of strength and dignity.

Why does she "smile at the future" (NASB)? The answer is simple: because she trusts God (v. 30) and works hard and wisely. As Christians our perspective should be eternal. We too should laugh and smile as we think of our glorious future in a post-resurrection era!

31:26 She opens her mouth in wisdom, and the teaching of kindness is on her tongue.

She doesn't talk about vain things. She "talks her walk," which is full of wisdom and kindness.

31:27 She looks well to the ways of her household, and does not eat the bread of idleness.

She is aware of her household. She knows the needs, the joys, the hurts, the finances, and the victories of her household. By not being idle, she is not only a catalyst for good things to happen to her family, but she is also a model and an inspiration to others in the family.

31:28 Her children rise up and bless her; Her husband also, and he praises her, saying:

Verses 12–27 provide an exposé on what the virtuous woman *does*. Verse 28 describes some of the *results* she attains. This is some of the fruit of virtuousness. She has worked hard and placed her family in such a lofty position within her heart that now her family willingly reciprocates her love and devotion. She will be adored. She will not be taken for granted.

31:29 "Many daughters have done nobly, but you excel them all."

In this verse we read of a husband's comparison of his wife to other women. A word of caution may be appropriate here. In a roomful of married couples who have healthy relationships, each man should be able to look around him, think about his wife's inner godly qualities as well as her external qualities (such as hard work, etc.), and conclude, "Thank you, God, for giving me such a wonderful helper suitable to me!" (See Genesis 2:18.) My caution is that *negative* comparisons could also be made, and these are seldom healthy or even productive in the relationship. We see that for this one man, the woman he has married excels all others. God's power and wisdom are revealed in the fact that this may be true for each man.

31:30 Charm is deceitful and beauty is vain, but a woman who fears the LORD, she shall be praised.

This verse demonstrates a great deal about biblical truth and practical living. This is the type of verse people read and agree with. Perhaps you read it, and found yourself nodding your head in agreement with the wisdom and clarity of the words. But the challenge is, do you *really* believe it?

Preachers often talk about people having head knowledge but lacking heart knowledge. Many areas of Christian living require heart knowledge, but because they involve inner qualities, such as courage or humility, they are difficult to measure. Beauty involves both inner and overt qualities, but clearly in this context, the author is referring to outer, physical beauty. This, then, provides us with a more overt test. What is your real attitude toward physical attractiveness? Do you agree with this verse, but still evaluate others based on their external appearance?

In an effort to provide greater clarity, I must point out that the verse does not mean Christians should not be beautiful. It is matter of balance, emphasis, focus, priorities, and perspective. This verse provides another way of saying, "Seek first His kingdom . . . and all these things shall be added to you" (Matthew 6:33). If you are following God, you are beautiful. The verse challenges us to think about our definition of beauty.

And what about charm? Is it wrong to be charming? Read the verse again carefully. When it talks about charm, it emphasizes deceitfulness. As believers, we should focus on what is true and lasting and of supreme importance. We are never encouraged to be deceitful. Nothing is more important than your walk with the Lord.

31:31 Give her the product of her hands, and let her works praise her in the gates.

The passage ends with another reminder of how valuable her work is. People will praise her, but so too will her works themselves.

Appendix A: Thoughts and Verses

This appendix is included for the leader of a small discussion group. When I was teaching through the book of Proverbs, I often included an interesting thought for the day or a memory verse that we would work on together before beginning the week's lesson. Sometimes we memorized the verse, and other times I read the verse aloud and asked everyone to simply meditate on it for a few moments.

Doing this allowed us to have a common focus point. Sometimes this would allow a mini-discussion before the regular lesson so that latecomers could find their seats. Use this appendix in any way you find useful. Perhaps you will find the memory verses of personal value. Add your own favorite quotes and verses to your lessons.

Thoughts for the Day

Most of us go through life praying a little, planning a little, jockeying for position, hoping but never being quite certain of anything, and always secretly afraid that we will miss the way. This is a tragic waste of truth and never gives rest to the heart.

A. W. Tozer, *The Knowledge of the Holy*

The idea of God as infinitely wise is at the root of all truth. It is a datum of belief necessary to the soundness of all other beliefs about God.

A. W. Tozer, *The Knowledge of the Holy*

The great curse of modern Christianity is that people will not be careless about things they have no right to be careful about, and they will not let God make them careful about their relationship to Him.

Oswald Chambers, *If Thou Wilt be Perfect*

Your character is what you are in the dark.

D. L. Moody

We are often hindered from giving up our treasures to the Lord out of fear for their safety; this is especially true when those treasures are loved relatives and friends. But we need have no such fears . . . . Everything is safe which we commit to Him, and nothing is really safe which is not so committed.

A. W. Tozer, *The Pursuit of God*

Thou hast formed us for Thyself, and our hearts are restless till they find rest in Thee.

Augustine

We have enough religion to make us hate, but not enough to make us love one another.

Jonathan Swift

A wise man will hear and increase in learning.

Solomon

Acquaint thyself with God. To regain her lost power the Church must see heaven opened and have a transforming vision of God.

A. W. Tozer, *The Knowledge of the Holy*

Compare the following proverbs to those you read in the Bible. In what ways are they the same? In what ways do they differ?

When you go to buy, use your eyes, not your ears.

Czech proverb

A skillful trade is better than an inherited fortune.

Welsh proverb

No one is ever hanged with money in his pocket.

Russian proverb

Learning is a treasure which will follow its owner everywhere.

Chinese proverb

Freiheit ist von Gott, Freiheiten vom Teufel. (Liberty is from God, liberties from the devil.)

Old German proverb

Do you agree or disagree with the following thought?
All life is an experiment. The more experiments you make the better.

Ralph Waldo Emerson

Memory Verses

Make your ear attentive to wisdom, incline your heart to understanding.

Proverbs 2:2

The fear of the LORD is the beginning of wisdom, and the knowledge of the Holy One is understanding.

Proverbs 9:10

The fear of the LORD is to hate evil.

Proverbs 8:13

Discuss: What does "fear of the Lord" look like? This verse shows us one of those ways.

Like a trampled spring and a polluted well is a righteous man who gives way before the wicked.

Proverbs 25:26

Like a city that is broken into and without walls is a man who has no control over his spirit.

Proverbs 25:28

To him who overcomes, I will grant to eat of the tree of life.

Revelation 2:7

Your time is always opportune.

John 7:6

Do not let your heart envy sinners, but live in the fear of the LORD always.

Proverbs 23:17

The righteous is concerned for the rights of the poor, the wicked man does not understand such concern.

Proverbs 29:7

Where there is no vision, the people are unrestrained, but happy is he who keeps the law.

Proverbs 29:18

A man's pride will bring him low, but a humble spirit will obtain honor.

Proverbs 29:23

Meditation Verses

Take a moment to read each verse and then ponder its meaning.

The fear of man brings a snare, but he who trusts in the Lord will be exalted.

proverbs 29:25

When the grass disappears, the new growth is seen.

Proverbs 27:25

He who walks blamelessly will be delivered.

Proverbs 28:18

He who trusts in the Lord will prosper. He who trusts in his own heart is a fool.

Proverbs 28:25–26

Appendix B: Sheol and Abaddon

This appendix is included for the reader who is interested in a deeper look at the concepts of Sheol and Abaddon.

We have seen several references to Sheol and Abaddon in the book of Proverbs (e.g., Proverbs 15:11). Other scriptures that may help us define this concept are provided here for your perusal.

"Fire is kindled in my anger, and burns to the lowest part of Sheol." (Deuteronomy 32:22)

"The departed spirits tremble under the waters and their inhabitants. Naked is Sheol before Him and Abaddon has no covering." (Job 26:5–6)

"Thou wilt not abandon my soul to Sheol; neither wilt Thou allow Thy Holy One to see the pit." (Psalm 16:10)

See also Acts 2:27 (Peter's sermon) and 13:35 (Paul's sermon). This is a reference to the Messiah. Resurrection and the immortality of the soul are Old Testament concepts.

"God will redeem my soul from the power of Sheol." (Psalm 49:15)

Through God's power, we have victory over Sheol.

"Put me like a seal over your heart . . . for love is as strong as death, [its ardor is as inflexible] as Sheol. Its flashes are flashes of fire, the very flame of the LORD. Many waters cannot quench love." (Song of Songs 8:6)

So we see that it is used in the poetry of scripture as well as didactic parts of scripture.

"Though they dig into Sheol, from there shall My hand take them; and though they ascend to heaven, from there will I bring them down." (Amos 9:2)

This passage, in reference to God's judgment, implies that those whom He deems worthy of judgment cannot hide in either Sheol or heaven.

Sheh-ole' is defined in Strong's dictionary[47] as the world of the dead. This world of the dead includes its accessories and inmates. Synonyms include the English words *grave, hell,* and *pit.*

Abaddon is defined as Hades (the Greek term), or the concept of destruction. It comes from the root *abad,* which means to lose oneself, to break, to destroy, or not to escape. In certain contexts, it may mean to fail, lose, perish, be void of, or simply to have no way to flee.

While they are both used as nouns, Sheol is more of a place, similar to the Nordic concept of the Netherworld. Abaddon is more the actual result of a destructive act. Admittedly, both words are somewhat vague, but that is, of course, the case with all concepts that deal with death and the afterlife.

In all likelihood, we will never fully understand these ideas, but we can rest assured because, as David wrote, "Where can I go from Thy Spirit? Or where can I flee from Thy presence? If I ascend to heaven, Thou art there; If I make my bed in Sheol, behold, Thou art there" (Psalm 139: 7–8).

Appendix C: Bread

$\mathcal{Q}$uite a few Proverbs deal with bread. It is a frequent metaphor. Because of this, I decided to include a short appendix about bread and how the Bible uses this word. While nothing in this appendix is earth-shattering, it is hoped that the interested reader will learn at least one new fact or idea.

An anthropologist I once met at SIL (Summer Institute of Linguistics) in Dallas, Texas, claims that the popular notion of hunter-gatherer societies is a physically nutritional impossibility. He claims such societies either traded for staples or actually did raise plants agriculturally. In essence, according to him, bread (or another similar staple, such as rice) is necessary for a civilization to exist. Obviously, this concept does not sit well with evolutionary anthropologists, whose theories of human development depend upon the idea of an intermediary society of hunters and gatherers that preceded agricultural civilizations.

Sharing bread demonstrates hospitality (e.g., Ruth 2:14). When taken in its most basic and literal usage, bread indicates life, e.g., "In all the land of Egypt there was bread" (Genesis 41:54). Concerning our basic need of bread, Jesus commanded us, saying, "Do not be anxious then, saying, 'What shall we eat?' . . . But seek first His kingdom" (Matthew 6:31, 33).

Even before the law, Melchizedek "brought out bread and wine" (Genesis 14:18). This may be a foreshadowing of the ceremony of communion. Under Levitical law, bread was used as a sacrifice (e.g., Leviticus 7:13). At the Last Supper Jesus used bread to symbolize His body. Throughout His ministry Jesus referred to Himself as the bread of life. In a radical statement, Jesus instructed His followers, "Do not work for the food which perishes, but for the food which endures to eternal life" (John 6:27).

Read John 6:30–63. What does the concept of "bread" as used by Jesus have to do with the idea of a bodily resurrection?

The book of Proverbs has quite a few references to bread. If holy communion consists of eating bread and drinking wine in remembrance of Jesus and His atoning sacrifice, then Proverbs 4:17 illustrates *unholy communion* metaphorically: "For they eat the bread of wickedness and drink the wine of violence."

Proverbs 6:26 also uses "bread" in a negative light: "For on account of a harlot one is reduced to a loaf of bread." But even in this humorous context, bread is symbolic of life. The verse ends by pointing out, "And an adulteress hunts for the precious life."

In Proverbs 9 we learn of two different types of bread, a bread of life and a bread of death. Wisdom beckons us, "Come, eat of my bread and drink of the wine I have mingled" (Proverbs 9:5 KJV). However, in Proverbs 9:17–18 we read, "Bread eaten in secret is pleasant. But he does not know that the dead are there" (see also Proverbs 20:17).

We have seen how God and Satan have both used bread as a tool (see notes for Proverbs 23:6–8). Proverbs 25:21–22 reveals how we can use bread as our own tool. By giving bread to your enemy when he is hungry, you can receive a reward from God and "heap burning coals on his head."

Notes

[1] *Webster's New World Dictionary* Copyright 1990 by Simon & Schuster

[2] Frankl, Viktor. *Man's Search for Meaning.* Boston:Beacon Press, 1959,1962,1984,1992.

[3] James 2:14–24.

[4] *Strong's Exhaustive Concordance of the Bible* Lynchburg: The Old-Time Gospel Hour Edition (no date of publication given)

[5] Luke 18:18–25.

[6] Calvin, John. *Institutes of the Christian Religion.* See *http://www.iclnet.org/pub/resource/text/ipb* e/epl-cvinst.html.

[7] Luther, Martin. *95 Theses.* See http://www.reformed.org/documents/95_theses.html

[8] Exodus 4:10–12.

[9] *The American Heritage Dictionary.*Boston: Houghton Mifflin Company, 1982.

[10] Voltaire. The *Great Quotes* by George Seldes, New Jersey: Castle Books, 1977.

[11] "Count Your Blessings" Text by Johnson Oatman, Jr. and Music by Edwin O. Excell *The Hymnal for Worship and Celebration,* Waco, Texas, Word Music, 1986.

[12] *The American Heritage Dictionary.* Boston: Houghton Mifflin Company, 1982.

[13] Donne, John. From "Devotions Upon Emergent Occasions" Meditation XVII, See Anderson, Buckler, Veeder *The Literature of England, Volume 1,* Palo Alto, California: Scott, Foresman and Company, 1979.

[14] Henry, Patrick. "Give Me Liberty or Give Me Death." See http://www.federalist.com/histdocs/liberty.htm

[15] The idea of the pen being mightier than the sword was used by Thomas Paine in the periodical "Common Sense" See http://www.publicbookshelf.com/public_html/Our_Country_vol_2/commonsen_if.html

[16] Pope, Alexander. An *Essay On Criticism* part 2, See Anderson, Buckler, Veeder *The Literature of England Volume One* Palo Alto: Scott, Foresman and Company, 1979.

[17] Lawrence Kohlberg see Crain, W.C. *Theories of Moral Development* Prentice-Hall (pp 118–136), 1985.

[18] Evolutionists argue that change happens little by little over many years. One problem with this idea is that many organs and body systems only work in a completed and "perfect" form. The human eye is an example. It cannot have "developed," because it can only function in a completed stage. This is called irreducible complexity. For a further explanation of irreducible complexity, read *Darwin's Black Box,* by Michael Behe New York: Touchstone, 1996.

[19] Plato's allegory of the cave presents us with the idea that we know only that to which we have been exposed to. As more truth is revealed to us, we see that there are realities beyond those which we previously were aware of. See *The World's Great Thinkers Man and Man: The Social Philosophers* see Plato's *Republic: Book VI.* Random House, 1947.

[20] Confucius, see http://jws2.ccccd.edu/mtarafdar/ConfIntro.html

[21] *The Complete Word Study Old Testament.* Chattanooga, TN: AMG Publishers, 1994.

[22] Esther 2:22

[23] Daniel 6:16–28

[24] Daniel 3:13–30

[25] *The Complete Word Study Old Testament,* p.1617

[26] *Webster's New World Dictionary* Copyright 1990 by Simon & Schuster

[27] Einstein http://www.ruleof72.net/rule-of-72-einstein.asp

[28] Christie, Agatha (from one of her novels)

[29] Piaget's theories include the idea that young children do not distinguish between abstract and concrete ideas. Abstract thinking is developmental. See Baruth, Leroy G. and Robinson, Edward H. III *An Introduction to the Counseling Profession* (p. 100–102) New Jersey: Prentice-Hall, Inc. 1987.

[30] Foxe, John *Foxe's Book of Martyrs* New Kensington, PA: Whitaker House, 1981.

[31] Phillips, J.B *Ring of Truth* London: Hodder and Stoughton, 1967.

[32] *Strong's Exhaustive Concordance of the Bible* Lynchburg: The Old-Time Gospel Hour Edition (no date of publication given) . . .

[33] Ezzo see http://www.gfi.org/java/faq_gkgw.jsp . . .

[34] Hebrew dictionary *The Complete Word Study Old Testament.* Chattanooga, TN: AMG Publishers, 1994.

[35] Likert scaling measures a person's attitudes, feelings or beliefs about an item being measured. Whenever you are asked to evaluate something on a scale from 1 to 10 (or any number) you have participated in a Likert scale. E.g. see *http://trochim*.human.cornell.edu/kb/scallik.htm

[36] Schaeffer, Francis. *The God Who Is There* Downers Grove: Intervarsity Press, 1968.

[37] *Webster's New World Dictionary* Copyright 1990 by Simon & Schuster

[38] Shakespeare, William. *Othello,* V.ii.337–343.

[39] Matthew 5:6.

[40] Kohlberg, Lawrence. see Baruth, Leroy G. and Robinson, Edward H. III *An Introduction to the Counseling Profession* (p. 106,107) New Jersey: Prentice-Hall, Inc. 1987.

[41] Donne, John. From "Devotions Upon Emergent Occasions" Meditation XVII, *The Literature of England,Volume 1,* Palo Alto, California: Scott, Foresman and Company, 1979.

[42] Tozer, A. W. *The Knowledge of the Holy.* New York: Harper and Row, 1961.

[43] Exodus 4–12.

[44] The Hebrew word is different in this verse.

[45] *The Complete Word Study Old Testament,* p. 2356.

[46] *The Complete Word Study Old Testament,* p. 60 in the Hebrew and Chaldee Dictionary.

[47] *Strong's Exhaustive Concordance of the Bible* Lynchburg:The Old-Time Gospel Hour Edition (no date of publication given) p. 111 of the Hebrew and Chaldee Dictionary.

To order additional copies of

Wisdom
for
Today's Decisions

Have your credit card ready and call:

1-877-421-READ (7323)

or please visit our web site at
www.pleasantword.com

Also available at:
www.amazon.com
and
www.barnesandnoble.com